CONTROVERSY

OF THE AGES

"The time is long past when we have needed a very careful, thoroughly documented analysis and response to the claims of young earth creationists. But with this book, I am delighted to say that that time has come. Its same thoughtful handling of evolutionary creationism makes *Controversy of the Ages* a critical read for evangelicals wending their way through the confusion. I am very enthusiastic about the scholarship, careful treatment, and irenic tone of this book and highly recommend it."

—J. P. MORELAND, Distinguished Professor of Philosophy,
Talbot School of Theology

"In addition to a well-informed history of evangelical moves for relating Genesis to geology and then to Darwinism, the authors have given us much more. They have provided trenchant evaluation of the argumentative strategies—theological, scientific, and philosophical. They show that of the various groups known to us today—the young earth creationists, the (non-Darwinian) old earth creationists, and the evolutionary creationists—none can be exempted from critique, and none deserves the place of exclusive privilege. This book deserves a wide readership, for it is informative, fair, and incisive. I rejoice that God spared Dr. Cabal from a terminal cancer to help write this!"

—C. JOHN COLLINS, Professor of Old Testament,
Covenant Theological Seminary

"When people ask for a good book to read about the age of the earth, I have a new favorite to recommend: *Controversy of the Ages*. With remarkable clarity, this book provides historical and theological context to the young-earth/old-earth controversy. But Cabal and Rasor move beyond mere description and prescribe the way to move forward—the Galileo approach. This is an important book, and it needs to be read by pastors, college and seminary students, and all who care about science and faith issues."

—KENNETH KEATHLEY, Senior Professor of Theology, Southeastern Baptist
Theological Seminary; coauthor of *40 Questions about Creation and Evolution*

"*Controversy of the Ages* is a welcomed addition to the issues swirling around the creation-evolution debate. The book is encyclopedic in scope, and the footnotes alone are a treasure trove of information. I appreciated the argument of the book; I appreciated even more the spirit of the book. I will be recommending this work for a long time."

—DANIEL L. AKIN, President, Professor of Preaching and Theology,
Southeastern Baptist Theological Seminary

"If I had the power to require every Christian parent, pastor, and professor to read two books on creation and evolution—ideally alongside their mature children, parishioners, and students—it would be *40 Questions about Creation and Evolution* (by Kenneth Keathley and Mark Rooker) along with the book you are now holding in your hands, *Controversy of the Ages*. Neither book intends to answer all of the questions definitively, but together they are like maps for Christians in the complex and confusing intersection of the Bible and science. We cannot bury our head in the sand, or outsource study of these issues to others. Cabal and Rasor help us sort through the issues and the options, modeling for us how to use proportion and perspective in our rhetoric and strategies of disagreement within the body of Christ. We live in perplexing days, but clear and clarifying books like this are a tremendous gift to the church. If the arguments and tone of this book are taken to heart, we will all be sharper, wiser, and kinder. I pray it is widely read."

—JUSTIN TAYLOR, author, managing editor of the ESV Study Bible, blogger at The Gospel Coalition

"Controversy of the Ages provides a concise and carefully researched history of the tensions between science and theology through the years. While offering a helpful overview of matters related to Copernicus, Galileo, and Darwin, among others, the book focuses on questions related to the age of the earth. With an informed understanding of young earth and old earth theories, as well as BioLogos and Intelligent Design proposals, Cabal and Rasor provide insightful analysis of these various perspectives based on an unapologetic commitment to the truthfulness of Scripture. As indicated by the subtitle, pastors, church leaders, and students will find an exemplary model of how to evaluate differing approaches to this important subject, doing so with conviction, kindness, and conciliatory civility. It is a privilege to recommend this rewarding volume."

—DAVID S. DOCKERY, President, Trinity International University

"Cabal and Rasor have provided an extraordinarily lucid and winsome guide to traversing the creation vs. evolution, and old-earth vs. young earth debates of our day. The authors endeavor to be fair, honest, and forthright in their description of the various views, and they practice what they preach, that is, they present a charitable approach to assessing the issues and positions involved in the complex web of these current debates. Readers will find this book enlightening, engaging, and greatly informative. But even more importantly, they will see a model for dealing with controversial issues in a way that honors Christ, seeks to know and uphold the truth, and shows charity toward others with whom we might differ. I'm deeply grateful for the wisdom this book puts forth and encourage all interested in these issues to consider carefully its weighty arguments and timely admonitions."

—BRUCE A. WARE, T. Rupert and Lucille Coleman Professor of Christian Theology, The Southern Baptist Theological Seminary

"At a time when Christianity is increasingly viewed with skepticism if not outright scorn, the people of God need to turn down the dial on needless intramural bickering. What I love about *Controversy of the Ages* is how Cabal and Rasor intelligently and winsomely put this thorny issue into historical perspective. Going back to the days of Copernicus, Galileo, and Darwin, the authors carefully explain how Christians with differing positions have wrestled with how to harmonize their understanding of what the Bible teaches with the discoveries of astronomers, geologists, and biologists (and vice versa). The Bible's inerrancy ought not to be confused with the fallibility of our interpretations. This extremely well-researched book is an excellent orientation to the topic for Christians of all ages, particularly pastors, theology students, and anyone who is interested in the physical sciences."

—ALEX CHEDIAK, Professor of Physics and Engineering, California Baptist University; author of *Thriving at College: Make Great Friends, Keep Your Faith,* and *Get Ready for the Real World!*

"In some circles young earth creationism is identified as orthodoxy, as if such a perspective is the only way a faithful Christian could interpret the early chapters of Genesis. Cabal and Rasor demonstrate conclusively that such a position reflects the dogmatism of its proponents and faces many significant objections. Here is a fair-minded and wise reflection on the age of the earth. I think pastors, students, and laypersons will learn much from this wise, mature, and reasoned approach."

—THOMAS R. SCHREINER, James Buchanan Harrison Professor of New Testament Interpretation, The Southern Baptist Theological Seminary

"Cabal and Rasor have thoughtfully and comprehensively outlined the complex history, theology, scientific foundations and philosophies surrounding the age of the earth controversy. While clearly stating their positions, they masterfully suggest a paradigm for a theological triage system that could encourage fellow Christians to discover the importance of unity rather than division. They humbly warn the reader not to miss the significance that old earth and young earth believers must be cautious of the encroaching beliefs of evolution in general and specifically theistic evolution throughout the culture as well as in the church. Whether you agree with their conclusions or not, everyone interested in this topic should appreciate the depth of their presentation and their attempts in calling for dialogue and for better understanding even in our differences."

—Tom Bary, Pastor, Neptune Baptist Church, Neptune, FL

"Unfortunately, the topic of the age of the earth and the 'days' of Genesis seems to bring out the very worst in some professing Christians. So I very much appreciate the irenic tone of Cabal's and Rasor's *Controversy of the Ages*—an even-handed assessment of the debate. These scholars have done careful work, and they make their case in a fair-minded way. Even if one may disagree with their perspective, they truly set the standard for discussing this shockingly divisive topic."

—Paul Copan, Professor and Pledger Family Chair of Philosophy and Ethics, Palm Beach Atlantic University

"I am more than happy to see the publication of this volume, and to recommend that it be given serious consideration by the evangelical world. There is no biblical doctrine more important than creation; thus it is crucial that all Bible believers speak with a unified voice on its main tenets. Even if we cannot agree on creation's every detail, I believe this book can help us to come closer together on its most important elements."

—Jack Cottrell, Professor of Theology, Cincinnati Christian University

"Listening to advocates on the age of the earth or human origins can be confusing because passionate believers in one viewpoint are not likely to present fairly opposing ideas, nor to point out the weaknesses of their own positions. After reading *Controversy of the Ages,* I have a much better handle on the differences, strengths, and weaknesses of old earth vs. young earth creationism. Thanks to Cabal and Rasor for their fair presentation of the evidence and irenic tone."

—Robert L. Plummer, Professor of New Testament Interpretation, The Southern Baptist Theological Seminary

"As a pastor and missionary engaged in cross-cultural ministry, I am so grateful for this book. Christians from many ethnic backgrounds must navigate each new wake of the intense Western debates over the age of the earth and human origins. The fresh insights in these pages may be just what they need to weed through the complexities of the controversy. Cabal's and Rasor's treatment of the issues is extensive, balanced, and passionate—yet they perform it with a demeanor that all Christians would do well to emulate."

—SEAN RYAN, Executive Director of Approach International

CONTROVERSY
OF THE AGES

WHY CHRISTIANS SHOULD NOT DIVIDE
OVER THE AGE OF THE EARTH

THEODORE J. CABAL
PETER J. RASOR II

LEXHAM PRESS

Controversy of the Ages: Why Christians Should Not Divide Over the Age of the Earth
© 2017 by Theodore J. Cabal and Peter J. Rasor II

Lexham Press, 1313 Commercial St., Bellingham, WA 98225
LexhamPress.com

First edition by Weaver Book Company

Print ISBN 9781683591368
Digital ISBN 9781683591375

Cover: LUCAS Art and Design
Interior Design: Nicholas Richardson
Copyediting: Line for Line Publishing Services

CONTENTS

PREFACE

I was no longer an evolutionist after my conversion to Christ. Believing in Christ and in the Bible came as a package deal to me in 1973, and Genesis seemed clearly to teach that humans did not evolve from lower life forms. Yet I cannot remember being concerned about the age of the earth. Anti-evolution old earth creationism (OEC) still dominated conservative evangelical and fundamentalist circles in those days.

But the young earth creationist (YEC) revolution soon ruled the scene, and I was swept into the movement. Books by Henry M. Morris and others from the Institute for Creation Research became my standard fare for science-theology issues. I not only taught their material as a pastor, I even wrote a pamphlet espousing their ideas.

Sometime in the early 1980s I became troubled by a trend in the movement. Much of its material seemed as much anti-old earth as it was anti-evolution. Though I had become a young earth creationist, the broadsides against OECs concerned me. Why were the unspoken motives of these fellow anti-evolutionists impugned? I also doubted sweeping but unsubstantiated claims that the loss of so much good in Western culture could be attributed to OEC. I began to wonder whether their scientific claims might suffer from similar rashness.

Though YEC leadership eventually shifted to Answers in Genesis, the trend intensified. I remained an anti-evolutionist (and still am), but eventually drifted back to non-dogmatic OEC. I became concerned that the age of the earth was the wrong place to draw boundaries between Christians. I decided to write a paper on the subject for a national Evangelical

Theological Society meeting in 2001. Chapter 7 recounts how response to that paper led ultimately to this book.

Even before I finished that paper, I was diagnosed with multiple myeloma, terminal cancer. Obviously I have lived longer than anyone expected. So in spite of years of chemotherapy, I began researching the issues. For much of a decade I participated in private annual meetings established to promote dialogue between OEC, YEC, and Intelligent Design leaders. Seemingly little rapprochement resulted. Eventually, a new player arrived on the scene. BioLogos added complexity to the situation with its advocacy of theistic evolution, or evolutionary creation as it prefers its view to be called. Despite sometimes serious differences, I have come to respect and care deeply about Christian friends in all these groups.

Eventually I knew it was time to write this book, but I could not. The debilitating effects of cancer treatments spared my ideas but not my writing ability. Peter Rasor became an answer to my prayers by agreeing to help with the writing and further research. Months of fruitful conversations, research and even trial chapters ensued. But then Peter was called to teach in a distant state. New responsibilities limited his ability to contribute. In God's mercy after several unexpected years of reprieve from treatments, my writing ability began to return. So I have written this book, but Peter kept the project alive when I could not.

Those coming to these pages hoping to find arguments for OEC or against YEC will be disappointed. Rather, the book provides perspective of the lines being drawn by Christians concerning the creation debate. Most leaders in creationist ministries will disagree with something I've written, but hopefully the book will make a contribution to clarifying the complex issues facing evangelicals today.

Jim Weaver deserves special thanks. His support as publisher has been extraordinary. I'm also especially grateful to the administration and trustees of The Southern Baptist Theological Seminary for granting me a sabbatical. Those months proved to be critical for finishing the research and writing.

—Theodore J. Cabal

Chapter 1

SCIENCE AND THEOLOGY AT WAR

> Who shall number the patient and earnest seekers after truth, from the days of Galileo until now, whose lives have been embittered and their good name blasted by the mistaken zeal of Bibliolaters?[1]
>
> —Thomas Huxley, "Review of *The Origin of Species*"

Thomas Huxley, Darwin's defender and "bulldog," wrote his review of *The Origin of Species* in 1860. A century and a half later similar sentiments abound. Contemporary creationists of all stripes face scorn, ridicule, and academic disenfranchisement in ways that would have surprised even Huxley. But was Huxley correct that science and theology have been locked in a brutal war ever since Galileo faced the Inquisition? The answer will not only shape our understanding of the relationship of science and theology but the age of the earth debate as well.

THE MYTHICAL CONFLICT THESIS

The year 1980 experienced "a watershed moment for science-themed television programming"[2] with the launch of the series "Cosmos: A Personal Voyage." As of 2009, the series remained the most widely watched

---

1. T. H. Huxley, "Review of *The Origin of Species*," *Westminster Review* 17 (1860): 556.
2. Dave Itzkoff, "'Family Guy' Creator Part of 'Cosmos' Update," *The New York Times,* August 5, 2011, http://www.nytimes.com/2011/08/05/arts/television/fox-plans-new-cosmos-with-seth-macfarlane-as-a-producer.html.

worldwide Public Broadcasting Service television show ever.[3] The engaging host, Carl Sagan, regularly took potshots at religion in the name of science and boldly began the series with a dramatic announcement: "The cosmos is all that is or ever was or ever will be." With just one sentence millions of people came face to face with philosophical naturalism, the view that nature is the ultimate reality. Whatever is natural is real; whatever is considered supernatural is unscientific, hence false. But though Sagan's proclamation had nothing to do with science, it didn't matter. The catchy presentations revealed to a popular audience so many fascinating features of the cosmos that surely this brilliant prophet of scientism must be right.

In March 2014, a reprise co-produced by Sagan's widow Ann Druyan, titled "Cosmos: A Spacetime Odyssey," launched to great fanfare. The "theology hinders science" motif stood out. In the first episode the new host, astrophysicist Neil deGrasse Tyson, depicted sixteenth-century Giordano Bruno as martyred by the church for daring to believe non-approved science. Little matter that Bruno's deplorable execution resulted from theological heresies rather than his scientific views—a recognized and appealing scientific expert had said so. The glaring historical distortion aside,[4] Tyson regards theology and science impossible to reconcile. In an interview by Bill Moyers concerning the series, Tyson professed, "All efforts that have been invested by brilliant people of the past have failed at that exercise. They just fail . . . the track record is so poor that going forward, I have essentially zero confidence, near zero confidence, that there will be fruitful things to emerge from the effort to reconcile them."[5]

Christians regularly believe and contribute to the idea of ongoing warfare between science and theology. Not long ago a prominent pastor in my town declared to his congregation that Galileo suffered persecution because he rejected the flat earth teachings of the church. Unfortunately, the Galileo affair had nothing to do with the shape of the earth. In fact,

3. "Cosmos: A Personal Voyage by Carl Sagan," http://www.cosmolearning.com/documentaries/cosmos/.

4. Casey Luskin, *Cosmos* Is Slammed for Its 'Inaccurate' and 'Revisionist' History of Giordano Bruno," Evolution News and Views, March 11, 2014, http://www.evolutionnews.org/2014/03/cosmos_slammed_083111.html.

5. "Transcript of Bill Moyers interview, Jan 17, 2014, part 2 with Neil deGrasse Tyson," Science, Religion and the Universe, http://billmoyers.com/episode/full-show neil-degrasse-tyson-on-science-religion-and-the-universe/.

virtually all Christian scholars in the Middle Ages acknowledged the earth's sphericity.[6] But more important, false ideas like these form part of the greater ongoing myth historians today call the "conflict thesis."

During the Darwinism debate of the late nineteenth century, the flat-earth myth gained traction as a component of the conflict thesis (sometimes called "warfare model" or "military metaphor").[7] The notion is simple: theology has always opposed the inevitable progress of science. To put it in Huxley's dramatic flair: "Extinguished theologians lie about the cradle of every science as the strangled snakes beside that of Hercules; and history records that whenever science and orthodoxy have been fairly opposed, the latter has been forced to retire from the lists, bleeding and crushed if not annihilated; scotched, if not slain."[8]

Two men, John William Draper and Andrew Dickson White, were chiefly responsible for propagating the warfare thesis. During the maelstrom of the Darwinism debate, Draper published his *History of the Conflict between Religion and Science*.[9] His thesis was simple: "Religion must relinquish that imperious, that domineering position which she has so long maintained against Science."[10] White's work, *A History of the Warfare of Science with Theology in Christendom*, was equally influential with a considerably more scholarly appearance than Draper's.[11] In his book, published in 1896 as the culmination of more than thirty years of research and publication on the subject, White criticized what he saw as stubborn, dogmatic theology restricting scientific advance. With the confidence of many intellectuals regarding Christianity already eroded by

---

6. Scholars of the Middle Ages commonly knew even the earth's approximate circumference. David Lindberg and Ronald L. Numbers, "Beyond War and Peace: A Reappraisal of the Encounter between Christianity and Science," *Church History* 55, no. 3 (1986): 338–54. For a detailed treatment of the pernicious myth that Europeans prior to Columbus believed that the earth was flat, see Jeffrey Russell, *Inventing the Flat Earth: Columbus and Modern Historians* (Westport, CT: Praeger, 1997).

7. Colin Russell, "The Conflict of Science and Religion," in *Science and Religion: A Historical Introduction*, ed. Gary Ferngren (Baltimore: Johns Hopkins University Press, 2002), 3–4.

8. Huxley, "Review of *The Origin of Species*," 556.

9. John William Draper, *History of the Conflict between Religion and Science* (New York: D. Appleton and Company, 1874).

10. Ibid., 367.

11. Andrew Dickson White, *A History of the Warfare of Science with Theology in Christendom* (New York: D. Appleton and Company, 1896).

Enlightenment philosophy and liberal theology, the current battle over Darwinism seemed to confirm that traditional theology inevitably deters scientific progress. The works of Draper and White powerfully catalyzed the mutual hostility theme into Western culture. The two "screaming titles . . . were to thunder through the decades, remaining audible more than a century later."[12]

Proclamations of Christianity's serious threat to science resound today especially through the popular works of the New Atheists such as Jerry Coyne. The title of his recent book says it all: *Faith Versus Fact: Why Science and Religion Are Incompatible*.[13] He claims Draper and White made a point needing to be heard still: religion fails to reveal truth of any sort. Though admitting science and theology may not have been at perpetual war, Coyne seems to think they should be.

In spite of Coyne's wish to ennoble the warfare model, its central thesis has been discredited for decades. Colin Russell, former president of the British Society for the History of Science, writes that for most of a century "the notion of mutual hostility (the Draper-White thesis) has been routinely employed in popular-science writing, by the media, and in a few older histories of science. Deeply embedded in the culture of the West, it has proven extremely hard to dislodge. Only in the last thirty years of the twentieth century did historians of science mount a sustained attack on the thesis, and only gradually has a wider public begun to recognize its deficiencies."[14] Contemporary historians of science recognize that "Draper takes such liberty with history, perpetuating legends as fact, that he is rightly avoided today in serious historical study. The same is nearly as true of White, though his prominent apparatus of prolific

---

12. David B. Wilson, "The Historiography of Science and Religion," in *Science and Religion: A Historical Introduction*, ed. Gary Ferngren (Baltimore: Johns Hopkins University Press, 2002), 16. A more mature twentieth-century work, J. Y. Simpson, *Landmarks in the Struggle between Science and Religion* (London: Hodder & Stoughton, 1925), continued the battle metaphor. See Russell, "The Conflict," 4.

13. Jerry Coyne, *Faith Versus Fact: Why Science and Religion Are Incompatible* (New York: Viking Press, 2015).

14. Russell, "The Conflict," 4. Cf. Wilson, "Historiography," 23. Wilson adds that "the conflict model is still widely accepted by academics (historians and scientists alike), though generally no longer by historians of science. A gulf in point of view thus marks the immediate setting of any scholarly treatment of the subject for a popular audience." Ibid., 15.

footnotes may create a misleading impression of meticulous scholarship."[15] The conflict thesis makes for interesting drama, but is "seriously deficient as history."[16]

The relationship between religion and science is best described as complex rather than conflicted. The interactions have been and can be supportive or in conflict or neutral.[17] More often than not, religious figures have been on both sides of disputes with no overall aim by any party involved in discrediting religion.[18] The conflict meme actually must ignore the historical fact that "Christianity has often nurtured and encouraged scientific endeavour, while at other times the two have co-existed without either tension or attempts at harmonization. If Galileo and the Scopes trial come to mind as examples of conflict, they were the exceptions rather than the rule."[19]

That Christianity "nurtured and encouraged" developments in modern science is well documented. Robert Boyle, Isaac Newton, Blaise Pascal, Marin Mersenne, Pierre Gassendi, and others demonstrated the symbiotic relationship between the two in the seventeenth and eighteenth centuries. The warfare model fails to describe the nineteenth century, particularly in Britain where the likes of Faraday, Joule, Maxwell, and Thomson (Lord Kelvin) sought to integrate science and Christianity. And in the twentieth century, "a number of distinguished scientists of religious persuasion were ready to join societies like the Victoria Institute in London or its

---

15. Russell, "The Conflict," 10.

16. David C. Lindberg, "Galileo, the Church, and the Cosmos," in *When Science and Christianity Meet*, ed. David C. Lindberg and Ronald L. Numbers (Chicago: University of Chicago Press, 2003), 33. Richard Olson quips that "history, like fiction, seems to demand conflict to make it interesting." Richard G. Olson, *Science and Religion, 1450–1900: From Copernicus to Darwin* (Baltimore: Johns Hopkins University Press, 2004), 4. For an excellent historical and philosophical overview of the history of science and religion, including presentist versus contextualist approaches, see Wilson, "Historiography," 13–29.

17. This describes the view of John Brooke, often considered today's most respected scholar working on the interaction between science and theology. Each case must be analyzed on its own merits. See Olson, *Science*, 24.

18. Richard H. Jones, *For the Glory of God: The Role of Christianity in the Rise and Development of Modern Science*, vol. 1 (Lanham, MD: University Press of America, 2011), 19–22, 139.

19. Gary Ferngren, "Introduction," in *Science and Religion: A Historical Introduction*, ed. Gary Ferngren (Baltimore: Johns Hopkins University Press, 2002), ix. Cf. Russell, "The Conflict," 8.

successors in Britain and the United States, which were dedicated to bringing together religious and scientific ideas."[20]

If battle imagery should be used at all, most debates pit proponents of one scientific theory versus another, which has no bearing on theology. Likewise, the overwhelming majority of the controversies in the history of theology have nothing to do with science. Battles between scientists and theologians have actually been rather sparse. If determined by how widespread in influence and how protracted, only two conflicts between science and theology qualify as world wars: the Copernican and Darwinian. Draper and White tacitly agreed by primarily stressing those two.[21] The Copernican controversy lasted almost two centuries and affected Catholics and Protestants alike. More important, a variety of understandings about the relationship between science and theology have impacted controversies ever since. And perhaps most reasonably educated people know that the Darwinian battle has impacted all streams of Christianity (and Western culture) ever since publication of *On the Origin of Species* in 1859, and shows no signs of abating. In a variety of ways, the shadow of Darwinism hangs over the subject matter of this book.[22]

EVANGELICAL FRIENDLY FIRE

Friendly fire is the wounding or killing of allied or neutral forces when intending to assault the enemy. Though unintended, it results from either improperly identifying the adversary or inaccuracy in the attack. But it still wounds or kills. Some of the most hurtful fire directed at Christians

---

20. Russell, "The Conflict," 8.

21. Terry Mortenson, *The Great Turning Point: The Church's Catastrophic Mistake on Geology—Before Darwin* (Green Forest, AR: Master Books, 2004), argues for three major science-theology conflicts by including the scriptural geologists' opposition to modern geology in the nineteenth century. But the relatively minor influence of the scriptural geology debate disqualifies it from being classified in the league with the Copernican and Darwinian controversies. I will survey the scriptural geologists briefly in chapter 6.

22. "Copernicanism (or the Galileo affair) is rather unique in that the issue is framed in relation to a single, pioneering figure." Obviously Darwinism "is quite exceptional in the history of modern natural science. . . . It is as though Darwin's own contribution has constrained the conceptual and empirical development of evolutionary biology ever after." Jean Gayon, "From Darwin to Today in Evolutionary Biology," in *The Cambridge Companion to Darwin,* 2nd ed., ed. Jonathan Hodge and Gregory Radick (New York: Cambridge University Press, 2009), 277–78.

involved in science and theology comes from fellow Christians. Evangelicals are especially adept at friendly fire.

But just what is an evangelical? The term has been somewhat difficult to define and describe. Diverse evangelical individuals include George Whitefield (1715–1770), John Wesley (1703–1791), Jonathan Edwards (1703–1758), Dwight L. Moody (1837–99), Billy Sunday (1862–1935), Carl F. H. Henry (1913–2003), and Billy Graham (1918–). In very general terms, evangelicals have been denoted by beliefs such as the centrality of Christ's sacrifice on the cross, the authority of the Bible, and living out the gospel in culture. Denominational groups considered evangelical reveal the wide diversity: black Baptists, Dutch Reformed, Mennonites, Pentecostals, Catholic charismatics, and Southern Baptists. And ironically, evangelicals have often been defined by their trans-denominationalism in support of evangelistic and cultural mission.[23]

The irony is in the way evangelical trans-denominational cooperation contributes toward friendly fire in science-theology[24] debates. On the one hand, trans-denominational teamwork is evident, but typically only in relation to one of three very different approaches to the science-theology relationship in general, and theology and evolution and the age of the earth in particular. Many subtypes exist within each camp, so when I refer to the main groups in this book, I will be most often using the following three terms to refer to these broad concepts. Young earth creationists (YECs) believe the creation days of Genesis 1 were 24 hours long and occurred 6,000 to 12,000 years ago. Approximately 4,300 to 5,300 years ago, Noah's flood radically altered the earth's surface and produced most of the geologic strata and fossils. YECs hold to biblical inerrancy.[25] Old

---

23. This broad description was taken from the Institute for the Study of American Evangelicals. Some consider these types of descriptions too broad to be helpful. See "Defining Evangelicalism," Institute for the Study of American Evangelicals, Wheaton College, http://www.wheaton.edu/ISAE/Defining-Evangelicalism, and "Defining the Term in Contemporary Times," Institute for the Study of American Evangelicals, Wheaton College, http://www.wheaton.edu/ISAE/Defining-Evangelicalism/Defining-the-Term.

24. I use the term "science-theology" instead of something like "science-Bible" because, as we will see in the following chapter, both science and theology involve interpreting data (nature and the Bible).

25. Terry Mortenson, "Young-Earth Creationist View Summarized and Defended," Answers in Genesis, February 16, 2011, https://answersingenesis.org/creationism/young-earth/young-earth-creationist-view-summarized-and-defended/.

earth creationists (OECs) believe the universe was created billions of years ago but reject human evolution, and universal common descent for that matter. OECs also believe in biblical inerrancy.[26] Evolutionary creationists (ECs) is the designation evolutionary evangelicals prefer over the older "theistic evolution."[27] They hold to an ancient creation and universal common descent, including human evolution, and hold a range of views on biblical inspiration.[28]

Loads of trans-denominational teamwork is evident in the support of these three types of creationist organizations in the form of millions of dollars per year. For several decades now groups dedicated to propagating a creationist viewpoint have been going at it full-time. The most recently available IRS Forms 990 for the three most influential ministries tell part of the story.

For the year 2014, Answers in Genesis (AiG) reported $32,424,557.[29] Without question, AiG is massively influential with its $27 million Creation Museum boasting "75,000 square feet of state-of-the-art exhibits, a high-tech Planetarium, full-size Allosaurus skeleton, stunning botanical gardens, petting zoo, zip lines, and more."[30] If assets serve as the criterion, the addition of the $100 million Ark Encounter in 2016 surely places AiG in the lead of all YEC (or any creationist) ministries.[31] And the ministry confidently agrees: "AiG, with 750 full-time and part-time/seasonal staff members, is the world's largest apologetics organization."[32] Particularly focused on providing answers to questions about the book of Genesis, AiG

---

26. These distinguishing views represent those of the most influential OEC organization, Reasons to Believe. See "Mission and Beliefs," Reasons to Believe, http://www.reasons.org/about/our-mission.

27. Denis O. Lamoureux, "Evolutionary Creation: A Christian Approach to Evolution," https://biologos.org/uploads/projects/Lamoureux_Scholarly_Essay.pdf.

28. These views represent the most influential EC organization, BioLogos. See "About BioLogos," http://biologos.org/about-us/.

29. I learned of this data from the excellent blog of leading YEC Todd Wood. See Todd Wood, "Creationist Finances Revisited," May 31, 2010, http://toddcwood.blogspot.com/search?q=institute+for+creation+research. You can search for this type of information at "990 Finder," Foundation Center, http://foundationcenter.org/find-funding/990-finder.

30. "Prepare to Believe," Creation Museum, https://creationmuseum.org/.

31. "Bigger Than Imagination," Ark Encounter, https://arkencounter.com/.

32. "History of Answers in Genesis," Answers in Genesis, https://answersingenesis.org/about/history/.

seeks "to expose the bankruptcy of evolutionary ideas, and its bedfellow, a 'millions of years old' earth (and even older universe)."[33]

Reasons to Believe (RTB) has been the leading OEC ministry for decades. In the year 2014, it reported $7,566,191 to the IRS on its Form 990. "RTB's mission is to spread the Christian Gospel by demonstrating that sound reason and scientific research—including the very latest discoveries—consistently support, rather than erode, confidence in the truth of the Bible and faith in the personal, transcendent God revealed in both Scripture and nature."[34] The best known OEC today and founder of the ministry, Hugh Ross, "has been on the frontier of making the biblical and scientific case against Darwinism for more than two decades. RTB scholars believe that God miraculously intervened throughout the history of the universe in various ways millions, possibly even billions, of times to create each and every new species of life on Earth."[35]

BioLogos, the newest of the three but the clear leader among EC ministries, reported $3,691,398 for 2014.[36] The organization has enjoyed remarkable growth since being founded in 2007 by Francis Collins, former director of the Human Genome Project and best-selling author. Its attractive and professional website offers numerous videos, essays, articles, blogs, and testimonials of evangelicals who have converted to evolutionary creationism. BioLogos holds conferences for evangelical leaders and scientists, workshops for middle and high-school teachers, and dialogues with Christians skeptical of evolution. The organization now provides grants for projects promoting evolutionary creation, with more than $3 million awarded in the past several years.[37] Many influential evangelicals such as Philip Yancey, Os Guinness, Tim Keller, N. T. Wright, and Andy Crouch have warmed to BioLogos and serve as endorsees.[38] BioLogos invites "the

---

33. "About," Answers in Genesis, https://answersingenesis.org/about/.

34. "Our Mission: Engage & Equip," Reasons to Believe, http://www.reasons.org/about/our-mission.

35. "FAQs," Reasons to Believe, http://www.reasons.org/about/faqs.

36. BioLogos also received a $2,028,238 Templeton Foundation grant running from 2008 to 2012 at its startup. "The Language of God: BioLogos Website and Workshop," John Templeton Foundation, https://www.templeton.org/what-we-fund/grants/the-language-of-god-biologos-website-and-workshop.

37. "Our History," BioLogos, http://biologos.org/about-us/our-history/.

38. "Endorsements," BioLogos, http://biologos.org/about-us/endorsements/.

church and the world to see the harmony between science and biblical faith as we present an evolutionary understanding of God's creation."[39]

Organizations like these use first-rate websites and various other social media to wield vast influence. And coupled with schools, pastors, and bloggers teaching their differing ideas, the opportunity for evangelical trans-denominational friendly fire has never been higher. Enormous amounts of time and energy (and money) are daily invested in the promotion of their ideas, and sometimes large doses of vitriol are expended toward creationists who disagree.

Non-specialists can find navigating this material especially difficult. Trying to understand just the material of one group is daunting, much less trying to grasp adequately the positions of the others. Extremely complex issues raise various questions. Just a small sample includes biblical issues (what is the relationship of Genesis 1 and 2?), theological (does the doctrine of original sin demand a historical Adam as father of the race?), scientific (has science demonstrated the age of the earth?), philosophical (are scientists allowed to argue for intelligent design?), and historical (how did believers understand the significance of extinct species?). In spite of these complexities, prominent and respected leaders urgently insist rank-and-file believers must choose their position to be faithful to truth.[40]

For instance, BioLogos declares: "Science makes it abundantly clear, we believe, that God has created through an evolutionary process and that there was never a time when there were just two individuals [Adam and Eve] on earth."[41] And another BioLogos article states that the apostle Paul erred because "he certainly assumed that Adam was a person and the progenitor of the human race. I would expect nothing less from Paul, being a first-century man. And again, God speaks in ways and uses categories that are available to human beings at that time. I don't expect Paul to have had a conversation with Francis Collins about the Genome Project and how

39. "Our Mission," BioLogos, http://biologos.org/about-us/.

40. Complicating matters further, scientists regularly expound on the Bible and theology while theologians seek to referee for readers various issues in cosmology, biology, and plate tectonics.

41. Darrel Falk, "BioLogos and the June 2011 'Christianity Today' Cover Story," May 31, 2011, http://biologos.org/blogs/archive/biologos-and-the-june-2011-christianity-today-cover-story.

common descent is essentially assured scientifically. I don't expect him to understand that."[42]

At the opposite end of the evangelical creationist spectrum, Ken Ham writes with great urgency:

> Bottom line—evolution is really *not* the problem as much as the age of the earth. Millions of years is the problem in today's world that has resulted in a loss of biblical authority in the church and culture and has led to an increasing loss of generations from the church.
>
> I personally believe that belief in millions of years is the lie of Satan in this present world that is used as one of the greatest attacks on God's Word. Yet the acceptance of millions of years permeates the church. Really, it is no different than the Israelites who adopted the idols of the pagan cultures and worshiped pagan Gods—often mixed in with what God's Word instructed them concerning holy days, sacrifices, etc. The church needs to wake up to the fact that when God's people accept the pagan religion of millions of years, they are helping the enemies of God attack His Holy Word.[43]

Here are voices of authority proclaiming with great certainty to untold numbers of people, yet with diametrically opposed views. Obviously the concerns are extremely important. How should a Bible-believing Christian respond to such complex disputes? Lines have been drawn, but are they in the correct places?

So much more than the age of the earth is involved in the issues at stake between these three groups. But the age of the earth has been the bone of contention for more than a half century among conservative evangelicals. The sheer daily investment of emotion spent debating these matters can render evangelicals unmindful of attacks by people like the New Atheists. Yet, though the scope of the controversy cannot compare to the great

---

42. "The Apostle Paul and Adam with Pete Enns," BioLogos, http://biologos.org/ resources/audio-visual/pete-enns-on-the-apostle-paul-and-adam.

43. Ken Ham, "Will Pastors Miss the 'Millions of Years' Point?" Answers in Genesis, January 11, 2012, https://answersingenesis.org/blogs/ken-ham/2012/01/11/will-pastors-miss-the-millions-of-years-point/. Emphasis his.

science-theology controversies, its being coupled with the Darwinian dramatically extends its significance. But should even the age and evolution questions be necessarily joined?

CONCLUSION

The prevalent notion that science and theology have been perpetually at war is a myth. Only two science-theology conflicts (the Copernican and Darwinian) qualify as major if judged by their influence over time and numbers of people. But the age of the earth controversy can seem quite major to those enmeshed in it. Three different evangelical viewpoints compete for allegiance with substantial resources to defend, debate, and even attack one another. Evangelicals find themselves confronted by voices of authority urgently declaring the importance of deciding where they stand on a variety of complex and important issues.

Sorting these matters out requires some historical investigation. The very first science-theology conflict is a good place to start because its impact continues to affect even the controversy before us. Illuminating lessons drawn from the first world changing science-theology debate can help us think more carefully about our own.

Chapter 2

THE COPERNICAN CONFLICT:
How to Go to Heaven or How the Heavens Go?

> I hold that the sun is located at the center of the revolutions of
> the heavenly orbs and does not change place, and that the earth
> rotates on itself and moves around it. . . . [but] they tried on
> their own to spread among common people the idea that such
> propositions are against the Holy Scriptures, and consequently
> damnable and heretical.[1]
>
> —Galileo, "Letter to the Grand Duchess Christina"

As onetime Librarian of Congress, director of the Smithsonian's
National Museum of American History, and recipient of the National
Book Award for a lifetime contribution to literature, Daniel J. Boorstin
had an impressive pedigree. Writing about the earliest days of the modern
scientific revolution, he declared that Martin Luther, Philipp Melanchthon
(Luther's collaborating Reformer), and John Calvin "carried a strong fun-
damentalist, anti-intellectual message."[2] When Boorstin declared these
Reformers were reflexively anti-science, people believed him.

And it wasn't hard to mine quotes seeming to support his view. After
all, one of the most cited Luther quotes was his opinion of Copernicus
and his new astronomy: the "fool [Copernicus] will overturn the whole

---

1. Galileo Galilei, "Letter to the Grand Duchess Christina (1615)," in *The Essential
Galileo,* ed. and trans. Maurice A. Finocchiaro (Indianapolis: Hackett, 2008), 111–12.

2. Daniel J. Boorstin, *The Discoverers: A History of Man's Search to Know His World
and Himself* (New York: Random House, 1983), 302.

art of astronomy. But, as Holy Writ declares, Joshua commanded the sun to stand still and not the earth."[3] Melanchthon's initial reaction to Copernican heliocentrism (a sun-centered and earth-moving universe) was to cite Scriptures such as Psalm 19:6 and Psalm 93:1 in which he believed the Bible clearly taught the sun moved but not the earth. He concluded: "Let us be content with this clear [*perspicuus*] testimony."[4] And as a text-book writer, Melanchthon's first edition of *Elements of the Knowledge of Natural Science* ridiculed geocentrism claiming "it is not decent to defend such absurd positions publicly."[5]

Unfortunately, Boorstin's immensely popular book got this story all wrong. Luther did informally opine on the new astronomy with his students. But that he discussed it at all is notable seeing that the intellectual community had hardly begun contemplating the seemingly wild theory. The overwhelming scientific consensus then and for the previous 1,500 years was on Luther's side, hardly an instance of poor secular scientists fending off theologians. All involved believed the Bible, not to mention the commonsense experience that the sun appears to be doing the moving. Luther would have been irrational to endorse Copernicanism at the time.

Even worse for Boorstin's work, the evidence suggests Calvin was not even aware of Copernicus. Boorstin's Calvin error can be traced to Andrew Dickson White who helped launch the mythical science-theology warfare thesis.[6] And one more item makes Boorstin's error worse still. One of the most interesting and providential aspects of the launch of modern science is that, under Melanchthon's leadership, it radiated from Wittenberg, the

---

3. Martin Luther, *Table Talk,* cited by Leopold Prowe, *Nicolaus Copernicus,* 3 vols. (Berlin: n.p., 1883–1884), 2:232, cited in Henry O. Taylor, *Philosophy and Science in the Sixteenth Century* (New York: Collier Books, 1962), 97.

4. Philipp Melanchthon, *Initia Doctrinae Physicae,* 217, in *Opera Omnia,* ed. Carl Bretschneider, Corpus Reformatorum, vol. 13 (n.p.: C. A. Schwetschke and Son, 1834), 656–57, quoted in Kenneth J. Howell, *God's Two Books: Copernican Cosmology and Biblical Interpretation in Early Modern Science* (Notre Dame: University of Notre Dame Press, 2002), 53.

5. Cited in Owen Gingerich, "The Copernican Revolution," in *Science and Religion: A Historical Introduction,* ed. Gary Ferngren (Baltimore: Johns Hopkins University Press, 2002), 99.

6. Edward Rosen, *Copernicus and His Successors,* ed. Erna Hilfstein (London: The Hambledon Press, 1995), 161–72. Rosen notes that White's work seems to be the basis for Bertrand Russell and others claiming similar errors regarding Calvin.

early intellectual center for teaching and publishing Copernicanism.[7] But before we see how, let's survey events that set the stage.

OF COURSE THE EARTH DOESN'T MOVE: COMMON SENSE, SCIENCE, AND THE BIBLE

Prior to the sixteenth century, Christians and non-Christians alike had every good reason to believe heavenly bodies orbited an unmovable earth lying at the center of the universe.[8] First, ordinary perception teaches the earth is at rest; the sun and planets do the moving. Second, the settled astronomy completely agreed. Nothing important for almost a millennium and a half challenged the *Almagest* of Claudius Ptolemy (AD 90–168).[9] This earth-centered science repeatedly proved itself competent to explain and predict heavenly data.

But most important for Christians, the Bible seemed clearly to teach dozens of times that the sun moves across the sky whereas the earth "shall never be moved" (Ps. 93:1)."[10] Perhaps the biblical passage cited most often to support this view was Joshua 10:12–13. In this historical narrative Joshua commands the sun and moon to stop their movements for Israel's military purpose: "And the sun stood still, and the moon stopped. . . . The sun stopped in the midst of heaven and did not hurry to set for about a whole day."[11] No one could even imagine understanding the Bible

---

7. Gingerich, "Revolution," 99.

8. Only a few thinkers historically thought otherwise, including Aristarchus of Samos (ca. 310–230 BC), Martianus Capella (fl. fifth century CE), and Nicholas of Cusa (1401–1464).

9. Stephen Toulmin and June Goodfield, *The Fabric of the Heavens: The Development of Astronomy and Dynamics* (New York: Harper & Row, 1961), 153.

10. Examples include Genesis 15:12, 17; 19:23; 28:11; 32:31; Exodus 17:12; 22:3, 26; Leviticus 22:7; Numbers 2:3; Deuteronomy 11:30; 16:6; 23:11; 24:13, 15; Joshua 1:4; 8:29; 10:12, 13, 27; 12:1; Judges 5:31; 8:13; 9:33; 14:18; 19:14; 2 Samuel 2:24; 3:35; 23:4; 1 Kings 22:36; 1 Chronicles 16:30; 2 Chronicles 18:34; Job 9:7; 26:7; Psalms 19:4, 5, 6; 50:1; 93:1; 104:19, 22; 113:3; Ecclesiastes 1:5; Isaiah 13:10; 38:8; 41:25; 45:6; 59:19; 60:20; Jeremiah 15:9; Daniel 6:14; Amos 8:9; Jonah 4:8; Micah 3:6; Nahum 3:17; Habakkuk 3:11; Malachi 1:11; Matthew 5:45; 13:6; Mark 1:32; 4:6; 16:2; Luke 4:40; Ephesians 4:26; James 1:11.

11. On the issue of biblical interpretation regarding astronomy in Galileo's day, see Richard J. Blackwell, "Galileo Galilei," in *Science and Religion: A Historical Introduction*, ed. Gary Ferngren (Baltimore: Johns Hopkins University Press, 2002), 110.

except geocentrically.[12] Under the guard of theology and science, not to mention everyday perception, alternatives to geocentrism were virtually unthinkable.

But even if geocentric astronomy "worked," its complex artificiality was almost unintelligible. Presuming a stationary earth with orbiting sun, moon, and planets forced mind-boggling contrivances to account for the heaven's movements. Making matters worse was having the system account for the puzzling behavior of planets apparently slowing down and moving backward (retrograde motion). The ancient solution, laden with off-centered orbits upon orbits, was so contrived that thirteenth-century King Alfonso X quipped that if such astronomy were true, he could have given God some good advice in creating the world.[13]

YES, THE EARTH DOES MOVE: COPERNICUS, KEPLER, GALILEO, AND NEWTON

In God's providence the birth of Nicolaus Copernicus in 1473 followed on the heels of Gutenberg's revolutionary printing press, enabling rapid dissemination of ideas. During the seventy-year lifetime of Copernicus the Renaissance would bloom in da Vinci and Michelangelo, Columbus would discover the new world, and Luther would ignite the Reformation with his ninety-five theses. On his deathbed Copernicus is said to have received a copy of his newly published magnum opus, *On the Revolutions of*

---

12. Though "geocentric" technically refers to earth-centered astronomy and "geostatic" to a non-moving earth, I use the terms synonymously to refer to the overall understanding of the day, that is, a non-moving earth at the center of the universe. Similarly for "heliocentric," "heliostatic" (sun-centered, motionless sun).

13. Nicholas Theodore Bobrovnikoff, *Astronomy Before the Telescope: The Solar System* (Tucson, AZ: Pachart, 1989), 90. Ptolemaic astronomy envisioned the sun and planets with circular orbits (deferents) around the earth. These non-rotating bodies also traveled along much smaller circles (epicycles) along the circumference of the deferent. To "save the appearances," meaning to account for the way things actually appear, the deferent needed to be centered not on the earth but on an arbitrary point (the eccentric). But even with circles on non-earth-centered circles, the strange retrograde motions of planets required de-centering the epicycles, too. So, Ptolemy had added another imaginary point (the equant) off-centered relative to the deferent around which the epicycle orbited. If you have trouble imagining all this complexity, you are not alone! For illustration of the Ptolemaic system, see http://faculty.fullerton.edu/cmcconnell/Planets.html.

the Celestial Spheres. Little could he have realized its 1543 publication now standardly dates the launch of the modern scientific revolution.[14]

The reconceived astronomy featured a daily rotating earth orbiting the sun at the center of the universe. Copernicus also discovered the true sequence of the planets, rightly explaining the optical illusion of their retrograde motion caused by the earth passing slower outer planets. Qualities elusive to the old astronomy such as simplicity, order, coherence, and intelligibility were had in spades by the new.[15] Copernicus himself described the view as "pleasing to the mind."[16] But his new model was hardly perfect with its allegiance to Aristotelian notions of "perfect" bodies in "perfect" circular orbits at constant speeds. In the end Copernicus could not do away with all of the old contrivances, and his system was not necessarily more accurate than the old. Final touch ups to the theory would be left for those coming after.

At his death a generation later, Tycho Brahe (1546–1601), the greatest observational astronomer of his day, bequeathed to his understudy the best observational data available before the invention of the telescope. Although Johannes Kepler (1571–1630) had already published an outspoken defense of Copernicanism, Tycho's data helped Kepler develop further evidence for heliocentrism. More important, Kepler's discovery of elliptical planetary orbits allowed him to discard the old contrived epicycles. With the publication of his laws of planetary motions (1609, 1619), scholars became increasingly aware of the superiority of Copernican theory.

Galileo Galilei (1564–1642) wrote Kepler in 1597 that he, too, was a Copernican, though he originally responded lukewarmly to Kepler's first correspondence.[17] And unlike Kepler, Galileo would not make public his

---

14. On "scientific revolution" as fundamental rather than rapid change, see Edward Davis and Michael Winship, "Early Modern Protestantism," in *Science and Religion: A Historical Introduction*, ed. Gary Ferngren (Baltimore: Johns Hopkins University Press, 2002), 119. The heliocentric principles of Copernicus without the mathematical proofs had previously circulated in 1514 in handwritten copies of his *Little Commentary*.

15. David C. Lindberg, "Galileo, the Church, and the Cosmos," in *When Science and Christianity Meet*, ed. David C. Lindberg and Ronald L. Numbers (Chicago: University of Chicago Press, 2003), 38.

16. Gingerich, "Revolution," 97.

17. Edward Rosen, "Galileo and Kepler: Their First Two Contacts," *Isis* 57, no. 2 (1966): 262–64. Cf. Maurice A. Finocchiaro, ed. and trans., *The Essential Galileo* (Indianapolis: Hackett, 2008), 5.

conversion to heliocentrism for more than a decade.[18] But the telescope's invention by Dutchman Hans Lipperhey in 1608 galvanized Galileo's commitment as a Copernican.[19] He quickly improved its design and became the first to train it systematically on the heavens. Suddenly he could see ten times more stars as well as mountains, valleys, and craters on the moon. His fame grew after publishing his discovery of the sun's moving spots and Jupiter's four orbiting moons. Suddenly not all heavenly bodies were understood to orbit the earth. Galileo especially contradicted the standard geocentric model in publishing his discovery that Venus has a complete set of phases, proof that it orbits the sun. And late in life Galileo's most substantive contributions to physics paved the way for the next and final phase of the theoretical justification of Copernicanism.

"Nature and Nature's laws lay hid in night: God said, *Let Newton be!* And all was light."[20] Alexander Pope's famous words expressed the significance of Isaac Newton's (1642–1727) work sounding geocentrism's death knell. *The Mathematical Principles of Natural Philosophy* (1687) "established his renown in science for all time."[21] In it Newton essentially ended significant scientific debate about heliocentrism by formulating (a) the three laws of motion and (b) the theory of universal gravitation, and then demonstrating that Kepler's three laws of planetary motion follow from (a) and (b). Kepler had identified his laws on the basis of Tycho's careful observations, but no one understood why they worked. Newton, however, demonstrated that objects on earth could be described using his laws of motion, and that Kepler's planetary laws were just special applications of these same laws. Newton supplied the quantitative corrections confirmed by observation for Kepler's approximately correct planetary laws. The publication of Newton's *Principia* truly united earth and sky,[22] settling the Copernican controversy once and for all.

---

18. Gingerich, "Revolution," 102. See also Lindberg, "Galileo," 42.

19. Lindberg, "Galileo," 41.

20. Alexander Pope, "Intended for Sir Isaac Newton, in Westminster Abbey" (1735). For more "Newton poetry," see "Isaac Newton poetry," Mathematical Institute at the University of St Andrews, http://www-groups.dcs.st-and.ac.uk/history/HistTopics/Newton_poetry.html.

21. Richard S. Westfall, "Isaac Newton," in *Science and Religion : A Historical Introduction*, ed. Gary Ferngren (Baltimore: Johns Hopkins University Press, 2002), 154.

22. Taylor, *Philosophy and Science*, 100–101.

PROTESTANT THEOLOGICAL RESPONSE TO THE
NEW SCIENCE: PROMOTION

Inevitably, the growth and promotion of Copernicanism created theological controversy. Apparently violating common sense, certainly upending long-established science, and seeming directly to contradict Holy Scripture, how could the new science not raise a stormy debate? Yet, Catholic theologians did not initially strongly oppose Copernicanism. Catholic Bishop Tiedemann Giese even encouraged Copernicus in 1539 to publish his theory.[23] The Catholic church's reform of the Gregorian calendar in 1586 was also based on tables calculated from the new astronomy. Sixty years would pass before *On the Revolutions* would land on the Index of banned books.[24] If anything, the first generation of Catholic intellectuals implicitly, if not explicitly, accepted the new astronomy on a limited basis.[25]

The initial German Protestant handling of Copernicanism was considerably more important. Were it not for the persistence of a young Lutheran astronomy professor at the University of Wittenberg, Copernicus's masterpiece might never have been published. In 1539, Georg Rheticus, at significant personal effort and cost, came to study with Copernicus just four years before the great astronomer's death. Rheticus fully embraced the new science, encouraged Copernicus to publish it, and was entrusted with the task.[26]

---

23. Christopher Kaiser, *Creation and the History of Science* (Grand Rapids: Eerdmans, 1991), 113.

24. Toulmin and Goodfield, *Fabric*, 161.

25. Richard G. Olson, *Science and Religion, 1450–1900: From Copernicus to Darwin* (Baltimore: Johns Hopkins University Press, 2004), 9. Rosen notes that lack of controversy surrounding publication of *On the Revolutions* resulted from Copernicus's death and Council of Trent distractions. Rosen, *Copernicus and His Successors*, 149-60.

26. Rheticus also introduced and exposited his teacher's work in his own 1540 publication, *First Account*, with the motto: "Free in mind must he be who desires to have understanding." This quote from the *Didaskalikos*, by second-century philosopher Alcinous, is also quoted by Rheticus later in the book. See Georg Rheticus, "Narratio Prima," in *Three Copernican Treatises*, trans. Edward Rosen (New York: Dover Publications, 1959), 108, 187. Kepler also utilized the saying in *Conversation with the Starry Messenger* (1610), his published endorsement of Galileo's *Starry Messenger* published earlier that year. See Howell, *God's Two Books*, 39. Discovered in 1973, a second narrative written by Rheticus addressed scriptural concerns regarding heliocentrism, noting how the sun's apparent motion can mislead. Gingerich, "Revolution," 99.

By far the key shaper of Protestant theological response to the new astronomy was Philipp Melanchthon, Luther's collaborating Reformer in both systematic theology and education. As already noted, Melanchthon initially ridiculed Copernicus in the first edition of his textbook, *Elements of the Knowledge of Natural Science*. But his later editions toned down the criticism.[27] And while never accepting heliocentrism, eventually Melanchthon viewed teaching the new astronomy important and Copernicus a "moderate" Reformer.[28] By 1553, Melanchthon wrote concerning the study of astronomy, "Let us therefore cherish the subject which demonstrates the order of the motions and the description of the year, and let us not be deterred by harmful opinions, since there are some who—rightly or wrongly—always hate the pursuit of knowledge."[29]

Under Melanchthon's leadership the "Wittenberg Interpretation" constituted a way astronomers read *On the Revolutions*.[30] These scholars touted the new theory's predictions and reduction of artificialities, and set the goal of translating Copernicanism into a geocentric model.[31] Especially promoting astronomy, Melanchthon reformed the German universities utilizing the Wittenberg Interpretation, which was eventually spread throughout Europe by many significant astronomers.[32] Notables included Erasmus Reinhold, who produced a new set of planetary tables (the Prutenic Tables) based on Copernicanism. Melanchthon's own son-in-law, Caspar Peucer, taught Copernican astronomy at Wittenberg. And Michael Mästlin, a Copernican at Tübingen especially influenced by Melanchthon,

---

27. Gingerich, "Revolution," 99.

28. Davis and Winship, "Early Modern Protestantism," 121.

29. Robert S. Westman, "The Melanchthon Circle, Rheticus and the Wittenberg Interpretation of the Copernican Theory," *Isis* 66 (1975):169-70. The Melanchthon quote is from William Hammer, "Melanchthon, Inspirer of the Study of Astronomy; With a Translation of His Oration in Praise of Astronomy (De Orione, 1553)," *Popular Astronomy* 59 (1951): 318.

30. Westman, "Melanchthon Circle," 166–67.

31. Ibid. Westman calls this "the "split" interpretation of Copernicus, which generally characterized its earliest reception in German universities and many parts of Europe. Ibid., 168. See also J. R. Christianson, "Copernicus and the Lutherans," *The Sixteenth Century Journal* 4, no. 2 (October 1973): 1–10.

32. See the excellent discussion in Howell, *God's Two Books*, 48–57. In pursuit of educational reform, Melanchthon wrote many textbooks in theology, classical studies, physics, and astronomy. During his lifetime he came to be called Praeceptor Germaniae (teacher of Germany). Westman, "Melanchthon Circle," 172.

taught Johannes Kepler whose work paved the way for the eventual full acceptance of heliocentrism.[33]

The generally positive attitude toward Copernicanism of first-generation Lutheran intellectuals opened the way for the next to make significant advances in astronomy. Tycho Brahe studied at the Melanchthon-influenced Lutheran university at Copenhagen and would develop a highly influential model mixing Copernicanism with the traditional view. Kepler's approach to science was nurtured by his Lutheran theological studies, and he felt no fear in revealing himself to be a devoted Copernican. In 1596, the Tübingen faculty even encouraged him to publish his *Mysterium Cosmographicum* with its clear and robust defense of Copernicanism.[34]

SECOND-GENERATION CATHOLIC THEOLOGICAL RESPONSE TO THE NEW SCIENCE: OPPOSITION

Compared to the Lutherans, second-generation Catholic theologians generally responded unfavorably to the new science, especially as promoted by Galileo. His *Sidereal Messenger* (1610) and *Letters on Sunspots* (1613) quickly landed him in the thick of the heliocentrism debate. Heavenly "imperfections" such as a scarred moon surface or a rotating sun implied by moving sunspots were troubling enough. But Galileo especially contradicted the standard geocentric model in discovering that Venus has a complete set of phases, proof that it orbits the sun. He then stepped completely over the edge in claiming that heliocentrism had been proven.

Making matters worse, Galileo also inserted himself into the theological fray at just the wrong time. With the Counter-Reformation in full swing, proper biblical interpretation stood at the forefront. The Council of Trent (1545–1563) had decreed that Scripture was not to be interpreted privately

---

33. Davis and Winship, "Early Modern Protestantism," 121.

34. The Tübingen faculty did have Kepler remove his chapter on biblical interpretation since he formally was not a theologian. Even so, he later inserted that chapter with the first and second laws of planetary motion in his *New Astronomy* in 1609. See Rosen, *Copernicus and His Successors*, 226–30. Kepler scholar Rosen concludes: "It cannot be too strongly emphasized that the Lutheran authorities at Tübingen University, far from compelling Kepler to suppress or conceal his adherence to Copernicanism, [even] required him to compose additional material expounding the new revolutionary astronomy." Ibid., 224–25.

but only in line with the fathers, the pope, and the bishops.[35] "Given the church's defensive frame of mind, it was in no mood to adopt a new and revolutionary model of the heavens."[36] Yet Galileo, not even a theologian, claimed the earth moves, the sun does not, and biblical interpretations to the contrary are wrong. For the first time in history, theology and science were set on a major collision course. The simmering controversy over Galileo's believing the earth rotates and orbits the sun would finally erupt into the most famous example of science and theology at war.[37]

In the first phase of the Galileo affair Cardinal Robert Bellarmine (1542–1621), the most authoritative theologian of the day, responded to Galileo. He served as chief opponent of the current wave of Protestants as well as a member of the Congregations of the Inquisition and the Index.[38] Highly regarded as calm and fair, Bellarmine had been friendly toward Galileo's heliocentrism when interpreted hypothetically. As a predictive tool, Bellarmine declared "no danger in it, and it suffices for mathematicians." But affirming "that in reality the sun is at the center of the world and only turns on itself without moving from east to west, and the earth is in the third heaven and revolves with great speed around the sun: this is a very dangerous thing, likely not only to irritate all scholastic philosophers [scientists] and theologians, but also to harm the Holy Faith by rendering Holy Scripture false."[39]

Galileo responded that no article of faith was at stake. Bellarmine disagreed: any biblical factual or historical claim about the natural world is an article of faith. One cannot reject biblical teaching regarding the number of Abraham's children any more than the virgin birth since both are spoken "by the Holy Spirit through the mouth of the prophets and the apostles."[40] As such, interpretation of biblical passages pertaining to geocentrism fall under church authority. Since the Bible is the highest standard of truth, and Copernicanism has not been proven, the traditional interpretation of

---

35. Blackwell, "Galileo," 107–108.

36. Ibid., 108.

37. Ibid., 105. See also ibid., 115, and Lindberg, "Galileo," 33.

38. Bellarmine was eventually canonized and declared a Doctor of the Church in 1931 by Pope Pius XI.

39. Robert Bellarmine, "Letter to Foscarini (1615)," in Galileo Galilei, *The Essential Galileo*, ed. and trans. Maurice A. Finocchiaro (Indianapolis: Hackett, 2008), 146.

40. Bellarmine, "Foscarini," 147.

the fathers settles the matter. And the Council of Trent, Bellarmine noted, especially prohibits biblical interpretation conflicting with the Greek and Latin fathers.[41] He surprisingly agreed with Galileo that if Copernicanism were truly proven, biblical interpretation would need to be adjusted accordingly.[42] But he had grave doubts it had been clearly demonstrated, and "in case of doubt, one may not abandon the Holy Scriptures as expounded by the holy Fathers."[43] Ironically, Bellarmine was correct. Even if the Ptolemaic ship was sinking, heliocentrism had not yet been proven.[44]

Believing Copernicanism contradicted so many biblical passages, Pope Paul V with his theologians condemned it as heretically false. Future books advocating Copernicanism were forbidden, but Galileo escaped the charge of heresy. Bellarmine issued a letter in 1616 enjoining him neither to believe nor defend that the earth moves rather than the sun.[45]

In 1623, Galileo again sought to advance heliocentrism when his friend, Maffeo Barberini (1568–1644), was elected Pope Urban VIII. As a cardinal, Barberini had been supportive of Galileo's overall scientific work, even penning a poem in his praise. Seizing a golden opportunity, Galileo consulted the new pope who conceded Copernicanism may accurately describe astronomical phenomena that from our perspective suggest an understanding conflicting with biblical teaching. But, he asked Galileo, could not God have arranged the heavens completely differently yet having the same phenomena? "And if this possibility exists, which might still preserve in their literal truth the sayings of Scripture, it is not for us mortals to try to force those holy words to mean what to us, from here, may appear to be the situation."[46]

---

41. The Council of Trent (1545–1563): "The Council decrees that, in matters of faith and morals . . . no one, relying on his own judgment and distorting the Sacred Scriptures according to his own conceptions, shall dare to interpret them contrary to that sense which Holy Mother church, to who it belongs to judge their true sense and meaning, has held and does hold, or even contrary to the unanimous agreement of the Fathers." Lindberg, "Galileo," 45, cited from "Decree of the Council of Trent, 8 April 1546," trans. Richard J. Blackwell, *Galileo, Bellarmine, and the Bible* (Notre Dame: University of Notre Dame Press, 1991), 183.

42. Olson, *Science and Religion,* 15. Cf. Blackwell, "Galileo," 111.

43. Bellarmine, "Foscarini," 164. See also Blackwell, "Galileo," 107–108.

44. See discussion in Blackwell, "Galileo," 111–12.

45. Ibid., 112–13.

46. Giorgio de Santillana, *Crime of Galileo* (Chicago: University of Chicago Press, 1955), 166, cited in Lindberg, "Galileo," 51.

Nevertheless, the pope granted Galileo permission to teach Copernicanism, but only hypothetically. Thus, in 1632, Galileo's *Dialogue on the Two Chief World Systems*, a "literary masterpiece," appeared.[47] Seeking to satisfy the pope's restriction to the hypothetical while refuting the standard objections to Copernicanism, Galileo presented the issues in classic (Platonic) dialogue form. A Copernican philosopher, Salviati, debates Simplicio, an Aristotelian-Ptolemaic philosopher. An open-minded layman, Sagredo, assesses both sides. The book ends with the pope's position: couldn't God's infinite power and wisdom produce physical phenomena in ways we cannot conceive? If so, then "it would be excessively bold if someone should want to limit and compel divine power and wisdom to a particular fancy of his."[48] Ill-advisedly, Galileo placed the pope's position in the mouth of Simplicio, ostensibly referring to an earlier Aristotelian philosopher, but widely viewed as a double entendre connoting *simpleton*.[49] And clever Salviati, the Copernican philosopher, obviously presented the far superior arguments.

The pope was furious and ordered the book's printing suspended. A special commission investigated, deeming the *Dialogue* to violate the 1616 decree forbidding books advocating Copernicanism. An inexplicable memorandum unbeknownst to the pope was produced from the files of the Holy Office. Its contents declared that Galileo had been specifically enjoined in 1616 never to believe, defend, or teach Copernicanism "in any way." Galileo had clearly violated this restriction, even though it was far more comprehensive than Bellarmine's original. Galileo was ordered to stand trial before the Inquisition.

Galileo produced during trial the less restrictive original Bellarmine letter, contending he had no memory of the inquisitor's newly discovered memorandum.[50] Asked whether he had the necessary permission

---

47. Blackwell, "Galileo," 114. Galileo wrote in Italian rather than Latin, ensuring wider readership.

48. Galileo Galilei, *Dialogue on the Two Chief World Systems*, in *The Essential Galileo*, ed. and trans. Maurice A. Finocchiaro (Indianapolis: Hackett, 2008), 270.

49. See Finocchiaro's comment, *Dialogue on the Two Chief World Systems*, 192 n. 5; Blackwell, "Galileo," 114.

50. The second document produced at the trial has been much discussed regarding its genuineness and the like. See Richard Blackwell, *Behind the Scenes at Galileo's Trial* (Notre Dame: University of Notre Dame Press, 2006), 1–28, and Blackwell, "Galileo," 113–14.

(imprimatur) to write such a book, Galileo shocked all by responding he sought none since his purpose was to *refute* heliocentrism. He then produced evidence of prior permission to publish the book. Galileo agreed to a plea deal for a lesser charge, confessing to having gone too far in the arguments for Copernicanism.[51]

Tragically, a deceptive and misleading trial report presented for judgment to the pope and cardinals omitted the plea bargain. The resulting verdict, "vehemently suspected of heresy,"[52] betrayed Galileo's arranged plea deal. The charge was second only to formal heresy in gravity. The sentence signed by the pope banned the *Dialogue,* forced Galileo publicly to abjure his error while kneeling, submit to house arrest, and never write or speak again on the earth's movement or the stability of the sun. For the rest of his life, Galileo "expressed nothing but contempt" for those who had betrayed him.[53]

WHAT CAN WE LEARN FROM THE FIRST GREAT SCIENCE-THEOLOGY CONFLICT?

Obviously, theologians exercised considerable caution in accepting the new astronomy since it apparently conflicted with the Bible. Draper-White warfare theorists will see this as confirmation of the regressive nature of theology. But for those who considered Scripture to be the Word of God, what other choice did they have? The Bible seemed clear and the interpretive tradition was obviously on their side. Various scientific problems with Copernicanism coupled with no clearly superior predictive accuracy contributed to the widespread delay in acceptance by astronomers for more than a century.[54] The only rational and faithful course for theologians, at

---

51. Lindberg, "Galileo," 55.

52. "Inquisition's Sentence (22 June 1633)," in *The Essential Galileo*, ed. and trans. Maurice A. Finocchiaro (Indianapolis: Hackett, 2008), 292. Three of ten cardinals did not sign the judgment. Blackwell, *Behind the Scenes*, 22.

53. Blackwell, *Behind the Scenes*, 22. See also Lindberg, "Galileo," 56–57.

54. See Toulmin and Goodfield, *Fabric*, 164, 175, and Herbert Butterfield, *The Origins of Modern Science: 1300–1800*, rev. ed. (New York: The Free Press, 1957), 67. Indeed, Copernicus's work had more in common with Aristotle and Ptolemy than with Kepler and Newton. "At first glance, it is not easy to tell a page of *On the Revolutions* from a page of Ptolemy's *Almagest.*" Toulmin and Goodfield, *Fabric*, 179.

least during the first couple of generations, was to resist reinterpreting the Bible.

The Theological Conservatism Principle

Let us call this caution with respect to apparently conflicting scientific theories the theological conservatism principle. In the business world the conservatism principle (or prudence concept) ensures reliable financial statements by requiring accounting for expenses or liabilities as soon as possible, but booking revenues or assets only when actually assured. Analogously, theologians erred on the side of caution when faced with abandoning traditional biblical interpretations, and only cautiously amended those interpretations over time when clear evidence demonstrated the tradition wrong. The historical stages of the Copernican controversy revealed three ways the conservatism principle was practiced, even though theologians may not have been conscious they were doing so. The three ways are comparable to marriage considerations.

The Two Can Never Wed

The first application of the conservatism principle can be seen in the way biblical interpreters kept the apparently conflicting new science at arm's length. No faithful biblical theologian could rightly conceive of wedding a scientific theory that seemed so clearly in opposition to Scripture. As we will see in upcoming chapters, conservative theologians have always exemplified this aspect of the conservatism principle—and they should. Since I personally practice the principle, I respect those who differ in the way they apply the same principle. If convinced there is no possible way a widely held scientific theory can be reconciled with Scripture, I see no necessary reason someone should be chided for refusing to adopt it.

The Two Can Court

Over time the old astronomy became less plausible and the new seemed less theologically threatening. In this second stage the conservatism principle prevented most theologians from adopting heliocentrism outright, but they began seriously contemplating alternative scientific theories that might not imperil traditional biblical understanding. Or they even considered creative ways to approach the new astronomy itself without imperiling traditional biblical interpretation.

One way theologians explored heliocentrism was to view it instrumentally rather than in realist terms. Lutheran theologian Andreas Osiander wrote the anonymous preface to *On the Revolutions* that mitigated its potentially shocking effect. He urged readers to consider the book's ideas as mathematical speculation with only hypothetical status. Astronomers' geometrical constructions, he claimed, are not intended to reveal heavenly physical truths. The idea was common at the time: astronomers develop mathematical hypotheses for calculating planetary positions whereas natural philosophers theorize what actually cause the phenomena.[55] Osiander's move freed the reader to explore the heliocentric model in a non-threatening way, and because he didn't sign the preface, most early readers assumed Copernicus wrote it.[56] By 1620, thirty to forty European scholars had studied *On the Revolutions*. Annotations from their extant copies indicate they overwhelmingly embraced Osiander's pragmatic proposal, ensuring wide scholarly interaction with the new science.[57] Melanchthon and the Wittenberg Interpretation he inspired also followed this antirealist strategy, which later spread even to Lutheran universities in other countries

---

55. Olsen, *Science and Religion*, 10.

56. Neither Copernicus nor Rheticus, his disciple tasked with publishing *On the Revolutions*, approved this particular preface. But due to Osiander's experience with mathematical texts, Rheticus assigned him the printing job. Osiander on his own initiative wrote the antirealist-instrumentalist preface that later infuriated Rheticus. "Today we find, in every copy that [Rheticus] ever held, a livid X slashed across that page in red crayon. And yet, that letter probably allowed Copernicus' ideas to spread and touch our world as few other ideas ever did." John H. Lienhard, "No. 2420: Rheticus and Copernicus," University of Houston, College of Engineering, http://www.uh.edu/engines/epi2420.htm. Fifty years later Kepler revealed Osiander as the actual preface author. Copernicus's original preface reveals his very realist intention to confront closed-minded readers up front: "Perhaps there will be babblers who claim to be judges of astronomy although completely ignorant of the subject and, badly distorting some passage of Scripture to their purpose, will dare to find fault with my undertaking and censure it. I disregard them even to the extent of despising their criticism as unfounded." Nicholas Copernicus, *On the Revolutions*, trans. and comm. Edward Rosen, in *Nicholas Copernicus: Complete Works* (Baltimore: Johns Hopkins University Press, 1992), 5. Copernicus died without knowing that Osiander's preface preceded his own.

57. André Goddu, *Copernicus and the Aristotelian Tradition: Education, Reading, and Philosophy in Copernicus's Path to Heliocentrism* (Boston: Brill, 2010), 420.

such as that at Gdańsk, Poland. Even Cardinal Bellarmine approved an instrumental approach in his interaction with Galileo.

Alternate and hybrid scientific models were equally significant in the long, slow courtship of Copernicanism. The great Lutheran astronomer Tycho Brahe developed the most significant of these synthesized approaches. Because of his open-minded view of the new science, he creatively adopted as much Copernicanism possible while remaining true to his understanding of the Bible. Tycho's geoheliocentric model envisioned the sun orbiting a motionless earth centered in the universe, but the rest of the planets orbited the sun. At Gdańsk professors debated and considered a dizzying array of astronomical alternatives, including Copernican, semi-Copernican or Tychonic, semi-Tychonic, and semi-Ptolemaic.[58] Even Catholic thinkers adopted the hybrid Tychonic model after *On the Revolutions* was placed on the Index of forbidden books.

In coming chapters we will find this courtship phase of the conservatism principle recurring frequently, even when its practitioners were unaware. Alternative theories can be useful for careful exploration of difficult but important challenges. Hybridized theories can be scientific or doctrinal or combinations of both, all usually serving to retain traditional biblical interpretations as long as they remain tenable. But to accommodate complex data, these "ad hoc modifications" typically combine facets of disparate models, often leading to suspicions about the stability or even orthodoxy of the new model.[59] Seasons like our age of the earth controversy when hybrids abound surely are confusing and contentious. And if particular scientific theories and biblical interpretations seem impossible to reconcile, this may signal they have no business courting.

The conservatism principle exemplified in the considerable time theologians took considering the new science points to the central methodological issue at stake: epistemological authority. How should human

---

58. Christine Jones Schofield, *The Geoheliocentric Planetary System: Its Development and Influence in the Late 16th and 17th Centuries* (unpublished dissertation, Cambridge University, Newnham College, 1964), 176–77; Edward Grant, *In Defense of the Earth's Centrality and Immobility,* Transactions of the American Philosophical Society (Philadelphia: American Philosophical Society, 1984), 5–20.

59. Hybrid scientific models are similar to Thomas Kuhn's "ad hoc modifications" of theories in his well-known *The Structure of Scientific Revolutions*, 2nd ed. (Chicago: University of Chicago Press, 1970), 78.

reason and perception relate to the authority of the Bible?[60] Specifically, should cosmological truths be established based on science or theology, or a combination of the two?[61] Ironically the key figure in the most famous science-theology conflict, Galileo, conceived and offered a proposal. His plan not only pertained to his own conflict but also to all such conflicts in the future. Who could have known more would come? Ironically, his own controversy would be settled after his lifetime through unconscious application of his proffered solution. Galileo's methodology for resolving science-theology conflicts is itself the embodiment of the conservatism principle.

The Two Can Wed on These Terms: Galileo's Proposal

Copernicanism did not correct the Bible, but scientific truth corrected biblical interpretation *and* science. But how? No leader announced a way to solve the controversy with everyone suddenly agreeing. No one then could have dreamed of winning support for a proposal that science should control biblical interpretation. What's clear is that the solution did not follow from interpreting scientific facts based on biblical study.

In fact, no conscious application of interpretive principles led to resolution of the Copernican controversy. Several generations of hard fought battles preceded the conclusion. Only after Newton's *Principia* was published in 1687 did the pieces come together such that the Copernican controversy could wind down. After that time, as we will see in chapter 10, the new astronomy (and physics) was taught in New England by Puritan pastors. Biblical language describing a moving sun and immobile earth was seen to be phenomenologically rather than technically descriptive.

So, though Galileo proposed a way to work through potential science-theology conflicts, I'm aware of no controversy ever settled by its intentional application. On the other hand, his idealistic proposal accurately describes the historical process by which conservative Christians have worked through science-theology debates until this day. Even when creationists have professed allegiance to a different approach, the historical

---

60. Lindberg, "Galileo," 58.
61. Ibid., 48, 58.

evidence reveals that the inherent process they practiced is what Galileo proposed.[62]

Seeing theological trouble brewing, Galileo spelled out his proposal in his "Letter to Castelli" (1613) and "Letter to the Grand Duchess Christina" (1615). He suggested an elegant interpretive procedure utilizing two fundamental assumptions and two interpretive steps to resolve science-theology clashes.

Galileo's Assumption 1:
Assume Biblical Inerrancy, Not Inerrant Interpretation

Galileo argued "that Holy Scripture can never lie, as long as its true meaning has been grasped."[63] He understood why theological geocentrists believed that "since in many places in the Holy Scripture one reads that the sun moves and the earth stands still, and since Scripture can never lie or err, it follows as a necessary consequence that the opinion of those who want to assert the sun to be motionless and the earth moving is erroneous and damnable."[64]

But Galileo also stressed "though Scripture cannot err, nevertheless some of its interpreters and expositors can sometimes err in various ways."[65] Not all of Scripture ought to be interpreted literally since this leads not only to "various contradictions but also serious heresies and blasphemies" such as attributing human body parts to God. Wise teachers provide reasons for interpreting biblical passages nonliterally, and wise readers recognize scriptural language is divinely accommodated to the capacities of ordinary people and should not be read as a scientific text.[66]

---

62. Many have understood Galileo to propose that science always trumps the Bible. But his proposal was very different. I have no interest in guessing how he would handle science-theology controversies today, just what he actually proposed.

63. Galileo, "Christina," 115.

64. Ibid.

65. Galileo Galilei, "Letter to Castelli (1613)," in *The Essential Galileo,* ed. and trans. Maurice A. Finocchiaro (Indianapolis: Hackett, 2008), 104. Galileo's assumption suggests familiarity with points Kepler previously made in the introduction to his *New Astronomy.* But as a Catholic, Galileo would have been foolhardy to cite a Lutheran. Gingerich, "Revolution," 102; Blackwell, "Galileo," 111.

66. Galileo, "Christina," 115.

Galileo's Assumption 2:
Nature and Scripture Cannot Disagree

Since God is the author of the book of nature and the book of Scripture, they cannot conflict when rightly interpreted. And when they apparently contradict, theologians should not necessarily be the only arbiters. Of course, theology is the queen of the sciences. Its subject matter is the salvation of souls, "which, surpassing all human reason, could not be discovered by scientific research or by any other means than through the mouth of the Holy Spirit himself." [67] But in matters such as geometry, astronomy, music, and medicine, theologians are not more expert than specialists in those fields. Galileo had illustrated his specialty in seeking to demonstrate the impossibility of a geocentric interpretation of Joshua's long day (Joshua 10). If the old astronomy were true, Joshua's command would have actually shortened the day.[68] In spite of the Council of Trent, Galileo rejected appeals to the fathers. The issues at stake are not articles of faith and the fathers wrote before the new discoveries.[69]

Galileo's Interpretive Step 1:
Traditional Biblical Interpretations Govern Unproven Science

For Galileo, biblical statements pertaining to scientific matters have authority over "any human works" supported by only "probable reasons."[70] Such human theories when apparently contrary to Holy Scripture "must be considered indubitably false" if not demonstrably proven.[71] Galileo's position here epitomizes the conservatism principle: if in doubt, stick with the Bible. The step also assumes that scientific theories can be errant interpretations of nature.

---

67. Ibid., 117.

68. Ibid., 141–43. See Blackwell, "Galileo," 110. Educated Christian geocentrists, a distinct minority today, both grant and resist Galileo's argument. See "Joshua's Long Day," http://www.geocentricity.com/astronomy_of_bible/jld/.

69. Galileo Galilei, "Galileo's Considerations on the Copernican Opinion, Part II," in *The Essential Galileo,* ed. and trans. Maurice A. Finocchiaro (Indianapolis: Hackett, 2008), 160–63.

70. Galileo, "Christina," 117.

71. Ibid., 126.

Galileo's Interpretive Step 2:
Proven Scientific Theory Requires Biblical Reinterpretation

This step follows from the second presupposition, that God's two books rightly interpreted cannot contradict. If the science is demonstrably true, then the conflicting biblical interpretation must be wrong. Step 2 actually protects against undermining the Bible by (mis)interpreting it to speak what is false.

Galileo believed he had already demonstrated the impossibility of a geocentric reading of Joshua's long day. But the geocentrists continued to insist on the traditional interpretation since they believed a multitude of passages are so clear they cannot be interpreted any other way. Galileo responded that traditional astronomy will become more widely discredited. So insistence on the traditional biblical interpretation and prohibiting the new science will confuse unbelievers and harm their souls by making it sinful to believe something proven true not essential to the faith. "For how can they believe our books in regards to the resurrection of the dead, the hope of eternal life, and the kingdom of heaven, when they catch a Christian committing an error about something they know very well . . . things they have already been able to observe or to establish by unquestionable argument?"[72] If the Holy Spirit never intended to reveal biblically the structure of the heavens, why should geocentrism be regarded as so important and heliocentrism so erroneous? In support, Galileo cited the late Cardinal Cesare Baronio that "the intention of the Holy Spirit is to teach us how one goes to heaven and not how the heaven goes."[73]

The Devil Is in the Details

Ironically, Galileo violated one of his own principles by arguing for reinterpreting Scripture before heliocentrism had actually been proven.[74] Even if Ptolemaic astronomy had been proven false, options such as Tycho's

---

72. Ibid., 138.

73. Ibid., 119. On Cardinal Baronius (1538–1607) and his possible conversation with Galileo, see Gingerich, "Revolution," 102, and Blackwell, "Galileo," 111.

74. Galileo Galilei, "Galileo's Considerations on the Copernican Opinion, Part III," in *The Essential Galileo,* ed. and trans. Maurice A. Finocchiaro (Indianapolis: Hackett, 2008), 166.

geoheliocentrism were rational alternatives to Copernicanism. The majority of qualified astronomers were not yet Copernicans, and Galileo's rhetorical brilliance could not mask heliocentrism's unproven status. Vatican theologians were backed into a corner with no choice but to reject the new science.[75]

Applying Galileo's hermeneutic has proven far more problematic than he ever imagined. Philosophers of science debate what even constitutes scientific rationality and justifies theory-change.[76] No doubt this problem explains not only why new scientific theories have not triumphed overnight, but also why theologians historically hold contrary science theories at arm's length. With the devil in the details of step 2, little wonder conservative theologians have intuitively thought the step illegitimate—even if they have historically practiced it, as we will see.

GOD AND HUMANS AT WORK IN THE GALILEO AFFAIR

Catholic-Protestant tensions lurk decisively in the background of the Galileo affair. Concerns regarding authority in biblical interpretation virtually guaranteed that the strong-willed Galileo would clash with the Vatican. In the end, Galileo's actual trial had more to with "disobedience and flagrant insubordination" than a science-theology conflict.[77] Arguably, one hundred years earlier or later, the Galileo affair likely would not have happened.[78]

Even if Galileo had been more diplomatic, he "might well have carried out a significant campaign on behalf of heliocentrism without condemnation."[79] His rhetorical gifts, perhaps the greatest in the annals of science,

---

75. Lindberg, "Galileo, 48–49. On the ambiguous and clever way Galileo referenced Copernicanism as proven, see J. Dietz Moss, "The Rhetoric of Proof in Galileo's Writings on the Copernican System," in *"The Galileo Affair: A Meeting of Faith and Science,"* ed. G. V. Coyne, M. Heller, and J. Zycinsky (Vatican City State: Specola Vaticana, 1985), 42–56.

76. John Worrall, "Theory-Change in Science," in *The Routledge Companion to Philosophy of Science*, ed. Stathis Psillos and Martin Curd (New York: Routledge, 2008), 281–91. Galileo can be forgiven for naïve standards of proof by today's standards (sensory experience, "necessary demonstrations," and "unquestionable argument"). See Galileo, "Letter to the Grand Duchess," 104–106, 138; and idem, "Galileo's Considerations on the Copernican Opinion, Part III," 166.

77. Lindberg, "Galileo," 54.

78. Blackwell, "Galileo," 108. Cf. Lindberg, "Galileo," 44–45.

79. Lindberg, "Galileo," 57.

could not ameliorate a "vehement and stubborn" demeanor.[80] His "arrogant, impetuous style seems, on balance, to have been more effective in stirring up trouble and making enemies than (as he had hoped) in calming the waters."[81] Galileo's personality and the pope's injured pride, coupled with misinformation regarding Galileo's 1616 restriction, proved key in the most (tragically) famous science-theology conflict.[82]

But a Christian knows God, not humanity, has the final say in the outworking of history. In God's providence Galileo's house arrest led him late in life to work on decades-old ideas that formed his *Discourses on Two New Sciences* (1638). "These writings were his most substantive contributions to physics in the long run, and in effect laid the groundwork for Newton's later theoretical justification of the Copernicanism which Galileo had been forbidden to discuss."[83]

CONCLUSION

As opposed to widespread misunderstanding, all involved in the Copernican conflict "called himself a Christian; and all, without exception, acknowledged the authority of the Bible."[84] Thus the Copernican "conflict was located as much *within* the church (between opposing theories of biblical interpretation) and *within* science (between alternative cosmologies) as *between* science and the church."[85]

---

80. Ibid., 47. Cited from Jerome Langford, *Galileo, Science, and the Church,* rev. ed. (Ann Arbor, MI: University of Michigan Press, 1966), 86–87. On Galileo's rhetorical gifts, see Lindberg, "Galileo," 41.

81. Lindberg, "Galileo," 47.

82. The pope later blamed Galileo for provoking Christendom's greatest scandal. Blackwell, *Behind the Scenes,* 27. Simultaneous human factors compounding turmoil surrounding Galileo's incendiary *Dialogue* were the Thirty Years' War, Spain's controlling half of Italy, and the pope facing much criticism on other fronts. Olson, *Science and Religion,* 17–18; Lindberg, "Galileo," 52–53. Lindberg concludes that "the outcome of the Galileo affair was a product not of dogmatism or intolerance beyond the norm, but of a combination of more or less standard (for the seventeenth century) bureaucratic procedure, plausible (if ultimately flawed) political judgment, and a familiar array of human foibles and failings." Ibid., 60.

83. Blackwell, *Behind the Scenes,* 27.

84. Lindberg, "Galileo," 58.

85. Ibid. Emphasis his.

A historical rationality in evidence by which Christians worked through the apparent science-theology conflict can be called the conservatism principle. This debate process revealed three logical responses that we will see repeated frequently in coming chapters. The basic intuition of the conservatism principle was "the two can never wed" response. When convinced no reconciliation of a scientific theory with Scripture was possible, theologians rightly rejected the theory. But when aspects of the new theory seemed plausible, theologians cautiously adopted "the two can court" approach. Traditional biblical interpretation might be retained but alternative scientific theories creatively explored. "The two can wed on these terms: Galileo's proposal" employed two assumptions (the Bible is inerrant, and biblical and natural truth cannot conflict) and two interpretive steps (unless conflicting scientific theory is proven, retain traditional biblical interpretation; and if the theory is proven, the traditional interpretation is in error).

Without question, this last interpretive step, though practiced to this day by even the most conservative Christians, is the most difficult to recognize as it happens—much less agree on how to employ it. And the way this lack of agreement is handled not only led to that which embarrasses Christians about the Galileo affair, but also to problems in our own day. Biblical Christians must make difficult decisions where to draw theological boundaries, but how they do so is crucial too.

Chapter 3

DARWINISM:
A New Kind of Controversy Altogether

> Can the mind of man, which has, as I fully believe, been developed
> from a mind as low as that possessed by the lowest animal, be
> trusted when it draws such grand [Darwinian] conclusions? [1]
> —Charles Darwin, *The Autobiography of Charles Darwin*

WORLDVIEWS, SCIENCE, AND DARWINISM

During the Copernicanism debate, all the key figures shared a bibli-cal worldview. The controversy ensued precisely because they sought biblical fidelity while facing a seemingly contradictory new theory. Yet Melanchthon spoke of cherishing astronomy for revealing God in his orderly heavens.[2] Kepler considered scientific work itself as worship of the living God. The creation's comprehensibility beckoned study because God desired to share his thoughts thereby.[3] He even viewed using the scientific discoveries of unbelievers as "stealing the golden vessels of the Egyptians

---

1. Charles Darwin, *The Autobiography of Charles Darwin: 1809–1882*, ed. Nora Barlow (London: Collins, 1958), 93.
2. Robert S. Westman, "The Melanchthon Circle, Rheticus and the Wittenberg Interpretation of the Copernican Theory," *Isis* 66 (1975): 169–70.
3. Christopher Kaiser, *Creation and the History of Science* (Grand Rapids: Eerdmans, 1991), 122–23, 126–27. Kepler considered *The Harmony of the World* (1619) his most important book. Astronomers consider its third law of planetary motion most significant, but Kepler devoted enormous energy to describing how planetary geometric relations in terms of nested polyhedra and musical harmonies reveal the Creator's wisdom. Johannes Kepler, *The Harmony of the World*, trans. E. J. Aiton, J. M. Duncan, and A. V. Field,

to build a tabernacle to my God from them, far, far away from the boundaries of Egypt."[4] Newton declared his scientific work as evidence for God, supplementing the rich natural theology tradition of his day.[5]

During Charles Robert Darwin's day (1809–1882) a biblical worldview was no longer considered requisite for science. Already preceding him were evolutionary ideas "firmly linked to materialism, atheism, and radical politics."[6] Materialists such as Georges-Louis Leclerc De Buffon (1707–1784) and Denis Diderot (1713–1784) contended that strictly natural forces might create life and produce species change. Darwin's grandfather, Erasmus Darwin (1731–1802), and Jean Baptiste Lamarck (1744–1829) presented comprehensive naturalistic theories of slow species transmutation. Some like Robert Chambers (1802–1871) sought to dissociate atheism from evolutionary thought, proclaiming the latter as an unfolding divine plan. The 1859 publication of Darwin's *On the Origin of Species*, however, dramatically changed everything with "a new and even potentially more materialistic mechanism of evolution."[7] Some of its doctrines eventually produced the most dramatic worldview shift ever caused by a scientific treatise.[8]

THE SHAPING OF DARWIN'S WORLDVIEW

Did Darwin view his theory as undermining belief in a personal God? Many writers rightly note that family tragedy and objection to certain

---

Memoirs of the American Philosophical Society, vol. 209 (Philadelphia: American Philosophical Society, 1997), viii and xxxviii.

4. Kepler, *Harmony*, 391.

5. John Locke later observed that he had known no one who knew Scripture better than Newton. Newton's manuscripts reveal he worked far more on theology than science; he even mastered the early church fathers. But these same theological manuscripts, only widely available to scholars since the late twentieth century, reveal his privately but vehemently held anti-Trinitarianism. Richard S. Westfall, "Isaac Newton," in *Science and Religion: A Historical Introduction*, ed. Gary Ferngren (Baltimore: Johns Hopkins University Press, 2002), 154–60.

6. Peter J. Bowler, "Evolution," in *Science and Religion: A Historical Introduction*, ed. Gary Ferngren (Baltimore: Johns Hopkins University Press, 2002), 221.

7. Ibid., 222.

8. C. Kenneth Waters, "The Arguments in the *Origin of Species*," in *The Cambridge Companion to Darwin*, 2nd ed., ed. Jonathan Hodge and Gregory Radick (New York: Cambridge University Press, 2009), 121.

Christian doctrines played a role in his eventual agnosticism. But it would be overstated to say his loss of faith and his science were unrelated.[9] Darwin denied his version of evolution was necessarily atheistic, but by 1868 believed it incompatible with a providential Creator. He also knew his theory raised momentous questions for human beings, as seen in the epigraph above. Philosophers still debate those questions: "Do our apparently unique capacities for language, reason and morality point to a divine spark within us, or to ancestral animal legacies still in evidence in our simian relatives?"[10] Eventually Darwin became more explicit in denying God any meaningful role in the world, permitting his name to support a group that sought "the extinction of faith in the Christian Confession" and the development of a humanistic religion. Darwin allowed publication of his agreement to "almost every word" of their doctrines.[11]

Darwin's Family and Educational Influences

Darwin's family did not view his grandfather Erasmus as a skeleton in their closet. Charles's father celebrated the name and books of the famous first "Darwinist." In turn, Charles revered his father Robert, "a man his children knew to be religiously no believer."[12] Charles's mother Susannah and

---

9. John Hedley Brooke, "Darwin and Victorian Christianity," in *The Cambridge Companion to Darwin,* 2nd ed., ed. Jonathan Hodge and Gregory Radick (New York: Cambridge University Press, 2009), 200, 205.

10. Jonathan Hodge and Gregory Radick, "Introduction," in *The Cambridge Companion to Darwin,* 2nd ed., ed. Jonathan Hodge and Gregory Radick (New York: Cambridge University Press, 2009), 1.

11. James Moore, "Charles Darwin," in *Science and Religion: A Historical Introduction,* ed. Gary Ferngren (Baltimore: Johns Hopkins University Press, 2002), 214. See also Jon Roberts, *Darwinism and the Divine in America: Protestant Intellectuals and Organic Evolution, 1859–1900* (Madison, WI: University of Wisconsin Press, 1988), 80. Theologians' suspicions that Darwin's theory itself had destroyed his faith seemed confirmed with the posthumous publication of *Life and Letters of Charles Darwin* (1887). See Roberts, *Darwinism,* 80, 99. The story of his deathbed conversion is false, but its rapid and widespread dissemination reveal the antipathy of American evangelicals toward Darwinism in the early twentieth century. See James Moore, *The Darwin Legend* (Grand Rapids: Baker, 1994), and idem, "Telling Tales: Evangelicals and the Darwin Legend," in *Evangelicals and Science in Historical Perspective,* ed. David N. Livingston, D. G. Hart, and Mark A. Noll (New York: Oxford University Press, 1990), 220–33; and idem, "Charles Darwin," 1–20.

12. Jonathan Hodge, "London Notebook: Programmes and Projects," in *The*

his sisters were Unitarians, believing in a Creator but rejecting the divinity of Christ. Unitarians promoted Enlightenment philosophical, scientific, and political ideas, earning them the distrust of conservative Christians. Grandfather Erasmus simply viewed Unitarianism "a featherbed to catch a falling Christian."[13] Undoubtedly both the male and female sides of his family shaped the complex relationship Charles had with Christianity his entire life.[14]

Charles studied medicine at the University of Edinburgh for two years before losing interest. But his introduction to marine invertebrate anatomy from Britain's leading invertebrate zoologist Robert Grant also familiarized him with theories undermining the fixity of species.[15] Darwin later recounted how on a walk the atheist Grant "burst forth in high admiration of Lamarck and his views on evolution. I listened in silent astonishment, and as far as I can judge, without any effect on my mind. I had previously read the *Zoönomia* of my grandfather, in which similar views are maintained, but without producing any effect on me. Nevertheless it is probable that the hearing rather early in life such views maintained and praised may have favoured my upholding them under a different form in my *Origin of Species.*"[16]

Accepting that Charles was not cut out to be a physician, his father recommended he consider becoming a clergyman. So Charles spent three years at the University of Cambridge preparing for Anglican ministry. There Darwin demonstrated competence in works such as William Paley's *Evidences of Christianity* as well as one of the four Gospels or the Acts of the Apostles in Greek.[17] Years later he noted he could translate the Greek New Testament "with moderate facility,"[18] and how the various works of Paley had delighted him. But he added, "I did not at that time trouble

Cambridge Companion to Darwin, 2nd ed., ed. Jonathan Hodge and Gregory Radick (New York: Cambridge University Press, 2009), 50.

13. Adrian Desmond and James Moore, *Darwin: The Life of a Tormented Evolutionist* (New York: W. W. Norton & Company, 1994), 5.

14. Phillip R. Sloan, "The Making of a Philosophical Naturalist," in *The Cambridge Companion to Darwin,* 2nd ed., ed. Jonathan Hodge and Gregory Radick (New York: Cambridge University Press, 2009), 22.

15. Moore, "Charles Darwin," 209; Hodge, "London Notebook," 49.

16. Darwin, *Autobiography,* 49.

17. Sloan, "The Making," 26.

18. Darwin, *Autobiography,* 57.

myself about Paley's premises; and taking these on trust I was charmed and convinced by the long line of argumentation."[19] He also "did not then in the least doubt the strict and literal truth of every word in the Bible," and soon persuaded himself "that our Creed must be fully accepted. It never struck me how illogical it was to say that I believed in what I could not understand and what is in fact unintelligible."[20] Later the irony of his Cambridge degree did not escape him when conservative clergy became some of his biggest foes.[21]

Though theology had little lasting impact, Darwin's scientific development at Cambridge was critical. The clergyman-geologist Adam Sedgwick took him on geological excursions, providing skills critical for his later work. John Herschel's *Introduction to the Study of Natural Philosophy* inspired Darwin to dedicate his life to search systematically for "true causes" in nature, not just mental hypotheses.[22] *The Personal Narrative* of Alexander von Humboldt provided Charles with a vision for "general theorizing on the grandest scale" by searching for relations between geology, geography, and biology.[23]

Five Years Exploring the World and Five Years Exploring the Implications

Recognizing Darwin's gifts and commitment, Sedgwick secured him an invitation for a five-year surveying voyage as the ship's resident naturalist. Darwin and the world would never be the same.[24] Journeying around the world on the HMS *Beagle*, Darwin studied and collected marine organisms and geological specimens. He encountered native peoples so different from his educated world, he wondered whether they had been that way since creation. Rereading Charles Lyell's *Principles of Geology* convinced Darwin to document geological changes in the earth's animate and inanimate

19. Ibid., 59.
20. Ibid., 57.
21. Ibid.
22. Sloan, "The Making," 28.
23. Ibid., 29.
24. Darwin himself recognized later the significance of his journey. Darwin, *Autobiography*, 76. Before the voyage, and during it, Darwin's reading of Lyell's *Principles of Geology* steeped him in what was later dubbed uniformitarianism. Extinctions in the fossil record should only be explained by forces operating today at the same intensities.

history, explaining them only by currently operating laws. Herschel, whom Darwin met at Cape Town, profoundly influenced Darwin by advocating natural rather than supernatural explanations for the appearance of new species in the fossil record.

Voyage documents reveal nothing of Darwin's thoughts on the transmutation of species, but reflections on his experiences soon after his return are revealing.[25] His publication of the *Beagle Diary* suggests that on the journey his analysis of extinct and living animals led him to accept common descent: "This wonderful relationship in the same continent between the dead and the living, to accept common descent will, I do not doubt, hereafter throw more light on the appearance of organic beings on our earth, and their disappearance from it, than any other class of facts."[26] The *Beagle Diary* made Darwin a public figure. His reputation as a naturalist grew further from his remarkable bird, fish, insect, and plant collections.

Darwin's five years after his arrival home seem just as important intellectually as the half-decade spent on the HMS *Beagle*. This productive but extremely private period is now called the notebook years. Darwin kept small leather-bound notebooks in which he developed his exceptionally consequential thinking on geology, the laws of life (including the transmutation of species), the theory of mind, and morality. He kept these theories secret, especially at first.[27] Evolution had become extremely controversial because radical naturalists wielded it "as a political weapon for attacking miracle-mongering creationists" believed to be strangling science.[28] Darwin became "a closet evolutionist."[29]

---

25. Sloan, "The Making," 38–39.

26. Charles Darwin, *Journal of Researches into the Natural History and Geology of the countries visited during the voyage round the world of H. M. S. Beagle* (London: John Murray, 1860), 173. The better-known title, *The Voyage of the Beagle*, came to be used after an edition in 1905.

27. Since the 1960s, study of these materials transformed scholarly understanding of Darwin. Instead of through the lens of his later autobiography or from his correspondence from this period, these notebooks reveal his private thoughts in their original contexts. See Hodge, "London Notebook," 41.

28. Moore, "Charles Darwin," 210–11.

29. Ibid., 211. Darwin's notebook strategy to deflect the consequences of his theory was to suggest a creator operating by natural law is superior to one fighting his own laws via miraculous creation. Hodge, "London Notebook," 61–62.

The Darwin of the notebooks is not just the scientist whose analysis of his fossil materials and journey notes led to writing *Origin of Species*. For example, in the notebook on mind, Darwin reveals that he has become a philosophical materialist. Brain function alone explains human thought, and free will is an illusion. The ramifications of this move were momentous. "Having subsumed mind materially and causally within his science at this time, Darwin never later had to construct new ways to secure the continuity between man and animals or between man and the lawful order of nature."[30] Because humans are animals fully explicable by science with no divine spark, even our belief in God results from the slow, gradual development of our animal ancestry.

In his later autobiography, Darwin reminisces how while on the *Beagle* he began doubting the Old Testament. The notebooks reveal Darwin abandoning Christianity altogether. Daydreaming a dramatic archaeological discovery might prove Christianity true, he eventually couldn't imagine any evidence able to convince him. By age 40 he had washed his hands of Christianity.[31] By life's end Darwin could "hardly see how anyone ought to wish Christianity to be true; for if so the plain language of the text seems to show that the men who do not believe, and this would include my Father, Brother and almost all my best friends, will be everlastingly punished. And this is a damnable doctrine."[32] Though the wonder of the universe kept him from atheism, his doubts about theism led to his professed agnosticism. Even in this conclusion, however, he was haunted by his famous doubt, wondering "can the mind of man, which has, as I fully believe, been developed from a mind as low as that possessed by the lowest animal, be trusted when it draws such grand conclusions?"[33] Late

---

30. Hodge, "London Notebook," 61–62.

31. Moore, "Charles Darwin," 216.

32. Darwin, *Autobiography*, 87. His wife Emma originally had this quotation deleted from the *Autobiography* since it seemed "raw" and few would think it Christian. And though she agreed that the doctrine of everlasting punishment was biblical, she could reject it because she rejected verbal biblical inspiration. Ibid., n. 1.

33. Ibid., 93, 94. He adds: "May not these [thoughts] be the result of the connection between cause and effect which strikes us as a necessary one, but probably depends merely on inherited experience? Nor must we overlook the probability of the constant inculcation in a belief in God on the minds of children producing so strong and perhaps an inherited effect on their brains not yet fully developed, that it would be as difficult for them to throw off their belief in God, as for a monkey to throw off its instinctive fear and hatred of

in life Darwin candidly assessed his final worldview. "Nothing is more remarkable than the spread of skepticism or rationalism during the latter half of my life."[34]

DARWINISM: A THEORY THAT SHAPED THE WORLD

Prior to the nineteenth century, belief in fixed species dominated the scientific landscape. Most thinkers held that stable species displayed design in their intricate features. For two centuries prior to the *Origin of Species*, the argument from design formed the backbone of Anglo-American apologetics, notably in William Paley's *Natural Theology* (1802). Scientists contributed by utilizing theological terms justifying their scientific inquiry.[35] John Ray's *The Wisdom of God Manifested in the Works of Creation* (1691) maintained that each species was created by God perfectly adapted to its environment. Robert Boyle contended that "there is incomparably more Art express'd in the structure of a Doggs foot, than in that of the famous Clock at *Strasburg*."[36]

But especially following Georges Cuvier's (1769–1832) work, awareness grew that significantly different species had become extinct in the past. And following them apparently new species appeared in the fossil record. Why would God allow any of his creatures to become extinct? Had God created new species at various times to replace them? And why did some of these extinct creations seem oddly similar yet so different from those living?

---

a snake." After his death Emma also had the monkey-snake illustration withdrawn from publication. Ibid., n. 2.

34. Ibid., 95. The notebooks reveal his very candid worries about his illnesses and about inbreeding since he married his first cousin Emma. But the notebooks reveal no concern for life after death. He suffered from headaches, stomach trouble, and insomnia such that Emma became not only mother to his ten children but also his "full-time nurse." Moore, "Charles Darwin, 212. A serious breakdown followed his father's death in 1848 from which he recovered several months later. But the death of his 10-year-old daughter Annie in 1851 led to his final break with Christianity. Hodge, "London Notebook," 62–63.

35. Roberts, *Darwinism*, 8.

36. Robert Boyle, *A Disquisition about the Final Causes of Natural Things: Wherein It Is Inquir'd, Whether, And (if At All) Withy What Cautions, a Naturalist Should Admit Them?"* (London: John Taylor, 1688), cited in Gregory Radick, "Independence, History and Natural Selection," in *The Cambridge Companion to Darwin*, 2nd ed., ed. Jonathan Hodge and Gregory Radick (New York: Cambridge University Press, 2009), 156.

Darwin answered with a bombshell in *On the Origin of Species* (1859).[37] His answers were averse to the notion of an active creator, but the earliest editions did not make this readily apparent. Eschewing the word "evolution" in the first five editions, Darwin readily employed "creation" or its cognates more than one hundred times.[38] Opposite the title page were two carefully selected quotes. The first by the influential William Whewell is "audaciously taken out of context"[39] from the well-known Bridgewater Treatises commissioned to explore God's design in nature. The quote can be interpreted that Whewell agreed with Darwin that God operated only through natural law.[40] The other from Francis Bacon reads, "let no man out of a weak conceit of sobriety, or an ill-applied moderation, think or maintain, that a man can search too far or be too well studied in the book of God's Word, or in the book of God's works; divinity or philosophy; but rather let men endeavour an endless progress or proficience in both."[41] Yet despite allusions to God and "creation" in the *Origin of Species*, Darwin not only abandoned the notion of fixed species, he also left no room for God's explicitly active involvement in evolutionary processes.

Scholars differ on the exact way to conceive Darwin's argument in the *Origin of Species*, but the main points are clear.[42] He explains that extinct

---

37. Alfred Russell Wallace (1823–1913) had been working on the same ideas as Darwin. Wallace, however, was not aware of it until much later when he met Darwin. Because he recognized Darwin had worked longer and with so much more depth, he allowed Darwin to take the lead in publishing *The Origin of Species*. See Alfred Russell Wallace, *Contributions to the Theory of Natural Selection, A Series of Essays* (London: Macmillan and Co., 1875), iv–v.

38. Moore, "Charles Darwin," 213; Jean Gayon, "From Darwin to Today in Evolutionary Biology," in *The Cambridge Companion to Darwin*, 2nd ed., ed. Jonathan Hodge and Gregory Radick (New York: Cambridge University Press, 2009), 279–80.

39. Janet Browne, *Charles Darwin: The Power of Place* (New York: Alfred Knopf, 2002), 80.

40. The quote: "But with regard to the material world, we can at least go so far as this—we can perceive that events are brought about not by insulated interpositions of Divine power, exerted in each particular case, but by the establishment of general laws." For a discussion whether Darwin quoted Whewell in context, see the comments at http://www.uncommondescent.com/intelligent-design/shoehorning-darwin-into-an-otherwise-legitimate-history-of-a-science-movement/.

41. A comprehensive resource for all things Darwin, including online access to various editions of *The Origin of Species*, can be found at Darwin Online, http://darwin-online.org.uk/.

42. The broader debate usually has to do with whether Darwin presented one long

species radically different from living species are nonetheless related. In evidence he notes that locations of living species contain fossils most similar, with the most recent fossils being most similar to living species.[43] Darwin also notes that his view explains why extinct species do not reappear. All species, extinct or not, are related by natural causes that have produced the necessary, and sometimes dramatic, transformations. How can natural causes do so much creative work?

Species grow at a geometric rate but are checked by environmental factors (lack of food, predators, etc.). Individuals with environmentally advantageous variations tend to survive better and leave more offspring. Offspring inheriting the superior adaptive variations eventually become the new local species. Darwin labeled this tendency "natural selection" in analogy with "artificial selection." The first four chapters of the *Origin of Species* carefully make the case that what humans intentionally do in plant and animal breeding also occurs naturally and unintentionally. But nature more comprehensively "selects" due to vastly greater time, thus producing radical transformations. Eventually descendant species may differ enough from each other and their progenitors to be different species. The same natural selective pressures that evolve new species may also eliminate intermediate varieties.[44]

Natural selection then produces two primary effects: (a) the transmutation of species, and (b) common descent, evolved species descending from earlier species. Darwin illustrated the branching off of species with his powerful but only illustration in the *Origin of Species*, the tree of life.[45] The buds represent existing species, and the limbs and trunk signify earlier species in the line of descent. Some branches become dead ends, indicating

---

argument as he thought, or whether the tree of life case is made apart from natural selection as its true cause. Waters, "The Arguments," 127, 141.

43. Charles Darwin, *The Origin of Species* (New York: Signet Classics, 2003 [1859]), 345–74.

44. See especially ibid., 60–127.

45. Ibid., 110. Contrast Darwin's ideas as powerfully illustrated in his tree of life diagram with Copernicanism, which was difficult for even sympathetic astronomers, including Galileo, to grasp. The Dutch Copernican Martin Hortensius believed the work would not have been so readily condemned if astronomers had presented its teaching more popularly utilizing visualizable material globes. See Robert S. Westman, *The Copernican Question: Prognostication, Skepticism, and Celestial Order* (Berkeley, CA: University of California Press, 2011), 141.

extinct species. Darwin's evolutionary model differed from others in that not only do species change, they also form new species. And he made clear the origin of his species differed fundamentally from traditional creation views. "I believe the animals are descended from at most only four or five progenitors, and plants from an equal or lesser number."[46] And ultimately natural selection could even explain how "all the organic beings which have ever lived on this earth may be descended from some one primordial form."[47] In this final case, Darwin is arguing for (c) universal common descent: natural selection produced an incredible array of life forms that long ago descended from a universal common ancestor. If one can trace far enough back to the roots of the tree, all living things, including humans, ultimately have come from the same root.

More than a century and a half after Darwin published *The Origin of Species* debates remain regarding how best to understand the details of contemporary Darwinism (Neo-Darwinism). But disputes about group versus individual selection or the role of mass extinctions do not mean a debate remains about Darwinism as such. The overwhelming academic consensus is that even if Darwin got some details wrong, his major "thinking about evolution has constantly been rectified rather than refuted."[48] Twentieth-century discoveries in genetics "constituted the major intellectual event in the history of theorizing about natural selection after Darwin,"[49] and many other fields have become part of the neo-Darwinian synthesis. The scientific community repeatedly reminds the public that "evolution" is not going away. But before examining evangelical interaction with Darwinism, the first-generation scientific reaction provides clues why conservative Christians have been slow to embrace it.

Initial Scientific Reaction to Darwinism

Darwin's ideas initially faced strong resistance both scientifically and philosophically. Lyell, Herschel, Whewell, Sedgwick, and many others resisted the notion that species are infinitely malleable. Actually, Darwin seemed

---

46. Darwin, *The Origin*, 502.
47. Ibid.
48. Gayon, "From Darwin to Today," 297.
49. Ibid., 288.

to dispose of the species concept altogether. Questions about the tempo of evolutionary change, as well as concerns about probability and chance in Darwinism were debated then (and now). Lyell refused to endorse Darwin's theory publicly. But other issues disturbed many intellectuals, including non-Christians, which continue to concern evangelicals today.[50]

The biggest initial controversy pertained to the descent of humans from lower animals. Darwin hinted in *The Origin of Species* that his theory would one day revolutionize the understanding of humanity. "In the future I see open fields for far more important researches. Psychology will be securely based on the foundation already well laid by Mr. Herbert Spencer, that of the necessary acquirement of each mental power and capacity by gradation. Much light will be thrown on the origin of man and his history."[51] Later he would write that "when I found that many naturalists fully accepted the doctrine of the evolution of species, it seemed to me advisable to work up such notes as I possessed and to publish a special treatise on the origin of man."[52] That special treatise became the *Descent of Man* (1871).[53]

Even a decade after publication of *The Origin of Species*, Lyell sought to persuade Darwin that his theory could not account for human moral and intellectual faculties.[54] But Darwin disagreed and presented a specific line of reasoning. He argued that human emotions are essentially those of animals. Dogs frightened by a parasol moved by the wind, natives trembling

---

50. See the excellent article on the philosophical problems of both Darwin's Darwinism and Darwinism today: James Lennox, "Darwinism," in *The Stanford Encyclopedia of Philosophy* (summer 2015 ed.), ed. Edward N. Zalta, http://plato.stanford.edu/archives/sum2015/entries/darwinism/.

51. Darwin, *Origin*, 506. "From the beginning of his theorizing about species, Darwin had human beings in view." Robert J. Richards, "Darwin on Mind, Morals, and Emotions," in *The Cambridge Companion to Darwin*, 2nd ed., ed. Jonathan Hodge and Gregory Radick (New York: Cambridge University Press, 2009), 96. Herbert Spencer (1820–1903) was not mentioned in this sentence in earlier editions of *The Origin of Species*. Spencer applied naturalistic evolution to everything from biology to psychology, ethics, sociology, and politics.

52. Darwin, *Autobiography*, 131.

53. Charles Darwin, *The Descent of Man, and Selection in Relation to Sex*, 2 vols. (London: John Murray, 1871). Darwin also treated the subject in other works, including *The Expression of the Emotions in Man and Animals* (London: John Murray, 1872).

54. Roberts, *Darwinism*, 51. Though initially Wallace published a paper (1864) contending that natural selection can explain human evolution, by 1869 he reversed course, holding supernatural intervention was necessary to account for the human mind. Ibid., 59.

before invisible spirits producing a lightning storm, and Christians fearful of God's wrath show little difference. The facial expressions of "children, adults, the insane, as well as in apes, dogs and cats . . . showed similarities across ages, sexes and mental capacities."[55]

Human morality, for Darwin, simply reflects further evolutionary development of animal emotions. Some thinkers could have accepted evolutionary continuity between animals and humans if traditional moral values were baked into nature such that they necessarily emerged in humans. But Darwin countenanced no such idea. "If, for instance, to take an extreme case, men were reared under precisely the same conditions as hive-bees, there can hardly be a doubt that our unmarried females would, like the worker-bees, think it a sacred duty to kill their brothers, and mothers would strive to kill their fertile daughters; and no one would think of interfering."[56]

---

55. Richards, "Darwin on Mind," 114.

56. Darwin, *Descent of Man*, 1:73. As Peter Bowler correctly observes of Darwin's view: "Our moral values are merely rationalizations of social instincts built into us because our ape ancestors lived in groups." Bowler, "Evolution," 225. Early concerns about Darwin's vision for humanity were exemplified in the famous exchange between Thomas Henry Huxley, a highly respected biologist, and the bishop of Oxford, Samuel Wilberforce. Wilberforce finished his anti-Darwinism message with a rhetorical flourish: "'I should like to ask Professor Huxley, who is sitting by me, and is about to tear me to pieces when I have sat down, as to his belief in being descended from an ape. Is it on his grandfather's or his grandmother's side that the ape ancestry comes in?' Then he took on a more serious tone and asserted that Darwinism is contrary to the Scriptures. Huxley responded: 'I should feel it no shame to have risen from such an origin. But I should feel it a shame to have sprung from one who prostituted the gifts of culture and of eloquence to the service of prejudice and of falsehood.'" From the notes of W. H. Fremantle as recounted by Francis Darwin in in *The Life of Charles Darwin*, ed. Francis Darwin (London: Studio Editions, 1995 [1902]), 238–39. Years later in a letter from Huxley to Darwin dated June 27, 1891, Huxley noted the bishop afterward never seemed to bear him malice and was always courteous whenever they met. Ibid., 240–41. Typically considered a classic science-theology conflict, Huxley's alleged thrashing of Wilberforce "has been exposed as more legend than fact." Christopher Rios, *After the Monkey Trial: Evangelical Scientists and a New Creationism* (New York: Fordham University Press, 2014), 8. See also J. Vernon Jensen, "'Debate' with Bishop Wilberforce, 1860," in *Thomas Henry Huxley: Communicating for Science* (Cranbury, NJ: Associated University Presses, 1991), 63–86. For a different take, see J. R. Lucas, 'Wilberforce and Huxley: A Legendary Encounter," *The Historical Journal* 22, no. 2 (June 1979): 313–30; Richard Harris, "Religion and Science—Old Enemies or New Friends?" *Modern Believing* 47, no. 1 (2006): 1, 22–27. The 1860 occasion was the prestigious scientific gathering, the British Association for the Advancement of Science, and Wilberforce was a Fellow of the Royal Society.

Another early worry pertained to natural selection, the central component of Darwin's theory. Couching the concept with the anthropomorphic
term "selection" might seem to imply the intelligent design of nature. From
the very start the rhetorical cast of Darwin's theory "constantly displayed
the teleological vocabulary of purpose, intention, and contrivance" when
actually natural selection serves as an "antonym both to artificial selection
and to supernatural supervision . . . advanced to dispel final cause from
biology."[57]

John Herschel, who had earlier inspired Darwin's search for "true
causes," tried to understand natural selection as an intermediate cause for
the appearance of new species, leaving room for God as the final cause.
The influential American botanist Asa Gray wrote an essay with the subtitle "Natural Selection Not Inconsistent with Natural Theology," seeking to persuade Darwin to assume variations are designed with favorable
goals. Gray believed Darwin's notion of "chance" was only a confession of
ignorance regarding the final cause, and any view that "things and events
in Nature were not designed to be so, if logically carried out, is doubtless
tantamount to atheism."[58] Darwin made clear in response to Gray that
divinely ordained beneficial variations would no longer be "natural" selection, believing that every aspect of the evolutionary process is "susceptible
to a natural explanation."[59]

So for roughly a quarter century the majority of attacks against
Darwinism "targeted the very existence of natural selection."[60] Darwin's
geology teacher Adam Sedgwick equated the theory's repudiation of
final causes as materialism. Herschel, Whewell, and John Stuart Mill,

---

57. David N. Livingstone, *Darwin's Forgotten Defenders* (Grand Rapids: Eerdmans,
1984), 105.

58. Asa Gray, "Essay: Natural Selection and Natural Theology: Natural Selection
Not Inconsistent with Natural Theology," Atlantic Monthly for July, August, and
October, 1860, The Darwin Correspondence Project, https://www.darwinproject.ac.uk/
essay-natural-selection-natural-theology.

59. Bowler, "Evolution," 227. For reasons such as this, geologist and seminary professor
George Frederick Wright (1838–1921), who had early on endorsed a Christianized version
of Darwinism, eventually became disillusioned with evolutionary theory. Mark A. Noll,
"Evangelicalism and Fundamentalism," in *Science and Religion: A Historical Introduction,*
ed. Gary Ferngren (Baltimore: Johns Hopkins University Press, 2002), 270.

60. Gayon, "From Darwin to Today," 287. See also Ronald L. Numbers, *Darwinism
Comes to America* (Cambridge, MA: Harvard University Press, 1998), 43.

the current major theorists of scientific method, agreed that the theory of natural selection at its "best . . . was not good enough, and certainly not as credible as the theory of creation by a designing intelligence. At worst, it was not a legitimate scientific theory at all."[61] Herschel argued that intelligence must continually direct organic change. Whewell compared Darwin's theory to that of the ancient atomist Democritus, asking if any persons "in modern times, assert that the world was produced by a fortuitous concourse of atoms?"[62] Just before his death, Mill emphatically argued that intelligent design alone could produce structures such as the eye. From the start these and many other thinkers opposing natural selection "correctly identified its materialistic implications. They saw that, in a universe governed solely by random variation and the survival of the fittest, the existing state of nature must be the outcome of trial and error, not of purposeful intention."[63]

Well into the early twentieth century many scientists rejected natural selection especially since it undercut "a purposeful process designed to enhance mental and moral progress."[64] Even some founders of the modern synthesis such as Julian Huxley (1887–1975) sought to find human values reflected in a progressive evolutionary process. But others such as George Gaylord Simpson (1902–1984) viewed Darwinism in strictly materialistic terms with no purpose or goals. By the mid-twentieth century, the revolution was complete; mainstream biologists regarded theories of purposeful evolution indefensible.[65]

Yet not all aspects of Darwinism met with scientific resistance for any length of time. Prior to the *Origin of Species*, most scientists had been hostile to theories of species transmutation. So immediately after the book's publication, much criticism focused on its advocacy since observation,

---

61. David L. Hull, "Victorian Philosophy of Science," in *The Cambridge Companion to Darwin*, 2nd ed., ed. Jonathan Hodge and Gregory Radick (New York: Cambridge University Press, 2009), 174. As is well known, even Thomas Henry Huxley doubted natural selection as a complete theory for organic evolution.

62. William Whewell, *Astronomy and General Physics Considered with Reference to Natural Theology* 7th ed. (London: Pickering: 1864,) xv, cited in Hull, "Victorian Philosophy of Science," 189.

63. Bowler, "Evolution," 226.

64. Ibid., 228.

65. Ibid., 231.

fossils, and domestic species seemed to confirm the immutability of species.[66] But if few scientists initially "rushed to embrace it,"[67] the rapid widespread acceptance of the transmutation of species "constitutes one of the most spectacular examples of a shift of paradigm."[68]

As mentioned earlier, Darwin's lone illustration in the *Origin of Species*, the tree of life diagram with thirty pages or so of explanation, "had an almost immediate effect upon the entirety of the biological community. Within a remarkably short period of time, it became the paradigmatic representation of organic evolution and its status as an established fact."[69] By 1875, the transmutation of species had become the "working hypothesis" of most scientists.[70] Just twenty years after publication of the *Origin of Species*, only two working North American naturalists were special creationists.[71] But the turn of the twentieth century, "it was "almost impossible to find significant biologists who plainly and explicitly denied the *existence* of evolution in the sense that species modify and are physically related with previous species through uninterrupted generations."[72]

For a century and a half now Darwin's tree of life has become the basis for the "whole industry of evolutionary biology."[73] Today "the typical question is *which* tree is the best one, not *whether* there is a tree in the first place."[74] And though Darwin's transmutation of species and universal common descent were separate notions, acceptance of the former led to

---

66. Roberts, *Darwinism*, 32, 44–46.

67. Ibid., 40.

68. Gayon, "From Darwin to Today," 282. Many scientists revealed in their personal reflections that they had already come to doubt the fixity of species, and were waiting for someone to marshal the facts and present them in such a way as to enable mass conversions to organic evolution. Numbers, *Darwinism*, 47. Of these scientists, "the ones who displayed liberal religious and political attitudes were significantly more likely to endorse Darwin's theories than those who did not." Ibid., 46.

69. Gayon, "From Darwin to Today," 282–83. See also Waters, "The Arguments," 127, 141.

70. Roberts, *Darwinism*, 84-85; Ronald Numbers, "Creationism since 1859," in *Science and Religion: A Historical Introduction,* ed. Gary Ferngren (Baltimore: Johns Hopkins University Press, 2002), 280.

71. Numbers, "Creationism," 278.

72. Gayon, "From Darwin to Today," 281; Numbers, *Darwinism*, 52.

73. Gayon, "From Darwin to Today," 282–83; Waters, "The Arguments," 127, 141.

74. Elliott Sober, "Metaphysical and Epistemological Issues," in *The Cambridge Companion to Darwin,* 2nd ed., ed. Jonathan Hodge and Gregory Radick (New York: Cambridge University Press, 2009), 313. Emphasis his.

rapid acceptance of the latter. The term "evolution" came to include both concepts. Thus even before widespread acceptance of natural selection as the explanatory mechanism for universal common descent, scientists commonly compared Darwin to Isaac Newton.[75]

Liberal Theological Reaction to Darwinism

Just because the scientific community hardly united around Darwinism initially, "it would be a mistake to imagine that all Christian theologians lined up against him."[76] Though by the end of the nineteenth century many American theologians argued Darwinism was irreconcilable with Christianity, liberals sought to "sanctify the theory of evolution in the name of Christianity" with theologies of progressive development.[77] Scientific delay in accepting natural selection allowed these theologians the common strategy of reconstruing Darwinism in the service of an evolutionary teleology.[78]

If players in the Copernican controversy sought to harmonize biblical interpretation and scientific theory, post-Darwin liberal theologians felt no such obligation. Though the idea of divine revelation in an inerrant Bible was not illogical, evolution itself replaced it as the "paradigm of divine activity" for many Protestant intellectuals.[79] Typically outspoken proponents of a developmental concept of religious knowledge and enthusiastic supporters of Darwinism were often one and the same. Liberals now commonly alluded to grounding Christian knowledge in Jesus Christ, not in the propositional truth of the Bible. In effect, however, human experience (consciousness, religious feeling, and the sense of obligation) viewed through an evolutionary lens formed the basis for formulating Christian doctrine.[80]

Theistic evolutionists justified this dramatic rejection of biblical authority by comparing their situation with earlier theologians facing Copernicanism. In reality, they had wearied of harmonizing Scripture and

---

75. Roberts, *Darwinism*, 86.
76. Brooke, "Victorian Christianity," 209.
77. Roberts, *Darwinism*, 116. Cf. ibid., 20, 122–23.
78. Brooke, "Victorian Christianity," 210; Livingstone, *Darwin's Defenders*, 48.
79. Roberts, *Darwinism*, 161.
80. Ibid., 126–28, 161, 166, 168–70.

science altogether. The conservatism principle was inverted. Biblical inerrancy now was suspect rather than evolutionary theory. If liberal theologians could not agree what constituted the set of biblical errors, virtually all of them united in outspoken support of German higher biblical criticism.[81]

Unconstrained by the need to ground doctrine biblically, time-tested essential Christian truths became time-bound traditional error needing full-blown reformulation. By definition, doctrines conflicting with modern thought were non-essential, necessitating rejection "as products of a cruder, more 'primitive' stage in man's evolving apprehension of divine truth."[82] The essence of Christianity, however, became increasingly difficult to identify. Indeed, if Christian truth is evolutionary, Christianity *du jour* must be superseded in the future. Along with species, Christian doctrines represented time-bound snapshots of developing but fluctuating thought.

Darwinism now functioned as "a substitute religion."[83] With supernaturalism deemphasized, theological emphasis fell on divine immanence. Evolution came to serve as the paradigm of divine activity, though God was hidden in the process. Evil itself now resulted from God's designing general laws while leaving the outcomes to chance. The doctrine of the historical fall was discarded; instead of humans degenerating from their innocent created estate, they evolved (fell) upward from their animal past with its beastly appetites. Evolutionary theologians transmuted even the redemptive death of Jesus to an emphasis on imitating his new way of life.[84]

Generally with orthodox doctrine no longer constraining them, liberal theologians believed the modern defense of Christianity must be reconstrued. Since traditional defenders of biblical inspiration impeded progress in science and undermined confidence in Christianity, they must be opposed. Evolutionary theologians believed they alone could hold court with the literate. For conservatives it seemed the new science had generated something new in the history of Christendom: the abandonment of Christianity in the name of Christianity.[85]

81. Ibid., 146–57.
82. Ibid., 171. See also ibid., 164–65, 172–73.
83. Brooke, "Victorian Christianity," 213.
84. Roberts, *Darwinism*, 136–45, 174–203, 211.
85. Ibid., 150–51. For a similar and now classic evangelical appraisal of liberal

A Reshaped Darwinian World

Unlike the Copernican controversy, the Darwinian brought about a trans-mutation of the Western worldview itself. As New Atheist Daniel Dennett writes, Darwinism is like a universal acid that "eats through just about every traditional concept, and leaves in its wake a revolutionized world-view, with most of the old landmarks still recognizable, but transformed in fundamental ways."[86] Within two decades "the vast majority of scientists and educated people had accepted the basic idea of evolution,"[87] but many of the same could not initially embrace the full implications of the theory. Religious liberals and secular radicals could not embrace a worldview focused on chance and suffering, so they compromised core aspects of Darwinism. But twentieth-century thinkers eventually became more comfortable with a non-purposive evolutionary world. By the middle of the century, biologists regarded theories of purposeful evolution indefensible: evolving life has neither goal nor any "inevitable trend toward higher levels of organization."[88]

Much more than biological landmarks were transformed. The very essence of humanity was reconceptualized. Before the ramifications of Darwinism were fully apparent, early radicals sought to develop an evolutionary morality.[89] But realization of those foundational implications in the late nineteenth century led to "a period of enormous, often convulsive, cultural change."[90] Twentieth-century intellectuals widely came to accept the materialistic significance of evolution, learning "to live with the idea that we are the products of a purposeless and, hence, morally neutral natural world."[91] The scientific community today largely accepts Darwin's view

---

Christianity written in 1923, see the work by Princeton Theological Seminary theologian J. Gresham Machen, *Christianity and Liberalism* (Grand Rapids: Eerdmans, 1923).

86. Daniel C. Dennett, *Darwin's Dangerous Idea: Evolution and the Meanings of Life* (New York: Simon & Schuster, 1995), 63.

87. Bowler, "Evolution," 223.

88. Ibid., 223. See also ibid., 226, 231. Cf. Michael Ruse, "Belief in God in a Darwinian Age," in *The Cambridge Companion to Darwin,* 2nd ed., ed. Jonathan Hodge and Gregory Radick (New York: Cambridge University Press, 2009), 370, and Sober, "Metaphysical Issues," 305.

89. Bowler, "Evolution," 224.

90. Roberts, *Darwinism,* 233.

91. Bowler, "Evolution," 220.

that morality (and human reason) are unguided outgrowths of animal instinct. Darwinian theories about the origin of human morality (evolutionary metaethics) are flourishing, while no evolutionary code of morality is anywhere in sight.[92]

Perhaps the landmark most defaced by the Darwinian acid is the very notion of God in relation to humanity. Once the door was opened to view everything in light of Darwinism, then "even religious sensibilities themselves can be fully explained by natural selection."[93] Darwinism's dethroning of the Judeo-Christian tradition has produced "a world without providential guidance, a world full of not only irony, but often also of tragedy, for it is a world that exhibits no purpose, moves toward no preordained goal, and provides no promise of human redemption."[94]

CONCLUSION

Unlike Copernicanism, the worldview producing and receiving Darwinism was virtually no longer constrained by biblical revelation. Everything about living things came under its purview. Life ceased being the product of a supernatural creation. The appearance of apparently new species in the fossil record no longer could serve as evidence of biblical creation. Late nineteenth-century American biologists, geologists, and anthropologists in the National Academy of Sciences largely shared the attitude that appeal to miracle such as special creation could no longer be considered legitimate

---

92. Alex Rosenberg, "Darwinism in Moral Philosophy and Social Theory," in *The Cambridge Companion to Darwin,* 2nd ed., ed. Jonathan Hodge and Gregory Radick (New York: Cambridge University Press, 2009), 365. Nonetheless, even naturalists such as Stephen Gould and Philip Kitcher have been nervous about sociobiology and evolutionary psychology theories often based "on the sketchiest evidence." Philip Kitcher, "Giving Darwin His Due," in *The Cambridge Companion to Darwin,* 2nd ed., ed. Jonathan Hodge and Gregory Radick (New York: Cambridge University Press, 2009), 459. Fields such as sociobiology and evolutionary psychology generally hold that "moral judgements are neither true nor false reports about the world." Rosenberg, "Darwinism in Moral Philosophy," 351. Seeing that humans do not and cannot live without acting as if objective moral values exist, little surprise that more than a century and a half later there is "probably more debate and discussion and controversy on these matters now than at any time since the *Origin.*" Ruse, "Belief," 387.

93. Brooke, "Victorian Christianity," 216.

94. Paul K. Conkin, *When All the Gods Trembled: Darwinism, Scopes, and American Intellectuals* (Lanham, MD: Rowman & Littlefield, 1998), xi.

science.[95] "The striking rapidity with which the scientific community cast its verdict in favor of a theory that shattered the traditional understanding of the history of life attested to the lack of commitment many natural historians felt toward the doctrine of special creation."[96]

Special creation was not the only casualty. With Darwinism as the catalyst, science itself was now considered legitimate only within the confines of methodological naturalism. Thus when theorizing without recourse to intelligent agency, the appearance of design and purpose in living creatures also must be explained without recourse to God. Of course, humanity earned no exemption: minds, morals, and even the origin of religion fell under the authority of evolution.

Many then and now share the conviction that the ultimate implication of Darwin's evolution is metaphysical naturalism, that everything interesting about the world reveals there is no God. Darwin's later acknowledged agnosticism certainly endorsed the notion that if God exists, he is hiding. His private notebooks reveal he had been a closet materialist long before writing *The Origin of Species*.

Liberal Christian theologians made rapid peace with evolution, even making it the centerpiece for God's work in the world. The conservatism principle was turned on its head, with the terms for all science-theology weddings dictated by Darwinism. The new theological hybrid models treated Christian theology in pragmatic and anti-realist fashion to conform to an evolutionary worldview. Human experience rather than the Bible became the ground of Christian knowledge.

In light of the above, evangelicals affirming evolution today face the challenge of how not to fall "into the syncretistic traps that characterized the modernist theologians of an earlier era."[97] Moreover, evolutionary creationists should expect deeply held misgivings from those practicing the conservatism principle. Just how much biblical Christianity can resist the universal acid?

---

95. Numbers, *Darwinism*, 25–30, 48.
96. Roberts, *Darwinism*, 85–86.
97. Rios, *Monkey Trial*, 187.

Chapter 4

AMERICAN EVANGELICAL RESPONSES TO DARWINISM:
Setting the Stage

> Evolutionary creation is an evangelical Christian approach to evolution. . . . Evolutionary creation contends that humans evolved from prehuman ancestors, and that the image of God and human sin were gradually and mysteriously manifested. Most importantly, evolutionary creationists enjoy a personal relationship with Jesus.[1]
> —Denis Lamoureux, "The Evolution of an Evolutionary Creationist"

Without question, evangelicals in the United States have had far more battles over evolution both with the culture and with each other than anywhere else in the world. Theories abound why, but one thing is clear. Emotions continue to run high on all sides about the related issues. Some even suggest that the biggest trial in the country's history, until the O. J. Simpson trial, underlies the passion about the subject.[2] The "monkey

---

1. Denis O. Lamoureux, "The Evolution of an Evolutionary Creationist," in *How I Changed My Mind about Evolution: Evangelicals Reflect on Faith and Science*, ed. Kathryn Applegate and J. B. Stump (Downers Grove, IL: IVP Academic, 2016), 142. Lamoureux is a featured and regular contributor to the webpage of BioLogos.

2. N. T. Wright, "A British Reflection on the Evolution Controversy in America," in *How I Changed My Mind about Evolution: Evangelicals Reflect on Faith and Science*, ed. Kathryn Applegate and J. B. Stump (Downers Grove, IL: IVP Academic, 2016), 134–36.

trial" dominated the news then as the "the trial of the century,"[3] and remains, alongside the Galileo affair, as a strategic symbol of the mythical battle between regressive (and repressive) theology and progressive science.

AMERICA'S GALILEO AFFAIR

During the 1920s, an American movement arose to ban the teaching of Darwinism from public schools just as high school enrollment almost doubled. Some states outlawed evolutionary textbooks, others prohibited its teaching outright. Though finding its greatest support in the South, people from all over the country backed the movement. Organizations such as the World's Christian Fundamentals Association helped provide leadership to the anti-evolution movement.[4] Darwinism seemed to be losing ground in public classrooms.

But the American Civil Liberties Union (ACLU) pushed back, offering assistance to anyone willing to challenge the anti-evolution law in Tennessee. The ACLU intended the resulting trial to test the statute forbidding the teaching of human evolution. John Scopes, who volunteered to be the guinea pig, was the ideal defendant. He was just 24 years old and boyish looking; his easy-going manner gave no appearance of being a radical. In truth, he shared the views of his father, who was a militant socialist and agnostic.[5] The 1925 conviction of Scopes in Dayton, Tennessee, for teaching Darwinism to his students actually mattered little, but the cultural impact has been lasting.

The well-known William Jennings Bryan (1860–1925), a religious conservative and onetime Democratic presidential nominee, was chosen as the special prosecutor. Privately Bryan admitted having no problem with possible speciation among animals.[6] But he had his reasons for having been a driving force behind anti-evolution laws. He especially viewed social Darwinism, and legitimately so in his day, as a danger with its view

---

3. Ronald L. Numbers, *Darwinism Comes to America* (Cambridge, MA: Harvard University Press, 1998), 76.

4. Ibid., 281.

5. Edward J. Larson, "The Scopes Trial," in *Science and Religion: A Historical Introduction*, ed. Gary Ferngren (Baltimore: Johns Hopkins University Press, 2002), 290.

6. Numbers, *Darwinism*, 82.

of the survival of the fittest.[7] Clarence Darrow (1857–1938), the most famous trial lawyer of his day, served as the ACLU's lead defense lawyer. Famous for defending labor organizers and political radicals, he was also well known for his militant opposition to biblically inspired laws. He believed Christianity dangerously created irrational, judgmental, and warring societies. Whereas liberal Christianity undermined the relevance of his anti-religious views, the anti-evolution movement provided him pertinence.[8] Darrow was more than happy to seat jurors who had never heard of evolution or couldn't even read. His goal was to try the statute, not acquit the defendant.

The most dramatic event came on the seventh day when Darrow cleverly led Bryan to submit to questioning about his biblical beliefs.[9] Bryan's

---

7. Larson, "Scopes Trial," 291. William Jennings Bryan could be forgiven for believing Darwinism led logically to eugenics. Wallace, co-discoverer of natural selection, believed a utopian human selection would lead to the superior intellectual, moral, and physical qualities of Europeans. Darwin sympathized, arguing in the *Descent*: "With savages, the weak in body or mind are soon eliminated; and those that survive commonly exhibit a vigorous state of health. We civilised men, on the other hand, do our utmost to check the process of elimination; we build asylums for the imbecile, the maimed, and the sick; we institute poor-laws; and our medical men exert their utmost skill to save the life of every one to the last moment. There is reason to believe that vaccination has preserved thousands, who from a weak constitution would formerly have succumbed to small-pox. Thus the weak members of civilised societies propagate their kind. No one who has attended to the breeding of domestic animals will doubt that this must be highly injurious to the race of man. It is surprising how soon a want of care, or care wrongly directed, leads to the degeneration of a domestic race; but excepting in the case of man himself, hardly any one is so ignorant as to allow his worst animals to breed." Charles Darwin, *The Descent of Man, and Selection in Relation to Sex*, 2 vols. (London: John Murray, 1871), 1:168. But Darwin did not feel humans should try to eliminate the weak since this would do damage to "the noblest part of our nature." Ibid., 169. Darwin's cousin Francis Galton, as founder of modern eugenics, worried that human evolution was headed in the wrong direction since inferior societal elements outbred everyone else. Darwin's son Leonard served as president of Britain's Eugenics Society in the early twentieth century. Even if most contemporary defenders of Darwin believe social Darwinism and eugenics are perversions of the theory, social applications continue to be disputed. Diane B. Paul, "Darwin, Social Darwinism and Eugenics," in *The Cambridge Companion to Darwin*, 2nd ed., ed. Jonathan Hodge and Gregory Radick (New York: Cambridge University Press, 2009), 219–22, 241. On the complex relationship of Christians to the eugenics movement, see Christine Rosen, *Preaching Eugenics: Religious Leaders and the American Eugenics Movement* (New York: Oxford University Press, 2004), 85–138.

8. Larson, "Scopes Trial," 291.

9. Numbers, *Darwinism*, 78.

own team tried to end the two-hour-long ordeal, but Bryan refused, declaring: "I am simply trying to protect the Word of God against the greatest atheist or agnostic in the United States" and "I want the papers to know I am not afraid to get on the stand in front of him and let him do his worst."[10] Darrow's strategic questioning, while giving little time for answers, effectively put the Bible on trial. Interrogations about Jonah and the whale, Adam's rib, and Cain's wife had little to do with the trial—but everything with the outside listening world's perception of science versus Christianity. The judge eventually stopped the debacle because of its irrelevance. Darrow then strategically waived his own closing that prevented Bryan's closing argument which contained his best thoughts prepared in advance and saved for last.[11]

---

10. Edward J. Larson, *Summer for the Gods: The Trial and America's Continuing Debate over Science and Religion* (New York: Basic Books, 1997), quote on 190 taken from the trial transcript, *The World's Most Famous Court Case: Tennessee Evolution Case* (Dayton, TN: Bryan College, 1990), 299.

11. Bryan's closing argument noted that Tennessee law did not prohibit teaching of evolution except in the case of human beings. He noted Darwin's *Descent of Man* traced human mind and morality back to animals. Bryan made much of the ill effects of Darwinism on Christian faith. He compared his protecting public school children from Darwinism to an earlier court case in which Darrow defended a teenage murderer. Darrow had argued that too early of an exposure to philosopher Friedrich Nietzsche's nihilism, as well as trashy murder novels, led the unstable male to commit murder. Others were actually more to blame for exposing the teen to these influences. Darrow went even further, noting biologically the young man also suffered from a criminal impulse descended from a remote ancestor, and that all biologists would agree about this. Bryan responded: "You cannot punish the ancestor—he is not only dead but, according to the evolutionists, he was a brute and may have lived a million years ago. And he says that all the biologists agree with him. . . . This is the quintessence of evolution, distilled for us by one who follows that doctrine to its logical conclusion. Analyze this dogma of darkness and death. Evolutionists say that back in the twilight of life a beast, name and nature unknown, planted a murderous seed and that the impulse that originated in that seed throbs forever in the blood of the brute's descendants, inspiring killings innumerable, for which the murderers are not responsible because coerced by a fate fixed by the laws of heredity! It is an insult to reason and shocks the heart. That doctrine is as deadly as leprosy; it may aid a lawyer in a criminal case, but it would, if generally adopted, destroy all sense of responsibility and menace the morals of the world. . . . No more repulsive doctrine was ever proclaimed by any man; if all the biologists of the world teach this doctrine—as Mr. Darrow says they do—then may heaven defend the youth of our land from their impious babblings." William Jennings Bryan, *The Last Message of William Jennings Bryan* (New York: Revell, 1925), 20. See also ibid., 8, 11, 16–20.

Just five days after the trial Bryan died during a Sunday afternoon nap. He had spoken that morning at a church in Dayton. His last message concerned the removal of teaching human evolution in public schools. The closing words of his message were drawn from his favorite hymn: "Faith of our fathers—holy faith / We will be true to thee till death!"[12] In the days after the trial, Darrow attended a local high school dance, smoking cigarettes and dancing with the students.[13] The trial and aftermath became an immediate sensation due to two hundred reporters covering the story, newsreel footage distributed rapidly to movie houses, thousands of miles of wires strung to convey updates from telegraph operators in the courtroom, and the pioneering use of live radio.

The Scopes trial has been frequently misunderstood because it can be manipulated to support a wide variety of interests.[14] Early assessment of the trial, though not unanimous, did not view it as a defeat for the anti-evolutionists. The American press initially considered little of significance resulted from it "beyond its having exposed Bryan's empty head and Darrow's mean spirit."[15] Most anti-evolutionists expressed outrage over the way Darrow had treated Bryan, and viewed Bryan's performance in heroic terms. Fundamentalist pastor J. Frank Norris compared Bryan's courage to the defiance of Moses to Pharaoh, Elijah to Ahab, Paul to Nero, and Luther to Pope Leo X.[16] Liberals also criticized Darrow at the time for his arrogance. Even the ACLU sought to remove him from the team, which appealed Scopes's conviction.[17]

---

12. Larson, *Summer for the Gods*, 199. The timing of Bryan's death moved some to regard him a martyr for the faith. Ibid., 203. "Scopes songs" became popular with lyrics concerning Bryan such as: "There he fought for what was righteous and the battle it was won / Then the Lord called him to heaven for his work on earth was done." Ibid., 205.

13. Ibid., 200.

14. Numbers, *Darwinism*, 76.

15. Larson, *Summer for the Gods*, 202.

16. Numbers, *Darwinism,* 82–83, 90.

17. Ibid., 83. Though evangelicals generally were not displeased with Bryan's performance, Henry Morris believed Bryan egregiously erred in expressing full confidence in the infallible Bible "but then to hedge on the geological question, relying on the day/age theory." Henry Morris, *A History of Modern Creationism* (San Diego: Master Books, 1984), 66. See also Numbers, *Darwinism*, 89, 206, on later young earth creationists who believe Price's failure to defend a young earth disastrously set back creationism. It is hard to understand how arguing for a young earth at the trial would have made any difference in the outcome.

The 1931 publication of the bestseller *Only Yesterday: An Informal History of the Nineteen-Twenties* started the idea that the trial intellectually defeated Bryan (and anti-evolutionism).[18] After *Inherit the Wind* in play (1955) and movie versions (1960), not to mention several television remakes, the utter defeat of Bryan became the standard storyline. For many, *Inherit the Wind* has become their only source and interpretation of the trial, but historical falsehoods abound. Scopes is jailed, the townsfolk are mean spirited, and Bryan appears as a fanatical buffoon or mindless leader of an anti-science mob. The enduring misimpressions of the trial due to *Inherit the Wind* have become "more a part of the folklore of liberalism than of history."[19] Yet the *National Standard for United States History* continues recommending the play and the movie for understanding Bryan and fundamentalist thinking—which historian Ronald Numbers compares to "recommending *Gone with the Wind* as a historically reliable account of the Civil War."[20]

By the end of the 1920s, anti-evolutionists had given up on removing the teaching of evolution from public classrooms.[21] And only a half-century later the shoe was on the other foot. Creationists found themselves unsuccessfully trying to turn Darrow's trial argument on its head, that teaching only one theory of origins is sheer bigotry.[22] The shade of the iconic "monkey trial" continues to cast a long shadow "as a protean source for legend-making: about Bryan and Darrow, about fundamentalism and modernism, about science and religion."[23] With substantive ideas in the background, and personalities and emotions at the fore, the Scopes trial lore perpetuates the science-theology warfare myth. The takeaway for secularists is that religious opposition to evolution is fool's work; bumbling fundamentalists have no business influencing the classroom.[24]

---

18. Frederick Lewis Allen, *Only Yesterday: An Informal History of the 1920s* (New York: Harper & Row, 1931).

19. This assessment was that of Joseph Wood Krutch, a correspondent at the trial. Joseph Wood Krutch, "The Monkey Trial," *Commentary* (May 1967): 83, in Larson, *Summer for the Gods*, 244. On the historical falsehoods, see ibid., 106, and Numbers, *Darwinism*, 85.

20. Numbers, *Darwinism*, 87. Cf. Larson, *Summer for the Gods*, 240–46.

21. Numbers, *Darwinism,* 89.

22. Ibid., 91.

23. Ibid.

24. Larson, "Scopes Trial," 292–97.

AMERICAN EVANGELICALS' INITIAL RESPONSE TO DARWINISM

Evangelical scientists in North America adapted to Darwinism in a variety of ways. Some continued to reject human evolution from lower life forms. Most considered Darwin's attack on design a serious problem, but no consensus response was forthcoming.[25]

Evangelical theologians, however, faced the constraints of the conservatism principle. Thorny problems abounded to anyone wanting to harmonize an inerrant Bible with Darwinism. Some evangelical theologians did court Darwinism, but most did not. I examine the most celebrated of the "evolutionary" evangelical theologians, B. B. Warfield, in chapter 9.

Around 1880, most American evangelical theologians recognized the transmutation hypothesis was settled among scientists. Theologians could no longer primarily recount evolution's scientific problems. Their new strategy was to demonstrate its incompatibility with Christianity itself.[26] These theologians correctly identified the materialistic implications of the *Origin of Species* suppressed by many of its initial supporters. Indicting Darwin's version "as the most extreme manifestation of the atheistical tendency inherent" in the basic idea of evolution, evangelical thinkers pointed out that "the natural world that produced us was reduced to a purposeless sequence of accidental changes."[27] And since Christian evolutionists proffered theological revisions radically beyond anything ever countenanced, traditional creationists felt obligated to denounce them nearly as much as outright enemies of Christianity. Grounding revelation in an evolving process rather than the Bible was unacceptable.[28]

Darwinism forced evangelical apologetics to shift from the reigning stronghold, the argument from design, to a defense of biblical inerrancy

---

25. David N. Livingstone, *Darwin's Forgotten Defenders* (Grand Rapids: Eerdmans, 1984), 49, 96, 98-99. Livingstone refers to Asa Gray, George Frederick Wright, and James Dwight Dana as "the alliance of evangelical evolutionists." Ibid., 70. Ironically, conservative theologians from 1859 to 1875 who rejected common descent relied heavily on the work of Harvard's Louis Agassiz, a Unitarian. Jon Roberts, *Darwinism and the Divine in America: Protestant Intellectuals and Organic Evolution, 1859–1900* (Madison, WI: University of Wisconsin Press, 1988), 37.

26. Roberts, *Darwinism*, 87, 90, 126.

27. Peter J. Bowler, "Evolution," in *Science and Religion: A Historical Introduction*, ed. Gary Ferngren (Baltimore: Johns Hopkins University Press, 2002), 223. See also ibid., 220.

28. Roberts, *Darwinism*, 214–16, 225–40.

itself.[29] Previously evangelicals carefully adjusted scriptural interpretation, but only after the painstaking conservatism principle had played itself out over time. Biblical inerrancy was never sacrificed on the altar of scientific consensus because "biblical considerations were paramount."[30] But Christians adopting Darwinism typically struggled to reconcile it with Scripture, and thus abandoned biblical infallibility. The Bible itself now was under siege due to Darwinism.

Christian evolutionists fundamentally altering the relationship between science and theology forced "clarification and articulation of epistemological priorities."[31] Conservatives retained an uncompromising view of biblical authority as the bulwark against the dangers of evolution. Three central points comprised this biblical epistemology: completeness, inerrancy, and clarity. Of course, humans can err in biblical interpretation. But as opposed to the view of some expositors, the populist approach argued that the plain meaning of the text is apparent to common sense. On the other hand, scientific data is more prone to misinterpretation since by nature its subject matter is less clear.[32] I examine especially in chapter 7 whether these evangelicals and those who followed actually practiced this hermeneutic, or if instead they continued practicing the conservatism principle. But clearly they were intuitively defending the core assumption of Galileo's proposal, the inerrancy of Scripture. That term was non-negotiable.

The most apparently unbiblical Darwinist doctrine, "a naturalistic account of the emergence of human beings from ape-like ancestors . . . reinforced doubts about biblical authority at a particularly sensitive time."[33] If species, including the human, were fluid and not essential, how could this square with the doctrine of our being made in God's image? And how can naturalism account for human intelligence, language, and morality? If Lyell and Wallace doubted natural selection can produce a human mind, why should theologians be expected to adopt the view? "Had the human 'soul' been added during the evolutionary process, or was

---

29. Livingstone, *Darwin's Defenders*, 189.

30. Roberts, *Darwinism*, 212–13.

31. Ibid., 236.

32. Ibid., 213, 217–21.

33. John Hedley Brooke, "Darwin and Victorian Christianity," in *The Cambridge Companion to Darwin,* 2nd ed., ed. Jonathan Hodge and Gregory Radick (New York: Cambridge University Press, 2009), 197.

it more appropriate to speak of our *being* souls rather than *having* them? What was the ground of moral values if the evolution of the moral sense could be explained simply in terms of survival value, without reference to the transcendent?"[34] And evangelicals were especially concerned regarding Darwinism's implications for the spiritual condition and salvation of the human race. Evolution seemed the antithesis to the biblical teaching that our innocent first parents' disobedience led to the fall of the race. Could Darwinian origins even square with the human need for a Savior? [35]

Evangelical Anti-Darwinian Champion: Charles Hodge

The theologians of Princeton Theological Seminary typically provided intellectual resources for defending evangelical orthodoxy and biblical infallibility in nineteenth-century America.[36] No one there did this more rigorously and influentially than Charles Hodge. Over the course of his career he trained approximately three thousand ministers, more than all other American theologians of the nineteenth century.[37] He addressed concerns regarding Darwinism that continue to resonate with most conservative evangelicals, and arguably he did so more articulately than any other theologian in his day. These concerns included the gap between the living and the non-living, the difference between plant and animal life, the differences between species, and the mental and moral difference between humans and animals.[38]

On this last issue he wrote: "It shocks the common sense of unsophisticated men to be told that the whale and the humming-bird, man and the mosquito, are derived from the same source. Not that the whale was developed out of the humming-bird, or man out of the mosquito, but that both are derived by a slow process of variations continued through countless

---

34. Ibid., 198. Emphasis his. See also ibid., 211; Livingstone, *Darwin's Defenders,* 49; and Roberts, *Darwinism,* 56–57, 104–105, 114–16.

35. Roberts, *Darwinism,* 21, 107–108.

36. Ibid., 222.

37. Ibid., 17.

38. Charles Hodge, *What Is Darwinism?* (New York: Scribner, Armstrong, and Company, 1874), 163. Hodge rejected the complete mutability of living things but rightly noted the difficulty of knowing just what constitutes a species.

millions of years. Such is the theory with its scientific feathers plucked off."[39]

But Hodge's biggest concern had to do with Darwin's central notion, the way Darwin used the word "natural."[40] Hodge rightly discerned that Darwin used "the word natural as antithetical to supernatural. Natural selection is a selection made by natural laws, working without intention and design. It is, therefore, opposed not only to artificial selection, which is made by the wisdom and skill of man to accomplish a given purpose, but also to supernatural selection, which means either a selection originally intended by a power higher than nature; or which is carried out by such power."[41] Darwinism comprises three elements: universal common descent, natural selection as its cause, and, most important, the rejection of purpose or design.[42] Hodge adduced ample testimony from friends and foes of Darwinism alike, not to mention Darwin himself, that it inherently disallows teleology. Therefore, "the denial of design in nature is virtually the denial of God. Mr. Darwin's theory does deny all design in nature, therefore, his theory is virtually atheistical; his theory, not he himself."[43] Hodge reiterated that though Darwinism is atheistic, he was not implying Darwinists are atheists.[44] Hodge attributed the remarkably rapid acceptance of Darwinian materialism due to a change in the "prevailing state of mind."[45] Its "essential harmony with the spirit of the age" stems from advocating a purposeless process producing from an unintelligent living cell "all the works of art, literature, and science."[46]

In his day, Hodge listed several factors that contributed unnecessary tension between some scientists and theologians. Some scientists

---

39. Charles Hodge, *Systematic Theology*, 3 vols. (Peabody, MA: Hendrickson, 2011 [1871–1873]), 2:14.

40. Hodge, *What Is Darwinism?* 40.

41. Ibid., 41.

42. Ibid., 50–53.

43. Ibid., 173.

44. Ibid., 176–77. Hodge noted that Asa Gray, contra Darwin, interpreted Darwinism theistically. Hodge, *Systematic Theology*, 2:16–18. On Gray's correspondence with Darwin, see Roberts, *Darwinism*, 38–39. On Darwin's most often cited response, see Charles Darwin, letter to Asa Gray, May 22, 1860, in *The Life of Charles Darwin*, ed. Francis Darwin (London: Studio Editions, 1995 [1902]), 236.

45. Hodge, *What Is Darwinism?* 149.

46. Hodge, *Systematic Theology*, 2:15.

discounted as knowledge anything that didn't derive from the five senses. Some scientists also failed to distinguish between facts of nature and the theories about those facts. And some scientists displayed a condescending attitude toward those who disagreed with them. These tendencies led some in science not only to "speculate, but dogmatize, on the highest questions of philosophy, morality, and religion."[47]

THE DECLINE OF AMERICAN EVANGELICAL INFLUENCE

Hodge considered his mid-nineteenth-century world in the throes of a rapid worldview change. But at least then most writers paid lip service to theological concerns. By the beginning of the twentieth century things had changed much more dramatically. Christianity had become increasingly a private matter with little relevance for the broader culture, and science played the primary role in the change. Conservative American theologians ascribed the Darwinian shift "not simply to a mistake in scientific judgment but to adherence to a world view antithetical to Christianity. From their vantage point, not only the effect but the very intent of the Darwinian hypothesis was to undermine belief in Christian theology. Darwinism, they believed, was embedded within a larger movement that was assuming an increasingly prominent role in philosophical discussions: scientific naturalism."[48]

American higher education was reshaped between the Civil War and World War I. The role of science was reduced from large-scale applications such as natural theology to narrower and more specialized and tightly controlled linkages between causes and effects. Moreover, since many phenomena once believed evidence of divine activity were now understood in fully natural terms, appeals to divine action were proscribed as explanations for gaps in scientific knowledge. Scientists now assumed invoking supernatural explanations to be slothful and anti-scientific. Methodological naturalism became the order of the day. "Nonbelief (though not unbelief) became science's reigning methodological principle."[49]

---

47. Hodge, *What Is Darwinism?* 139. See his discussion on 125–39.
48. Roberts, *Darwinism*, 63. See also ibid., xviii.
49. Jon H. Roberts and James Turner, *The Sacred and the Secular University* (Princeton, NJ: Princeton University Press, 2000), 31.

So "naturalistic description, which had begun as one of the products of scientific analysis, became increasingly a postulate of such analysis. And inevitably, methodology edged into metaphysics."[50] Darwinism played an especially significant role in convincing scientists that everything, including human beings, falls under the purview of this approach to science. Darwin's close supporter, Thomas Huxley, had "coined the term *agnosticism* to denote the critical state of unbelief generated by a scientific approach to nature,"[51] a term Darwin eventually applied to himself regarding religion. Though most scientists were not consciously anti-religious, their new vision resulted in bringing virtually everything under the domain of naturalistic explanation. American culture became increasingly agnostic or secular.

With the origins of matter, life, and mind now under the domain of science and not theology, the social sciences rose in importance during this time as a way of studying humanity, including religious practices. Between the two world wars, the modern university education largely excluded theology as a source of knowledge. The promise of unlocking a progressively better future would be based on the arts and sciences. From a "Christian point of view, the humanities emerged in the long run as more than passive abettors in the deconstruction of the religious framework of knowledge; ironically, they proved to be active undercover agents, a fox welcomed into the henhouse" with the effect of eventually "sapping Christianity, indeed undermining any conviction of objective truth transcending human beings."[52] Traditional Christianity had "lost its central place within higher education, and evangelical Protestants were displaced from their role as the major intellectual arbiters of American culture."[53]

The supplanting of Scripture as a source of warranted knowledge fit well with modern theological liberalism but bode poorly for evangelicals. Only the inner life of humanity could be considered the rightful place to ground religious knowledge.[54] "Modernist Christianity," in breaking with the conservatism principle, fully embraced secular developmental philosophies and evolutionary views of the Bible and religion. *The Fundamentals*

---

50. Ibid., 29.
51. Bowler, "Evolution," 220.
52. Roberts and Turner, *The Sacred*, 119. See also ibid. 14, 36.
53. Ibid., 19.
54. Ibid., xi, 1–13, 28.

(1910–1915), the now famous treatises giving rise to the term "fundamentalism," were written by evangelicals to raise awareness of these convergent threats.

The evolutionary approach to all of life seemed at root to blame. Not surprisingly, evangelicals leading the culture war generally referred to themselves as "anti-evolutionists," with the term "creationist" mostly coming into play later in the century.[55] Some hoped to combat Darwinism based on agreement regarding the interpretation of Genesis, but most evangelicals considered this largely unimportant. If American evangelicals held a variety of approaches to Genesis, they united around the need to contest evolution.[56] Believing their worldview under siege, many American evangelicals not only refused to court any aspect of Darwinism, they sought to banish it outright. The anti-evolutionism movement, culminating in the Scopes trial, would be the result.

AMERICAN EVANGELICALS AND EVOLUTION: MID-TWENTIETH CENTURY TO THE PRESENT

With the loss of institutional and societal influence, American evangelicals found themselves by the middle of the twentieth century disenchanted with their lack of cultural engagement. Retreat no longer seemed an option. Evangelicals sought to renew their influence intellectually. The formation in 1942 of the National Association of Evangelicals appeared promising that evangelicals were uniting to engage a secular world.[57] Another facet of this engagement led to the formation of the American Scientific Affiliation (ASA) in 1941.

---

55. Numbers, *Darwinism*, 52, 80. At the time of publication of Darwin's *Origin* in 1859, the term "creationists" referred to those who believed God specially created the soul of every human at conception rather than the soul being inherited from parents (traducianism).

56. Numbers, *Darwinism*, 53. See also Ronald L. Numbers, "Creating Creationism: Meanings and Uses Since the Age of Agassiz," in *Evangelicals and Science in Historical Perspective*, ed. David N. Livingstone, D. G. Hart, and Mark A. Noll (New York: Oxford University Press, 1990), 235.

57. George M. Marsden, *Reforming Fundamentalism: Fuller Seminary and the New Evangelicalism* (Grand Rapids: Eerdmans, 1987), 8–11; Christopher M. Rios, *After the Monkey Trial: Evangelical Scientists and a New Creationism* (Bronx, NY: Fordham University Press, 2014), 41.

The American Scientific Affiliation: Evolutionary Opposition and Affirmation

Five evangelical Christian scientists met to form the ASA at the invitation of the president of Moody Bible Institute. These men devoted "themselves to the task of reviewing, preparing, and distributing information on the authenticity, historicity, and scientific aspects of the Holy Scriptures in order that the faith of many in the Lord Jesus Christ may be firmly established."[58] Evincing the conservatism principle, the original ASA doctrinal statement affirmed biblical inerrancy and the impossibility of contradiction between Scripture and genuine scientific facts.[59] Originally a new kind of fundamentalism with anti-evolutionary assumptions, its membership came to include evangelical theologians such as Carl F. H. Henry. Examples of the rejection of universal common ancestry can be found in early articles of the ASA's journal by luminaries such as Bernard Ramm and Russell Mixter.[60]

But though the founders of the ASA were personally anti-evolutionary, the organization did not identify itself as such, which "resulted in considerable confusion among those who attempted to identify the group as friend or foe."[61] In fairly short order, it became apparent that the ASA was not a foe of evolution. Henry proposed in the 1940s an ASA volume to coincide

58. Terry Gray, "The History of the American Scientific Affiliation (Part One)," May 12, 2016, http://biologos.org/blogs/ted-davis-reading-the-book-of-nature/evolution-and-christian-faith-seventy-five-years-of-conversation-in-the-american-scientific-affiliation/.

59. Rios, *Monkey Trial*, 43; Numbers, *Darwinism*, 3–4.

60. Advocating rejection of theistic and naturalistic evolution's notion of "vertical" evolution, see Bernard Ramm, "The Scientifico-Logical Structure of the Theory of Evolution," *Journal of the American Scientific Affiliation* 1, no. 3 (June 1949): 10-15, http://www.asa3.org/ASA/PSCF/1949/JASA6-49Ramm.html. Ramm was professor of apologetics at the Bible Institute of Los Angeles (Biola) at the time. See also Russell Mixter, "The Science of Heredity and the Source of Species," *Journal of the American Scientific Affiliation* 1, no. 3 (June 1949): 1–6, http://www.asa3.org/ASA/PSCF/1949/JASA6-49Mixter.html.

61. Rios, *Monkey Trial*, 45. Working in a different context than American anti-evolutionists, a more progressive and heterogeneous group of British evangelicals formed in 1950 the Research Scientists' Christian Fellowship, now Christians in Science (CiS). The group set out to expose not Darwinism, but naturalistic materialism. Biblical authority was viewed as pertaining to matters of faith and conduct, not history and science. On J. I. Packer's early controversy with the group over the historic fall and worries about drifting toward modernism, see Rios, *Monkey Trial*, 93–99, 104. The ASA and CiS now are considered sister organizations.

with the centennial of Darwin's *Origin*, assuming the book would oppose Darwinism. By the time of publication in 1959, *Evolution and Christian Thought Today* revealed the general pro-evolution consensus and direction the ASA had assumed.[62] Within two decades leaders of the organization came to affirm theistic evolution.[63] By the 1960s, the ASA was the most prominent evangelical society in the United States defending evolution, "becoming one of the most appreciated and most abhorred organizations within American evangelicalism."[64] By the 1990s, members of the ASA predominately held to "uncompromising evolution" rather than one of the more limited versions held by some earlier evangelicals.[65]

Eventually the early ASA consensus faded regarding the impossibility of contradiction between Scripture and genuine scientific facts. Within the lifetime of its founders, some ASA leaders came to believe the Bible contained errors in historical and scientific details. These errors were believed to pose no problems for God's saving purposes since they were not the intentional teachings of Scripture.[66] Discussions ensued in the ASA journal likely unimaginable to the founders such as whether a historical Adam existed or if the first evolved humans necessarily sinned due to their

---

62. Russell Mixter, ed., *Evolution and Christian Thought Today* (Grand Rapids: Eerdmans, 1959). See Rios, *Monkey Trial*, 53–60.

63. Rios, *Monkey Trial*, 2.

64. Ibid., 42; see also ibid. 122. Terry Gray contends that the decisive turning point toward embracing evolution occurred a bit later: "During the first three decades of the ASA, many members held an either/or attitude concerning creation and evolution: it's one or the other, not both. . . .Two publications in 1971 by the editor of the ASA journal, Stanford materials scientist physicist Richard H. Bube, signaled the beginning of the end of the older attitude. The titles of his articles adequately summarized Bube's position: 'We Believe in Creation' and 'Biblical Evolutionism?' While some members had already dropped hints of embracing evolution as a God-directed means of creation, most earlier writings depicted evolution as a stark alternative to biblical creation." Terry Gray, "The History of the American Scientific Affiliation (Part 3)," May 26, 2016, http://biologos. org/blogs/ted-davis-reading-the-book-of-nature/the-history-of-the-american-scientific-affiliation-part-3#sthash.b9KKRpQE.dpuf.

65. Numbers, *Darwinism*, 14.

66. Rios, *Monkey Trial*, 145–46, 150–52. Gray presents the case a bit less starkly: "Some have done this by adopting some form of limited inerrancy. Others interpret alleged scientific errors in the Bible as prescientific phenomenological claims employing the language of appearances." Terry Gray, "The History of the American Scientific Affiliation (Part 4)," June 2, 2016, http://biologos.org/blogs/ted-davis-reading-the-book-of-nature/ the-history-of-the-american-scientific-affiliation-part-4#sthash.gprzFLtN.dpuf.

animal ancestry.[67] The ASA today distinguishes itself by "belief in orthodox Christianity, as defined by the Apostles' and Nicene creeds," and "a
commitment to mainstream science, that is, any subject on which there is
a clear scientific consensus."[68] A fair description of the ASA might be to say
its members generally seek to relate prevailing natural science and methodological naturalism with Christian doctrine while opposing naturalistic
assumptions such as philosophical naturalism.[69]

To accuse the ASA of theological liberalism would be neither fair nor
accurate. Unlike classic theological liberals, authors of ASA journal articles typically seek to reconcile science with orthodox theology. And unlike
theological liberals, often contributors to the ASA journal develop hybrid
science-theology models taking the Bible seriously. But the ASA has abandoned the Galileo proposal of assuming biblical inerrancy. Traditional
evangelicals will contend that taking Scripture seriously without a firm
commitment to biblical infallibility will produce theological instability at
best. And conservatives will continue to resist most ASA Darwinian theological models as evangelically inconsistent.

Henry Morris and the Institute for Creation Research: Anti-Evolutionism and More

Not all members of the ASA were pleased with its eventual evolutionary direction. Henry M. Morris (1918–2006) joined the ASA in 1948

---

67. ASA journal examples debating various theological issues assuming no historical
Adam or an Adam evolved from lower life forms include Denis O. Lamoureux, "Beyond
Original Sin: Is a Theological Paradigm Shift Inevitable?" *Perspectives on Science and
Christian Faith* 67, no. 1 (March 2015): 35–49; George L. Murphy, "Roads to Paradise
and Perdition: Christ, Evolution, and Original Sin," *Perspectives on Science and Christian
Faith* 58, no. 2 (June 2006): 109–18; Daniel C. Harlow, "After Adam: Reading Genesis
in an Age of Evolutionary Science," *Perspectives on Science and Christian Faith* 62, no. 3
(September 2010): 179–95; and John A. McIntyre, "The Real Adam and Original Sin,"
Perspectives on Science and Christian Faith 58, no. 2 (June 2006): 90–98. Responses to
McIntyre include: David Wilcox, "The Original Adam and the Reality of Sin," *Perspectives
on Science and Christian Faith* 58, no. 2 (June 2006): 104–105, and James P. Hurd, "Reply
to the Real Adam and Original Sin," *Perspectives on Science and Christian Faith* 58, no. 2
(June 2006): 102–103.

68. "Who Are We?" American Scientific Affiliation, http://network.asa3.
org/?page=ASAAbout.

69. Rios, *Monkey Trial*, 60, 183.

because it held promise, but became distraught over the evolutionary turn.[70] Attempts in the 1950s to include versions of theistic evolution as a legitimate creationism model "provoked a backlash among the increasingly outspoken advocates" of young earth creationism (YEC).[71] Collaboration between Morris and another disaffected ASA member, John C. Whitcomb (1924–), led to the 1961 publication of *The Genesis Flood*.[72] The book fired a shot across evangelicalism's bow that, not only was theistic evolution wrong-headed, but a unified recent creation and flood geology approach was "the only orthodox understanding of Genesis."[73]

The Genesis Flood birthed a movement, striking an immediate chord with those concerned about evolutionary evangelicals. If the ASA seemed to submit biblical interpretation to science, Morris and Whitcomb claimed they were taking the Bible literally, making sure to accommodate science to fit Scripture. Following the lead of Morris and Whitcomb, evangelicals getting on board with the new movement not only were characterized by anti-evolutionism, but also anti-old earth creationism. YEC quickly became the standard view among conservative evangelicals. "In substantial, though undetermined, numbers they abandoned the once-favored day-age and gap theories, which allowed for the antiquity of life on Earth, accepting instead the strict creationism of flood geology, which limited the history of life to no more than 10,000 years and affirmed creation in six twenty-four-hour days."[74]

Previous old earth creationist models, not to mention theistic evolution, had typically offered seemingly looser connections between biblical exegesis and science. With flood geology, evangelicals now could oppose theistic evolution while offering an apparently clear, tight science-theology model. And YEC evangelicals were energized and excited. The importance of the extremely influential movement launched by publication of *The Genesis Flood* cannot be overstated. By the 1980s, a new standard of "virtual orthodoxy" dominated among conservative evangelicals with the

---

70. Morris, *A History of Modern Creationism*, 136.

71. Numbers, *Darwinism*, 55.

72. John C. Whitcomb and Henry M. Morris, *The Genesis Flood: The Biblical Record and Its Scientific Implications* (Phillipsburg, NJ: P & R, 1961).

73. Numbers, *Darwinism*, 55.

74. Ibid., 5. Numbers overstates the exact limits of creation at ten thousand years. Some YECs entertain a slightly older creation date.

term "creationism" almost exclusively associated with young earth flood geology.[75]

Anti-evolutionists who viewed the ASA as a lost cause launched in 1963 their counterpart, the Creation Research Society (CRS), with its own scholarly journal. Though initially the group did not agree on the geological effects of the flood or the age of the earth, it eventually came largely to embrace flood geology due to the influence of Morris.[76] Members, however, have only been required to subscribe to the following: the inerrancy of the Bible, including its historical and scientific assertions, and that Genesis origin accounts factually present historical truths; God's direct creation of the original kinds, with subsequent biological changes limited to within those kinds (i.e., rejection of universal common descent); the Genesis flood as a historical worldwide event; the special creation and subsequent fall of Adam and Eve as the basis of the necessity of accepting Jesus Christ as the only Savior.[77]

Morris formed in 1972 the Institute for Creation Research (ICR) with an emphasis on research, education, and communication. Within a short time ICR's influence exploded. In little more than a decade it had published fifty-five books, with those of Morris translated into ten languages.[78] Eventually ICR became the unquestioned worldwide leader for young earth creationism, "endeavoring to impact the lives and ministries of pastors, teachers, students, and families with the wonders of God's creation."[79] ICR would dominate the YEC world in influence for decades until the death of Morris in 2006 and the meteoric rise of Answers in Genesis.

By the early 1980s, the young earth creationist movement swayed public opinion such that efforts were made to grant it equal time in public

---

75. Numbers, "Creationism," 284, 287. See also Rios, *Monkey Trial*, 115, and Numbers, *Darwinism*, 56.

76. Donald B. DeYoung and Kevin L. Anderson, "The Creation Research Society: Fifty Years of Service, 1963 to 2013," *Creation Research Society Quarterly* 50, no. 1 (Summer 2013): 4–12. See also Rios, *Monkey Trial*, 66.

77. "History and Aims," Creation Research Society, https://www.creationresearch. org/index.php/about-crs/history-and-aims. DeYoung and Anderson, "The Creation Research Society," 5, however, claim that the society's "tenants [sic] include a recent supernatural creation" and "24-days of biblical Creation."

78. Rios, *Monkey Trial*, 115.

79. "Who We Are," Institute for Creation Research, http://www.icr.org/who-we-are. See also Numbers, "Creationism," 286.

science classrooms.[80] Since flood geology ("creation science") as a science issue could be distinguished from biblical teaching ("biblical creationism"), proponents of the equal time push argued they were not promoting religion in the classroom.[81] Anti-evolutionists during the 1920s such as William Jennings Bryan had sought to ban the teaching of Darwinism in public schools; these young earth creationists sought only to include in public school curricula this alternative scientific explanation of the world.[82] But evolution had become an American educational centerpiece since the 1960s. If the scientific establishment was forced to pay attention to anti-evolutionism for the first time since the 1920s, it nonetheless quickly rose up to defeat it.[83]

I survey the historical and conceptual background of YEC in chapter 7. But in this look at the evangelical response to evolution since the mid-twentieth century, the most significant development has clearly been the rise of YEC. The young earth creationist movement continues with enormous momentum more than a half-century after *The Genesis Flood*. Today, when evangelicalism and evolution are discussed, YEC is likely the first connotation coming to mind. Though hotly debated by evangelicals, the cluster of ideas associated with YEC has become the new standard by which evangelical anti-evolutionism is measured.

EVANGELICALS ENGAGING EVOLUTION TODAY: FOUR DIFFERENT WAYS

Conservative American evangelicals largely remain nervous about evolution. But arguably they are generally more easily confused than their predecessors as to just what constitutes the evolutionary problem. No longer is the issue before them just the rejection of universal common descent and human evolution. Four influential and popular groups associated with evangelicalism today present four divergent ways of relating to evolution. Three of them I introduced in the first chapter.

---

80. Numbers, *Darwinism*, 7.
81. Rios, *Monkey Trial*, 106.
82. Numbers, *Darwinism*, 56.
83. Rios, *Monkey Trial*, 110.

Answers in Genesis: Young Earth Creationism

If Henry Morris was the inspiration and conceptual founder of the modern
YEC movement, Ken Ham (1951–) has been the superior organizer and
popularizer.[84] "The president, CEO, and founder of Answers in Genesis-US,
and the highly acclaimed Creation Museum, and the world-renowned
Ark Encounter, Ham is one of the most in-demand Christian speakers in
North America."[85] He moved to the United States from Australia in 1987
to work with Morris's Institute for Creation Research. He founded his
own YEC ministry in 1994, renamed Answers in Genesis (AiG) in 1997.
In 2007, AiG opened its Creation Museum near Cincinnati, Ohio, on 70
acres. "The brainchild" of Ham, the 75,000-square-foot museum attracted
2.7 million visitors in its first nine years.[86] He was also the "visionary
behind a popular, full-size Noah's Ark," opening in 2016 with more than
"300,000 awe-struck visitors and 200 media" in its first ten weeks.[87] Ham's
2014 debate with Bill Nye "the Science Guy" made him "internationally
known."[88]

But even if AiG has become the undisputed leader in YEC ministries,
specific details about what it stands for and opposes can be difficult to sort
out. Though it makes clear that the ministry seeks "to expose the bankruptcy of evolutionary ideas, and its bedfellow, a 'millions of years old'
earth (and even older universe),"[89] just what's involved in those "evolutionary ideas" can be complex. I examine just what AiG considers "evolutionary" science in chapter 7. And based on the age of the earth alone, AiG's
strident approach to fellow anti-evolutionary evangelicals who believe in

---

84. Morris was himself an effective popularizer. ICR had its own creation museum in
San Diego before AiG's. Launched in 1992, the "10,000 sq. ft. showcase," the Creation
and Earth History Museum, was developed by ICR for sixteen years before being sold to
new owners when ICR moved its headquarters to Texas in 2008. "Museum History Past,
Present and Future," Creation & Earth History Museum, http://creationsd.org/museum_
history.html. ICR currently has plans for its own new creation museum. "ICR Discovery
Center for Science and Earth History," Institute for Creation Research, http://www.icr.
org/discoverycenter/.

85. "Ken Ham: Speaker, Author, President, CEO, and Founder of Answers in
Genesis," Answers in Genesis, https://answersingenesis.org/bios/ken-ham/.

86. Ibid.

87. Ibid.

88. Ibid.

89. "About," Answers in Genesis, https://answersingenesis.org/about/.

biblical inerrancy can be bewildering. But my examination of those issues must await chapters 7, 8, and 9.

Reasons to Believe: Old Earth Creationism

Reasons to Believe (RTB) has been the major old earth creationist (OEC) ministry for decades. Led by astronomer Hugh Ross (1945–), RTB "is dedicated to demonstrating, via a variety of resources and events, that science and biblical faith are allies, not enemies. While in college, [Ross] committed himself to faith in Jesus Christ. After his study of big bang cosmology convinced him of a Creator's existence, curiosity led him to test religious 'holy books' for scientific and historical accuracy. Only the Bible passed the test, therefore persuading him of Christianity's validity."[90] Having earned a Ph.D. in astronomy from the University of Toronto, Ross "founded Reasons to Believe in 1986, to bring scientific evidence for Christianity to light."[91] By means of numerous books, articles, videos, and podcasts, as well as speaking at several hundred universities and as many churches, Ross has sought to "spread the Christian Gospel by demonstrating that sound reason and scientific research—including the very latest discoveries—consistently support, rather than erode, confidence in the truth of the Bible and faith in the personal, transcendent God revealed in both Scripture and nature."[92]

For the first hundred years after *The Origin of Species* the majority of evangelical anti-evolutionists were old earth creationists as we will see in chapter 6. Many believed the seeming appearance of new species in the fossil record provided evidence of creation. As opposed to evolutionists, these "progressive creationists" believed the evidence revealed God's direct creation occurred many times interspersed over long periods of time. RTB is the best known proponent of progressive creationism today: "RTB scholars believe that God miraculously intervened throughout the history of the universe in various ways millions, possibly even billions, of times to create each and every new species of life on Earth."[93]

---

90. "Dr. Hugh Ross: President & Founder," Reasons to Believe, http://www.reasons.org/about/who-we-are/hugh-ross.

91. Ibid.

92. "Our Mission: Engage & Equip," Reasons to Believe, http://www.reasons.org/about/our-mission.

93. "FAQs," Reasons to Believe, http://www.reasons.org/about/faqs.

Because of these positions and their prominence, Ross and RTB often bear the brunt of anti-old earth blows from some YECs. Progressive creationists like Ross are often referred to as "evolutionists," or as "semi-creationists," or perhaps the most common word used to describe OECs like Ross, "compromisers."[94] But Ross has fired back at his accusers, too, calling them the "hyperevolutionists."[95] I shall offer critique of RTB's ministry in chapter 9.

BioLogos: Evolutionary Creationism

Young earth creationists have had very influential ministries like ICR and AiG for decades. And OECs have had RTB. But only recently did theistic evolutionists, or to use the preferred term among evangelicals, evolutionary creationists (ECs), develop their "premier organization producing resources on multiple platforms, which celebrate the compatibility of evolutionary creation and biblical faith. These resources are not just for scientists, but also for pastors, small groups, parents, and anyone else interested understanding what science and the Bible reveal about the development of life."[96] BioLogos may be the youngest of the evangelical friendly organizations seeking to engage evolution, but it has dramatically risen in influence in a short period of time.

---

94. Douglas Kelly claims that progressive creationists can legitimately be termed "evangelical evolutionists." Douglas Kelly, *Creation and Change: Genesis 1.1–2.4 in the Light of Changing Scientific Paradigms,* reprint (Fearn, Scotland: Christian Focus Publications, 1999), 142. In a December 2001 letter to supporters of the ICR, John Morris refers to old earth advocate Hugh Ross as a "semi-creationist." John Morris, "Do Creationists Really Believe in Evolution?" http://www.icr.org/article/do-creationists-really-believe-evolution/. And the title of the following book says it all: Jonathan Sarfati, *Refuting Compromise: A Biblical and Scientific Refutation of "Progressive Creationism" (Billions of Years) as Popularized by Astronomer Hugh Ross,* 2nd ed. (Powder Springs, GA: Creation Book Publishers, 2011).

95. Hugh Ross says, "Those who have leveled some of the most stinging criticism at old-earth creationists, accusing them of being theistic evolutionists . . . are actually forced by their own interpretation to be hyperevolutionists. Their apparent faith in the efficiency of natural-process biological evolution actually exceeds that of nontheists." Hugh Ross and Gleason L. Archer, "The Day-Age View," in *The Genesis Debate: Three Views on the Days of Creation,* ed. David G. Hagopian (Mission Viejo, CA: Crux Press, Inc., 2001), 126–27.

96. "What Is BioLogos?" BioLogos, http://biologos.org/resources/audio-visual/what-is-biologos#sthash.3C656CgM.dpuf.

Evangelical Francis Collins (1950–) founded BioLogos in 2007, and its website has only been up since 2009. His stature as former leader of the Human Genome Project and now director of the National Institutes of Health earned immediate attention and credibility for the new ministry. Since its inception, "BioLogos has experienced tremendous growth in the numbers of fully committed followers of Christ who resonate with our efforts and have joined the conversation. Our website now includes over 1,200 blog entries and receives nearly two thousand 'hits' a day. Nearly a million people have visited our website since its launch and many of them have returned, for a total of over two million visits."[97] BioLogos has sought conversations with evangelicals "skeptical of evolution," including Southern Baptist leaders and Reasons to Believe.[98] But in spite of the group's irenic conversations with anti-evolutionist evangelicals, significant theological concerns about BioLogos remain as we will see in chapters 8 and 9.

Intelligent Design: Anti-Evolutionism without Theology

Finally, though the movement known as intelligent design (ID) is not composed strictly of evangelicals, it has received much evangelical attention in the past quarter century. But some mistakenly assume ID, rather than old earth creationism, to be the evangelical counterpart to young earth and evolutionary creationism.[99] Some of its leaders have written theological books and articles.[100] But in spite of a rather more traditional

---

97. Deborah Haarsma, "New Leadership for The BioLogos Foundation," BioLogos, January 28, 2013, http://biologos.org/blogs/deborah-haarsma-the-presidents-notebook/new-leadership-for-the-biologos-foundation#sthash.kFekMrZ1.dpuf. Unlike traditional evangelical creationist ministries, which have often been founded and led by one major figure, BioLogos has had three different presidents in its short existence.

98. "Our History," BioLogos, http://biologos.org/about-us/our-history/#sthash.nwzVq4gc.dpuf. For one of these dialogues, see *Creation and Evolution: A Conversation between BioLogos and Reasons to Believe*, ed. Kenneth Keathley (Downers Grove, IL: InterVarsity Press, forthcoming).

99. For example, see these three discussed as alternatives by Tyler O'Neil, "Reasons Christians Can Believe in Evolution," June 28, 2016, PJ Media, https://pjmedia.com/faith/2016/06/28/4-reasons-christians-can-believe-in-evolution/.

100. For example, William Dembski, *The End of Christianity: Finding a Good God in an Evil World* (Nashville: B & H, 2009).

anti-evolutionism featured in the influential 1991 book *Darwin on Trial*[101] by father of the movement Phillip E. Johnson, ID essentially "refers to a scientific research program as well as a community of scientists, philosophers, and other scholars who seek evidence of design in nature. The theory of intelligent design holds that certain features of the universe and of living things are best explained by an intelligent cause, not an undirected process such as natural selection."[102] So, although contending for design in nature puts ID at odds with orthodox Darwinism today, not all ID proponents reject universal common descent. And the movement has neither statement of faith nor stated position on the Bible. Since ID is neither representing evangelicals nor even Christianity per se, we will not focus on its ideas henceforth. But its influence in evangelical circles in the past couple of decades, in spite of any salutary contributions, makes matters even more confusing for rank-and-file evangelicals trying to sort out young earth, old earth, and evolutionary creation.[103]

CONCLUSION

Most American evangelicals in principle have resisted Darwinism, even if often unclear just what is involved. The conservatism principle in no other controversy has been more clearly at work. So much about evolution seemed so unbiblical. Universal common descent, including humans, not to mention the Darwinian model of the origin of human intelligence and morals, has from the first repelled evangelicals. Most felt the only faithful option was to defend the Bible in its conflict with evolution.

Evangelicals became characterized by their anti-evolutionism. But it seemed just as they stood in the gap against Darwinism, they themselves

---

101. Phillip E. Johnson, *Darwin on Trial* (Downers Grove, IL: InterVarsity Press, 1991).

102. "Definition of Intelligent Design," http://www.intelligentdesign.org/whatisid. php.

103. Making matters even more confusing is the ongoing debate, sometimes heated, between ID proponents and ECs at BioLogos. Obviously, advocates for design won't agree with traditional anti-teleology Darwinians like most at BioLogos. Cf. Robin Parry, "God Is More Than an Intelligent Designer," BioLogos, March 31, 2016, http://biologos. org/blogs/brad-kramer-the-evolving-evangelical/god-is-more-than-an-intelligent-designer#sthash.OWpUlzIK.dpuf with "Did a Commenter at BioLogos Find a Damning Error in Meyer's Signature in the Cell? Nope," Evolution News & Views, October 3, 2016, http://www.evolutionnews.org/2016/10/did_biologos_fi103185.html.

went from cultural guardians to cultural goats. Evangelicals not only lost their academic influence, but they watched as the conception of science itself changed. No longer used to provide evidence for God, any assumption of the miraculous or design was ruled out in advance (methodological naturalism).

Evangelicals sought to reinvigorate their academic involvement, but their new American Scientific Affiliation itself soon became largely committed to theistic evolution. In response, the modern young earth creationist movement was born. Its surprising rise to dominance among evangelicals testified to their ongoing concerns about evolution. Today evangelicals are likely to reject evolution, with 57% believing "humans and other living things have always existed in their present form."[104]

But if American evangelicals are generally uneasy about evolution, they also can be forgiven for being less than clear about just what is the problem. Influential but competing evangelical ministries today have arisen to exhort evangelicals what to think about extremely complex matters. Which authority should they trust?

BioLogos has many warm-hearted evangelicals promoting it. But the group is fully comfortable with modern evolutionary theory, and thereby are much less inclined to invoke God in the evolutionary process than even the secularists of Darwin's day. Do they really practice the conservatism principle?

Reasons to Believe rejects the anti-design universal common descent that ECs accept. But it is comfortable with millions of years of animal death before Adam's fall. Answers in Genesis argues that all OECs are virtually as dangerous as ECs. Yet as we will see in chapter 7, leading YECs today are typically more amenable to the adaptive effects of natural selection (providentially directed) than first-generation secularists. Ironically, OECs often stress the transmutation of species less than YECs.

Anti-evolutionists a century ago in some ways had it easier. Their differences seemed smaller and their concerns much clearer. Too many options today may be stressful, but high-powered ministries won't easily let evangelicals remain blissfully on the sideline.

---

104. David Masci, "On Darwin Day, 5 facts about the evolution debate," Fact tank: News in the Numbers, February 12, 2016, http://www.pewresearch.org/fact-tank/2016/02/12/darwin-day/.

Chapter 5

FLOOD, FOSSILS, AND STRATA:
Geology and the Age of the Earth

"Some drill and bore
The solid earth, and from the strata there
Extract a register, by which we learn,
That He who made it, and revealed its date
To Moses, was mistaken in its age."[1]

—William Cowper, "The Task"

In the early eighteenth century, about the time New England Puritan ministers were teaching the new astronomy, some also announced the discovery of fossilized evidence of human giants killed by Noah's flood. A giant tooth weighing nearly five pounds on the banks of the Hudson River provided the evidence, though it actually had belonged to a mastodon.[2] Mastodon fossil remains were so puzzling they were referred to as the American *incognitum*. Early American gentry were very familiar with the puzzling phenomenon, and frequently collected its bones and speculated about its identity. A salt lick in Kentucky came to be known as "Big Bone Lick" due to the discovery there in 1739 of *incognitum*'s bones.

---

1. William Cowper, "The Task," cited in J. Mellor Brown, *Reflections on Geology* (Edinburgh: The Edinburgh Printing and Publishing Co, 1838), 24, in *Creationism and Scriptural Geology, 1817–1857*, 7 vols., ed. and intro. John M. Lynch (Bristol, England: Thoemmes Press, 2002), vol. 1.

2. Paul Semonin, *American Monster: How the Nation's First Prehistoric Creature Became a Symbol of National Identity* (New York: New York University Press, 2000), xiii, 3, 10–12, 15, 25. Cotton Mather was one of those proclaiming this alleged biblical confirmation.

Before the Revolutionary War, bones from the site were sent to Paris, London, and Philadelphia. Recipients included George Washington, Thomas Jefferson, Benjamin Franklin, and French naturalist Georges-Louis Leclerc Buffon. Even during the Revolutionary War, Washington and Jefferson bothered to collect their bones from battlefields.[3] Within a few decades, most rightly held that the bones were from some type of elephant like the mammoth whose frozen carcass had been discovered in Siberia. Jefferson, as the nation's foremost authority on these bones, even believed the animal still lived in the Northwest Territories. Most Americans were not yet aware that any of God's creatures had ever become extinct. Debates ensued whether *incognitum* had been carnivorous. Speculation about its potential savagery made its extinction God's blessing on the human race.[4]

Fascinating fossil discoveries like *incognitum* would become key to the growing understanding of the earth, and why some would eventually believe it was old. Ussher's famous biblical chronology from the mid-seventeenth century dated creation to 4004 BC.[5] Students of the earth at that time felt no compulsion in challenging such work.[6] Why should they? The earth's age had been uncontroversial, and recent creation was assumed much the same way geocentrism had been.

No one set out to determine scientifically the age of the earth. Pragmatic concerns such as mining and digging wells provided incentive to learn about its interior. But following the Copernican revolution, questions also arose regarding the earth's nature since it now was understood to be a planet. The new science of the heavens inspired seventeenth- and

---

3. Ibid., 2. Jefferson even had Daniel Boone deliver a request to George Rogers Clark during the Revolutionary War to procure some of the *incognitum*'s teeth from Big Bone Lick. Ibid., 9.

4. Ibid., 3, 7–8. Early on the animal's giant tusks were incorrectly depicted facing downward, giving the impression of a ferocious carnivore. Ibid., 364.

5. On the many others in antiquity who produced biblical chronologies, see François Ellenberger, *History of Geology*, vol. 2, *The Great Awakening and Its First Fruits—1600–1810*, ed. Marguerite Carozzi (Rotterdam: A. A. Balkema, 1999), 36, and Martin J. S. Rudwick, *The Meaning of Fossils: Episodes in the History of Palenotology*, 2nd ed. (New York: Science History Publications, 1976), 70.

6. Davis A. Young and Ralph F. Stearley, *The Bible, Rocks and Time: Geological Evidence for the Age of the Earth* (Downers Grove, IL: InterVarsity Press, 2008), 47.

eighteenth-century "theories of the earth" regarding the earth's surface and interior.[7]

Many geologists in the late sixteenth and early seventeenth centuries, much like Johannes Kepler, viewed their work as a religious duty since they were respecting the Creator's handiwork.[8] The late seventeenth- and early eighteenth-century British geologists often understood geology to reveal God's glory. They correlated the creation order of Genesis 1 with the fossil sequence in the strata as evidence for the truth of the Bible.[9] During the first couple of centuries of geological theorizing, most claimed their views were in full accord with the biblical creation and flood.[10] Theologians especially supported early geological work.[11] With an emphasis on God's work in history, the biblical worldview framed an understanding of the finite, linear flow to earth history.[12]

THEORIES OF THE EARTH

Early modern scientific thinking about the earth was naturally influenced by the Bible. But important questions still did not admit of ready-made answers. For instance, what was the nature of the interior of the earth? Was it the biblical "great abyss," or was it filled with a liquid or fire?[13] One theory, however, was standard.

Diluvialism: Early Flood Theories

In the seventeenth and eighteenth centuries, the most influential early theory was diluvialism, explaining phenomena in light of the flood. Though some Christians had historically suggested the flood as cause of some of

---

7. Ellenberger, *History,* 2:359.

8. Ibid., 2:84.

9. Ibid., 2:341.

10. Ibid., 2:13.

11. M. Kölbl Ebert, "Geology and Religion: A Historical Perspective on Current Problems," in *Geology and Religion: A History of Harmony and Hostility,* ed. Martina Kölbl Ebert (London: The Geological Society, 2009), 1.

12. Martin Rudwick, *Earth's Deep History: How It Was Discovered and Why It Matters* (Chicago: University of Chicago Press, 2014), 29, 101.

13. Ellenberger, *History,* 2:16–22.

the earth's features,[14] these new theorists sought more explicitly scientific explanations. And like the central figures in the geocentrism controversy, these thinkers typically sought to understand puzzling physical features in light of the Bible.[15] The theories were diverse, controversial, and creative.

Seventeenth- and eighteenth-century Protestants discussed scientifically reasonable, discoverable, and usually massive geological effects of the flood. They often speculated that the deluge produced the inclination of sedimentary layers, but differed widely otherwise. Some argued the waters collapsed the earth's crust, with mountains remaining as points not sunken down. Others conjectured that the earth entirely dissolved in the flood and was then redeposited as the present strata. Some reasoned that the land and oceans had been completely rearranged.[16]

Thomas Burnet (1635–1715) calculated that the volume of water in the oceans could not have covered the mountains during the flood. Therefore, there must be a subterranean reservoir of water.[17] The cracking open of the crust not only released that water but also broke up the smooth surface and created a tilt in the earth's axis. This brought about the origins of seasonal climates. And because the sun was not created until the fourth day, the first three days could have been of undetermined length, thus allowing an extended history of the earth. Burnet's theories were controversial enough, but he also provoked trenchant criticism by discounting the biblical flood as literal history.[18]

John Woodward (1665–1728), regarded as the "Grand Protector of the Universal Deluge," agreed with Burnet regarding a hollow earth filled with water. But he condemned Burnet for not maximizing the flood's effects. The desolating waters, according to Woodward, would have broken the entire landmass into particles. The deposition of the rock layers represents the heavier particles on bottom and the lightest on top. The resulting strata

14. For the names, see François Ellenberger, *History of Geology,* vol. 1, *From Ancient Times to the First Half of the XVII Century,* ed. Marguerite Carozzi (Rotterdam: A. A. Balkema, 1996), 59, 99–102, 137–38, and Peter J. Bowler, *The Earth Encompassed: A History of the Environmental Sciences* (London: Norton, 1992), 174.

15. Ellenberger, *History,* 2:15; Rudwick, *The Meaning of Fossils,* 87–88.

16. Ellenberger, *History,* 2:43–45.

17. Michael Leddra, *Time Matters: Geology's Legacy to Scientific Thought* (Hoboken, NJ: Wiley-Blackwell, 2010), 104.

18. Ibid.

were also broken and dislocated in places, with virtually no significant modification of the earth's surface since the flood.[19]

William Whiston (1667–1752) also believed the water necessary to cover the earth had been trapped in its core. A comet traveling perilously close tilted the earth on its axis, releasing the deadly interior waters. Getting double-duty from comet theory, Whiston postulated a comet also had affected the chaos of Genesis 1:1–2. Edmund Halley (1656–1742), of comet fame, earlier had theorized that a comet induced the earth to tilt, causing the flood. But Halley's theory didn't require as much water, speculating that the tilting sloshed the oceans out of their basins over the continents. Louis Bourguet (1678–1742), like Woodward, hypothesized that the flood's complete dissolution of the earth re-hardened into various sedimentary layers.[20] But he added mountain formation coupled with a novel use of the now accepted heliocentrism: the earth's daily rotation stirred the dissolved landmass into the final contours of mountain ranges.[21]

The seventeenth and eighteenth centuries also produced theorists approaching diluvialism in quite the opposite fashion; they minimalized the flood's effects. Based on biblical teaching alone, some argued against a violent deluge; the olive branch brought to Noah by the dove implied an olive tree survived the catastrophe. Others argued that the flood's short duration could not have caused the multitude of fossil layers.[22] Some diluvialists posited the flood universally killed all humans but limited the flood geographically because of the absence of catastrophic geologic effects.[23]

Catholic thinkers accentuated the flood's supernaturalism and deemphasized observable effects such as marine fossils discovered inside mountains. Some argued that interpreting the deluge scientifically demeaned its miraculous nature. Others worried providing flawed proofs would create doubts in the minds of believers and strengthen skeptics. But Voltaire ridiculed it nevertheless: "All is miracle in the history of the deluge. . . . It would

19. Gabriel Gohau, *A History of Geology*, rev. and trans. Albert V. Carozzi and Marguerite Carozzi (New Brunswick, NJ: Rutgers University Press, 1990), 55–56; and Ellenberger, *History*, 2:114–30. See also Rudwick, *The Meaning of Fossils*, 77–80, 82–87, and Leddra, *Time Matters*, 105.

20. Gohau, *History*, 55; Ellenberger, *History*, 2:36.

21. Ellenberger, *History*, 2:138–40.

22. Ibid., 2:46–47, 51.

23. Ibid., 2:47.

be senseless to explain it; these are mysteries one believes by faith; and faith consists in believing what reason does not believe, which is another miracle."[24] Catholic censors denouncing physical explanations of the flood safeguarded their theology, but opened the door for Enlightenment geologists to abandon the Bible altogether.[25]

Even if flood theorists found little consensus, attempts to understand the geo-historical effects of the flood contributed to the rise of modern geology.[26] But by the mid-eighteenth century, extensive European fieldwork led to widespread doubts that the flood primarily caused all the rock sequences and fossils. Before 1770, flood theories predominated, but afterward a "critical mass" regarding theories of the earth was reached.[27] From 1770 to 1800, a variety of important ideas began to coalesce.[28] One of the major sources of the new ideas came from well-digging and especially mining.

In 1605, just three years before Dutchman Hans Lippershey (1570–1619) unveiled a telescope that fascinated Galileo, another important event took place in Holland. An Amsterdam well dug more than 200 feet deep revealed fascinating alternating layers of silts, sands, and clays. This evidence of remarkable stratification would be studied by scholars for the following century.[29] And the end of the seventeenth century would witness impressive advances in mapping stratigraphic cross-sections for the use of miners. With its attempts to understand the substructure of the vast underground, mining in Europe played a critical role in the development of geology.[30]

Reformation advancements in university education like those we saw associated with Melanchthon included mining. The 1556 publication of Georgius Agricola's *De Re Metallica* (*On the Nature of Metals*) with its clear description of the rock layers provided the authoritative text for most of the following two centuries.[31]

---

24. Voltaire, "Flood" (1764), in idem, *Philosophical Dictionary,* n.p., quoted in Ellenberger, *History,* 2:46. See also ibid., 2:45–47.

25. Ellenberger, *History,* 2:141.

26. Leddra, *Time Matters,* 115.

27. Ellenberger, *History,* 2:3, 38.

28. Ibid., 2:3; Rhoda Rappaport, *When Geologists Were Historians, 1665–1750* (Ithaca, NY: Cornell University Press, 1996), 136.

29. Ellenberger, *History,* 2:82–83.

30. Gohau, *History,* 99–110; Ellenberger, *History,* 1:160.

31. Ellenberger, *History,* 1:164–72. See also Rudwick, *The Meaning of Fossils,* 23.

But mining knowledge really exploded in the second half of the eighteenth century. The Industrial Revolution necessitated locating and extracting abundant resources such as coal and iron.[32] Journeys devoted to searching for distant mineral deposits multiplied, with many romanticized publications resulting with the word *Voyage* in their titles.[33]

The study of the origin and distribution of minerals and rocks became a distinct scientific field.[34] Teaching in a major mining academy, Abraham Gottlob Werner (1749–1817) focused on the structure and content of the earth's subsurface. Though he didn't create this new science, Werner coined its name, "geognosy." Geognosy provided methodical accounts of the earth's architecture, "both global and local, vertical and horizontal, dividing it, in a hierarchical manner, from great systems to elementary lithostratigraphic units. Of significance, geognosy gave a name to each subdivision. It fixed their sequential order of superposition, which it tried also to trace laterally step by step."[35]

Neptunism: Oceans Do the Work

Werner also speculated about rock origins, with his theory called "Neptunism."[36] Named after the Roman god of the sea, the theory conjectured that the terrestrial subsurface crystallized from oceans. As the standard model in the latter half of the eighteenth and early nineteenth centuries, Neptunism largely ended the dominance of diluvialism.[37] Some such as Richard Kirwan (1733–1812) viewed Neptunism through a biblical lens, thinking of the initial watery chaos of Genesis 1:2, as well as the flood waters receding into caverns in the earth.[38] But as an Enlightenment deist, Werner felt no obligation to the Bible and did not accept the biblical flood.[39] Without submission to external authority, he sought to project his ideas as a rational and objective examination of the evidence. Nonetheless,

---

32. Leddra, *Time Matters*, 247–48.
33. Ellenberger, *History,* 2:179.
34. Ibid., 2:262; Leddra, *Time Matters*, 37–39.
35. Ellenberger, *History,* 2:264.
36. Ibid., 2:262–63.
37. Leddra, *Time Matters*, 83.
38. Davis A. Young, "Scripture in the Hands of Geologists (Part Two)," *Westminster Theological Journal* 49 (1987): 257–304, 260–61.
39. Leddra, *Time Matters*, 84.

its reductionism regarding geological mechanisms legislated erroneous expectations that various homogenous strata would be discovered throughout the earth.[40]

Plutonism: Heat Does the Work

Neptunists tried to make oceanic sedimentation responsible for too many geologic features. Plutonism, named after the Greek god of the deep earth, held that interior heat generates not only volcanic rocks but also produces granites and uplifts in the surface.[41] James Hutton (1726–1797) theorized that subterranean heat uplifted new continents that over time eroded and were deposited into the oceans, only to have the endless cycle begin again.[42] Hutton argued that so many cycles had already passed that no current rocks could be considered original.[43]

Hutton fell into his own reductionist outlook. Whereas other theories viewed the earth as in steady decay, Hutton construed the earth as a kind of self-replenishing heat engine deduced from first principles rather than field observations.[44] Controversially he assumed all geologic features have resulted from past natural processes still operating today at the same rates. This view, later called uniformitarianism, directly challenged the idea that short-lived, violent events produced most geologic effects, that is, catastrophism.[45] Many Christians deemed uniformitarianism unacceptable since it undermined supernatural activity such as creation and the flood.[46]

CHARLES LYELL'S UNIFORMITARIANISM: REJECTING THE SUPERNATURAL

Charles Lyell's (1797–1875) famous book that Darwin devoured, *Principles of Geology*, contended that geology would never become a science until it relied solely on observable processes to explain the past. He employed his

---

40. Ellenberger, *History,* 2:289.
41. Leddra, *Time Matters,* 86.
42. Gohau, *History,* 112–13; Leddra, *Time Matters,* 87.
43. Leddra, *Time Matters,* 91.
44. Ibid., 119.
45. Ibid., 95.
46. Ellenberger, *History,* 2:11.

legal training to present a sustained case against catastrophism, usually associated with progressive creationists.[47] Linking geology with the Bible disturbed Lyell. So he sought to remove supernatural causes and to discredit a universal flood.[48] He emphasized, then, Huttonian uniformitarianism to attack diluvialism, but took it to a whole new level.[49] Committed to no change over time, Lyell proposed that dinosaurs might one day reappear or great numbers of mammals would be discovered in the earlier strata.[50] Most geologists, however, accepted the evidence of fossil changes in rock sequences and found Lyell's approach unrealistic.

Lyell's dogmatism runs counter to contemporary geology, which accepts frequent small and infrequent large geologic events. Lyell's view precluded acceptance of catastrophic mass extinctions (such as the so-called big five).[51] Gradualism, that major changes always come by slow, incremental steps, has come to be rejected. On the other hand, actualism, the unity of historical processes, with its emphatic rejection of supernatural explanations, is still accepted.[52]

But if some like Werner, Hutton, and Lyell sought to liberate geology from biblical connections, many theorists continued to search for correlations with the Bible. But just how to understand the evidence in correlation with the flood was requiring considerably more creative hybrid theories. Earlier theorists developed numerous models to account for the missing volume of flood water. Now much greater knowledge of the earth's interior was forcing similar moves. For reasons we will see shortly, the burgeoning knowledge of the earth's strata led to an increasing marginalization for all-encompassing flood theories in the last half of the eighteenth century.

---

47. Rudwick, *The Meaning of Fossils*, 180–97; Reijer Hooykaas, *Selected Studies in History of Science* (Coimbra, Portugal: Por ordem da Universidade, 1983), 562; Leddra, *Time Matters*, 122.

48. Martin Rudwick, *Worlds Before Adam: The Reconstruction of Geohistory in the Age of Reform* (Chicago: University of Chicago Press, 2008), 201–206, 253–65, 297–314; Bowler, *The Earth Encompassed*, 239, 242; Ellenberger, *History*, 2:345.

49. Bowler, *The Earth Encompassed*, 241; Leddra, *Time Matters*, 121–23.

50. A. Hallam, "Lyell's Views on Organic Progression, Evolution and Extinction," in *Lyell: The Past Is the Key to the Present*, ed. D. J. Blundell and A. C. Scott (London: Geological Society Publishing House, 1998), 134; Bowler, *The Earth Encompassed*, 286; Leddra, *Time Matters*, 123.

51. Leddra, *Time Matters*, 125–26.

52. Ibid., 125, 130.

But Christian diluvialists persisted into the nineteenth century, though the difficulties sometimes led to in-house quarrels over what specific effects the flood had on the earth.[53]

A remarkable revival of diluvialism was born around the beginning of the nineteenth century with a new burst of resourceful hypothesizing. Because current processes (e.g., erosion) could not explain all the earth's surface features, the flood (or running waters for those not concerned to correlate their theory with the Bible) became the most likely explanatory cause as the last of a number of earth-shaping events.[54] Even after glaciology began to be understood several decades later, the notion of running waters, often cataclysmic, as the cause of many surface features remained an ongoing theory.[55] Perhaps other catastrophes better explained the earth's internal features. But in 1822 geologist William Conybeare (1787–1857) even coined a term "diluvium," for the flood's water-born debris, the last great geologic catastrophe shaping the earth's surface.

William Buckland (1784–1856), pioneering geologist at Oxford University, also was a theologian concerned to demonstrate the Bible's trustworthiness in light of geological discoveries. His conviction that the flood explained all the internal rock formations had waned after studying volcanoes.[56] But his study of surface features prompted his dramatic announcement in 1823 that he had confirmation of the universal flood.[57] Buckland correctly identified recently discovered fossils in Kirkdale Cave (North Yorkshire, England) as non-native: hyena, elephant, and hippopotamus. He originally supposed they had been swept there from afar by the flood, but evidence eventually led him to believe the animals lived there before being destroyed by the deluge. This radical idea, that Great Britain had once featured a vastly different ecological system, was quite

---

53. Rappaport, *When Geologists Were Historians*, 178.

54. Martin Rudwick, "Biblical Flood and Geological Deluge: The Amicable Dissociation of Geology and Genesis," in *Geology and Religion: A History of Harmony and Hostility*, ed. Martina Kölbl Ebert (London: The Geological Society, 2009), 105.

55. Ellenberger, *History*, 2:49.

56. Leddra, *Time Matters*, 113.

57. Buckland's book was titled *Reliquiae Diluvianae* (*Relics of the Deluge*), subtitled *Or, Observations on the Organic Remains Contained in Caves, Fissures, and Diluvial Gravel, and on Other Geological Phenomena, Attesting the Action of an Universal Deluge.* Bowler, *The Earth Encompassed*, 239.

controversial.[58] But a major figure had reincorporated the flood into geology.

DISCOVERIES THAT LED TO OLD EARTH THEORY

Buckland may have led the renewed charge to defend the biblical flood, but like virtually all geologists at the time, including Christians, he believed the evidence pointed to a very old creation. That same evidence had prompted him to seek flood evidence on the earth's surface. Difficulties long associated with correlating biblical and earth history pertained largely to the evidence of life contained in rocks.

Fossil Theories

Originally "fossil" (Latin *fossilium*) meant anything dug up from the ground,[59] and generally the Greeks and Romans showed little interest in them.[60] The ancients easily identified fossilized animal bones that had contemporary analogues. But enormous fossil bones were another story and likely contributed to stories of giant human bones both ancient and modern (e.g., *incognitum*).[61]

Inorganic Views

By the end of the Middle Ages most believed fossils spontaneously formed in rocks. The view from their perspective was hardly irrational: how could living things have ever made their way inside rocks? Theories of causation for these included tricks or "sports" of nature, mysterious natural forces, astral fertilizations of the soil, satanic creations, and even God's ancient experiments.[62]

---

58. Bowler, *The Earth Encompassed*, 238–39; Leddra, *Time Matters*, 110–11; Rudwick, *Worlds Before Adam*, 73–88. Robert Hooke (1635–1703) had earlier suggested that the enormous size of some of fossils in Great Britain indicated that England once must have been in a torrid zone. Ellenberger, *History*, 2:88–91.

59. Rudwick, *The Meaning of Fossils*, 1.

60. Ellenberger, *History*, 1:264.

61. Leddra, *Time Matters*, 173. Detailed lists of giant bone discoveries can be found in writers such as Herodotus and Pliny. See Ellenberger, *History of Geology*, 1:27.

62. Ellenberger, *History*, 1:158.

During the Copernican controversy, the church showed little interest in fossils. Though Luther basically attributed them to the flood, marine fossils discovered on land were paid little attention. Speculations regarding fossil causes included a type of fatty matter was fermented by heat; seeds or germs sunk through pores into rocks; underground passages carried seeds to mountaintops to be watered by snow; and even that God created fossils as puzzles to test believers' faith. The prevailing view in the sixteenth century and even into the seventeenth was that the strange rock-encased forms had spontaneously generated.[63] Fossils were just unique rocks that formed without ever having been part of any animal or plant.[64]

Theorists admitted fossils often looked similar to living things or other slightly different fossils, even referring to them as analogues. British naturalist Martin Lister (1638–1712) zealously explored the English countryside, collecting fossils and mapping their distribution. He reportedly trekked halfway across England to follow the trail of just one fossil in a particular rock layer.[65] Yet writing at the end of the seventeenth century, Lister denied that fossil shells were really shells. They were only resemblances found in unique rocks, *Lapides sui generis*.[66] How could they have come from living animals if they were of the same material as the surrounding rock?[67]

Modern Organic Views

But if only a few such as Leonardo da Vinci (1452–1519) had once recognized the organic origin of fossil shells, around 1660 fossils began regularly to be considered as evidence from the living past.[68] Robert Hooke (1635–1703) affirmed the organic origin of fossils in 1665 even though some had no living analogues.[69] He likened fossils to divine archaeological objects serving as archives of the past. And because written in stone, they provide

---

63. Ibid., 1:122–24, 173–78; Butterfield, *Origins*, 235.

64. Gohau, *History*, 59.

65. Ellenberger, *History*, 2:96–97.

66. Ibid., 2:97.

67. He also puzzled over why the fossils of similar "creatures" differed from place to place as well as from living examples. Ellenberger, *History*, 2:98–99.

68. Rudwick, *The Meaning of Fossils*, 39; Ellenberger, *History*, 1:130.

69. Ellenberger, *History*, 2:86–87.

even more lasting monuments than Egyptian pyramids.[70] Other observers such as flood theorist John Woodward (1665–1728) accepted the organic origin of fossils and noted they not only differed from their analogues today, but analogues also differed from place to place.[71] By the middle of the seventeenth century, publications throughout Europe described fossils, even though systematic classification terminology had not yet been developed.[72] Bernard Le Bovier de Fontenelle (1657–1757) foresaw the need for paleontological maps indicating fossil geographical distribution with their resemblances to present-day flora and fauna.[73]

Carolus Linnaeus (1707–1778), the father of modern taxonomy, laid the foundation for the modern description of fossils. His *Systema Naturae* classified the plant and animal kingdoms. Linnaeus conceived of orders containing a number of genera that contained the closely related species. He introduced the modern technique of assigning every species two Latin names, the first term for genus, the second for species.[74] For more than a century afterward the overwhelming majority of scientists considered the species a largely unchanging biological reality until Darwinism rendered them more like snapshots in time.

So eighteenth-century geologists overwhelmingly accepted the organic origin of fossils and believed they likely resulted from the flood.[75] Theories abounded as to how the fossils of marine animals were discovered on high mountains. Diverse notions of the flood, with or without the lowering of

---

70. Ibid., 2:88–91.

71. Ibid., 2:92, 114–30. See also Rudwick, *The Meaning of Fossils*, 77–80, 82–87.

72. Ellenberger, *History*, 2:74–75.

73. Ibid., 2:189, 192.

74. Bowler, *The Earth Encompassed*, 163–64. Robert Hooke had utilized the word "species" to denote a larger grouping than the word does today. He felt the evidence pointed to development and transformation within the species, but not toward a full-blown evolutionary tree. Ellenberger, *History*, 2:94. Interestingly, Linnaeus proposed an idea that sounds similar to a model currently suggested by some leading young earth creationists I examine in chapter 7. He argued that the Garden of Eden was located on a tropical island mountain. The mountain's height produced a sequence of climates (biomes) from polar to tropical especially suited for the various created life forms that spread out as dry land appeared, and then again later after the flood waters receded. David N. Livingstone and Charles W. J. Withers. *Geography and Enlightenment* (Chicago: University of Chicago Press, 1999), 81; Leddra, *Time Matters*, 153.

75. Young and Stearley, *The Bible, Rocks and Time*, 70.

the oceans or the raising of the ground were all much discussed.[76] Discovery of tropical animal fossils in temperate zones (e.g., Kirkdale Cave) as well as gigantic flora and fauna fossils were just some of the enigmas confronting thinkers at the dawn of geology.[77] During this period passion arose in Great Britain for inventorying minerals, rocks, and especially fossils.[78] John Woodward carefully collected and catalogued an immense collection of fossils still preserved today at Cambridge.[79] Later a network of fossil dealers sold rare specimens to wealthy clients. The famous tongue-twister "she sells seashells, by the seashore" was based on the life of Mary Anning (1799–1847), discoverer of important fossils and collector for famous geologists.[80]

Strata: The Layers Reveal Their Secrets

While the organic origin of fossils was being settled, problems for recent creation and traditional flood theories were mounting. The challenges had to do not only with the types of fossils being discovered, but where they were discovered: in rocks. The fossil-embedded layers revealed unanticipated keys to the earth's past.

Nicolas Steno (1638–1686), often viewed as the father of geology, sincerely desired to demonstrate agreement with his discoveries and the creation and flood of Genesis. He also devoted an entire year to studying ancient shell deposits and the geological structure of Tuscany. He became convinced that Tuscany once lay under water, and that the flood provided the satisfactory explanation. The publication of Steno's studies in 1669,

---

76. Ellenberger, *History,* 2:29–32. Athanasius Kircher (1602–1680) analyzed the common suggestions that fossils are "sports of nature" in which the rocks present all manner of images ranging from animals to letters of the alphabet to images of Christ. He explored the possibilities, including chance processes in which our imaginations "see" things by filling in details. He also considered other theories that regarded plant fossils as having originated from germinated seeds. But he concluded that ancient marine animals provided the basis for fossil shells. Ellenberger, *History,* 2:75-81. Edward Lhwyd (1660–1709) postulated that fish fossils inside rocky masses as seen in cliffs might be explained by the flood waters causing fish to infiltrate very small spaces in the ground, thus reaching the interior of the earth. Ibid., 2:111.

77. Ibid., 2:33

78. Ibid., 2:85.

79. Ibid., 2:114–30. See also Rudwick, *The Meaning of Fossils,* 77–80, 82–87.

80. Bowler, *The Earth Encompassed,* 114.

the *Prodromus* ("forerunner" of a work never published), is regarded as one of the most important texts in the history of science. [81] Unlike others who theorized from a chair, his originality lay in allowing objects to reveal their history and mode of production, whether large (regional structures) or small (fossils or crystals). One of his handwritten manuscripts displays his attitude: "They sin against the greatness of God, who do not wish to observe the actual works of nature but, satisfied by reading the writings of others, imagine and fabricate various hypotheses."[82] The birth of stratigraphy is associated with Steno's recognition of what later would be called the principle of superposition: due to the order in which they were deposited, older layers of rock generally lie under the younger.[83]

Steno's discovery had been recognized before. Miners had long defined certain beds as markers helping them navigate layers of rock. The strata were often labeled by letters or numbers because they generally followed in order. Then fossils themselves were termed "medals" or "monuments" as ways of indexing and dating the various strata.[84] By the latter half of the eighteenth century, the contents of these strata were being catalogued as archives of earth's history.[85] So when the "father of English geology," William Smith (1769–1839), displayed his fossil collection, he grouped similar types together according to the strata in which they were found and coined the term "stratigraphy."[86] He also identified and named many of the Mesozoic rock units and created a geological map of much of England and Wales.[87]

But these discoveries presented a problem for theorists seeking a comprehensive flood explanation of the strata. Why were the fossils found in the strata with such regularity that the layers could be indexed by them? Should not the flood have thoroughly mixed rather than thoroughly sorted the animals and plants of that world? Some pondered why no human fossils were mingled in the strata. The problem led Johannes Jakob Scheuchzer

---

81. Rudwick, *Earth's Deep History,* 46; idem, *The Meaning of Fossils,* 49–53; Ellenberger, *History,* 1:156, 190–92, 199, 211, 214, 224–27, 249–50; Rudwick, *Earth's Deep History,* 46; idem, *The Meaning of Fossils,* 49–53.

82. Steno, "Chaos," cited in Ellenberger, *History,* 1:200.

83. Leddra, *Time Matters,* 29; Ellenberger, *History,* 1:193, 222.

84. Ellenberger, *History,* 2:52–61.

85. Ibid., 2:61–62.

86. Rudwick, *Worlds Before Adam,* 35–45.

87. Leddra, *Time Matters,* 44–45.

(1672–1733) to seek diligently for *homo diluvia testis*, a (fossilized) human witness of the flood. In 1726, he dramatically announced just such a find, claiming it a clear flood relic confirmable by even the most exacting anatomist. The "ancient sinner" fossil was celebrated and reproduced in numerous publications. Georges Cuvier, however, carefully and conclusively demonstrated in 1812 that it belonged to an extinct giant salamander.[88]

Another problem had to do with the kind of fossils entombed in the rocks. I've already alluded to the controversy raised by Buckland's discovery of tropical animal fossils in England. Further finds of that sort raised the question: Did the earth in the past have very different ecologies? Stranger still were the discoveries of fantastic creatures such as the dinosaurs. William Buckland described in 1824 for a rapt public the gigantic carnivore from the Jurassic rocks. He named it Megalosaurus (great lizard), the first published description of a dinosaur.[89] He and fellow clergyman William Conybeare also conveyed details about the remarkable flying reptiles. Non-scientists developed tremendous interest in the historical past by identifying and collecting fossils.[90] By the latter half of the nineteenth century, dramatic paleontological discoveries opened the door to a vastly richer understanding of the past.

But if the strange fossil world was being increasingly better understood, Christians were increasingly being faced with the challenge of making sense of the extinctions. The sheer number of extinct animals raised concerns how all of them could have fit on the ark.[91] Early assumptions even made it theologically difficult to accept the possibility of extinctions. If God created species for his glory, why did he allow them to become extinct before humans had ever seen them?[92] Did extinctions imply an imperfect creation from the start?[93] Some sought to escape the problem by theorizing only near complete extinctions, that "lost" species might still live somewhere yet unexplored (e.g., Jefferson's suggestion about *incognitum*).[94] The

88. John Reader, *Missing Links: In Search of Human Origins* (New York: Oxford University Press, 2011), 52–54. A clear picture of the fossil on p. 53 hardly looks human.

89. Bowler, *The Earth Encompassed*, 284.

90. Gohau, *History*, 92; Ellenberger, *History*, 2:344.

91. Rudwick, *The Meaning of Fossils*, 37.

92. Young and Stearley, *The Bible, Rocks and Time*, 59–60.

93. Ellenberger, *History*, 2:93.

94. Ibid., 2:319.

great John Ray in the late seventeenth century frankly admitted he had no easy answer and retreated to the widely held inorganic fossil view to avoid the extinction problem.[95]

Most vexing of all was the question why the strata revealed occasional extinctions followed by sudden appearances of quite different creatures. Georges Cuvier (1769–1832), the father of modern paleontology, recognized that strata characterized by unique fauna were replaced by distinctive younger fauna and could thus be dated relative to one another. This principle would come to be called the law of faunal succession.[96] He observed that "modern" species diminish farther down in the strata, whereas the older strata contain extinct species with no modern counterparts.[97] He noted that reptiles predated mammals, and marine mammals predated terrestrial mammals.[98] William Buckland in 1821 noted that continental Europe had faunal succession similar to that of Britain.[99] By the middle of the nineteenth century, similar patterns discovered in British and continental European biostratigraphy were corroborated on other continents, leading to the virtually complete understanding of the stratigraphic column during that century.[100]

The Flood Column Becomes a Creation Column

Late seventeenth- and early eighteenth-century British geologists often understood the fossil sequence as evidence for creation, and sought to correlate the strata with the first chapter of Genesis.[101] But since the seventeenth century, the primary lens for understanding the geologic

---

95. Bowler, *The Earth Encompassed*, 157–58. See also Rudwick, *The Meaning of Fossils*, 63–66, and Ellenberger, *History*, 2:101–102.

96. Rudwick, *The Meaning of Fossils*, 101–115, 127–32; Leddra, *Time Matters*, 41.

97. Robert Hooke (1635–1703) had affirmed in 1665 that many extinct creatures had no living analogues. Ellenberger, *History*, 2:86–87.

98. Leddra, *Time Matters*, 154; Rudwick, *Worlds Before Adam*, 11–24. See also Rudwick, *The Meaning of Fossils*, 101.

99. Young and Stearley, *Bible, Rocks and Time*, 102.

100. Leddra, *Time Matters*, 14; Young and Stearley, *Bible, Rocks and Time*, 111–12. The Grand Canyon, for example, exemplifies an extensive sequence of strata. But "no part of the earth's surface has had sedimentary rocks deposited upon it throughout the planet's history." The column is idealized based on what a complete column would look like. Bowler, *The Earth Encompassed*, 214.

101. Ellenberger, *History*, 2:341.

column had been the flood. Yet diluvialists had never agreed on an over-all theory of the earth nor had they been convincing in their handling of the growing challenges presented by advancing geological knowledge. Unanticipated from a flood standpoint, fossils were found sorted according to strata rather than mixed. Human fossils were never found in the old strata, but strange creatures like the dinosaurs were. Extinctions were followed by new and different species. If the flood seemed unable to account for the challenges, and neither spontaneous generation nor evolutionary approaches were acceptable, the only tenable option remaining for most people, not just Christians, was to accept that God had progressively created many new life forms following various extinctions in the earth's past.[102] The flood column came to be viewed primarily as a creation column.

Cuvier resisted any evolutionary implication of the evidence. He insisted that similar organisms resulted not from common ancestry but common function, and that Lamarck (like Darwin later) had to posit transitional forms not found in the fossil record.[103] So though his religious convictions made him uncomfortable with the notion of repeated creations, Cuvier accepted that the evidence supported "progressionism," a cycle of catastrophe-divine creation-catastrophe, with each new divine creation becoming more complex.[104]

Though not all of the Christians contributing to the rise of modern geology held a progressive creationist view (some held to an old earth gap theory), virtually all were both old earth creationist and anti-evolutionary. William Conybeare viewed Lamarck's evolutionary theory as "monstrous."[105] Adam Sedgwick (1785–1873), William Buckland (1784–1856), and Hugh Miller (1802–1856) also strongly rejected Lamarckianism. They believed that the absence of missing links in the fossil record argued against the gradual transformation of organisms over time.[106] Miller and

102. Ibid., 2:317. Georges-Louis Leclerc Comte de Buffon (1707–1788) proposed a materialistic version of spontaneous generation to explain the appearances of new species seen in the fossils. Ibid., 2:230–31.

103. Bowler, *The Earth Encompassed*, 216, 282; Leddra, *Time Matters*, 154–55.

104. Ellenberger, *History*, 2:99–100, 321; Young and Stearley, *Bible, Rocks, and Time*, 93–94.

105. Leddra, *Time Matters*, 157.

106. Tess Cosslett, ed., *Science and Religion in the Nineteenth Century* (New York: Cambridge University Press, 1984), 4.

Sedgwick were especially outraged with Robert Chamber's (1802–1871) proposal of an animal ancestry for humans in his *Vestiges of the Natural History of Creation* (1844).[107]

By the early nineteenth century, the same evidence that led the overwhelming majority of Christian geologists to view the strata as a creation column also convinced them the earth was very old.[108] By the middle of that century, Darwin presented the same evidence as an evolution column through the world-changing lens of the *Origin of Species*. And those who resisted Darwinism and theological liberalism (surveyed in the previous chapter) like Hodge or the fundamentalists or William Jennings Bryan were old earth creationists. They wore the primary anti-evolutionist mantel for a full century.

But even though the fossil column had come to be viewed as a creation column, Christian geologists continued to look for the effects of the flood. Some such as William Buckland continued to use the flood as explanation for the carving and shaping of the earth's surface features. But Louis Agassiz (1807–1873), an early influential pioneer in the study of glaciers and later a decidedly anti-Darwinist, demonstrated that glaciers best explained surface features rather than diluvialism. Even though he eventually convinced Buckland and others of his view, most geologists rejected it in continued support of diluvialism. By the 1850s, however, the majority began to consider seriously ice age theory.[109] Modern geology, and, as we will see, even leading young earth creationists hold that the superficial features of northern Europe and North America have been extensively shaped by glaciation.[110]

The gradual dissociation of flood explanations for various geologic features was not acrimonious among the majority of Christian geologists

---

107. Cosslett, *Science and Religion*, 5. Miller, in his *The Testimony of the Rocks* (1857), used Cuvier's theory of progressive creationism as a means of buttressing natural theology, refuting atheism, and rejecting common descent and even uniformitarianism. See Cosslett, *Science and Religion*, 67–69, 72, 81.

108. Michael Roberts, "Adam Sedgwick (1785–1873): Geologist and Evangelical," in *Geology and Religion: A History of Harmony and Hostility,* ed. Martina Kölbl Ebert (London: The Geological Society, 2009), 166.

109. Rudwick, *Worlds Before Adam*, 517–34; Leddra, *Time Matters*, 113–14. Agassiz convinced Adam Sedgwick in 1831 that superficial materials were not the work of the flood but glaciation. Bowler, *The Earth Encompassed*, 226.

110. Bowler, *The Earth Encompassed*, 224.

and theologians. A vocal but largely uninfluential minority, the scriptural geologists, protested old earth creationism and the move away from flood geology, as we will see in the following chapter. For the most part, amicable biblical interpretation generally developed alongside the new understanding in the developing science.[111] Some attempted hybrid models incorporating the notion of a geographically local flood destroying all humans other than those saved on the ark.[112] But perhaps most conservative Christians continued to accept a geographically universal flood without attempting scientific correlations until the rise of modern flood geology.

Later Dating Methods Strengthening Old Earth Theory

Dating methods moved from relative and inexact to increasingly more exact methods. Early estimates based on such things as erosion and sedimentation rates were very inexact. A great many types of dating methods developed over time such as measuring starlight or the number of ice cores in glaciers. Radiometric dating gets the most attention since it has also permitted the development of absolute rather than relative dating methods for rocks and the earth.[113]

Other aspects central to modern geology also seemed to corroborate the ancient age of the earth. One such critical concept is now central even in many leading young earth creation models: the notion that a supercontinent(s) broken up and moved by plate tectonics led to our present continents. As early as 1596, Abraham Ortelius (1527–1598), geographer and creator of the first modern atlas, noted the similarities in the coastlines of

111. Martin Rudwick, "Biblical Flood and Geological Deluge: The Amicable Dissociation of Geology and Genesis," in *Geology and Religion: A History of Harmony and Hostility,* ed. Martina Kölbl Ebert (London: The Geological Society, 2009), 103.

112. As early as the seventeenth century, the great flood theorist John Ray noted that local flood theory solved a number of baffling geological problems so long as it extinguished all human beings other than Noah's family. Rappaport, *When Geologists Were Historians,* 136.

113. Bowler, *The Earth Encompassed,* 403–404; Leddra, *Time Matters,* 47; Ellenberger, *History,* 2:350–51. "The scientists and laboratories involved in radiometric dating take great care" to account for a wide variety of factors that can influence the dating of rocks. See the list of those factors in Leddra, *Time Matters,* 51.

the Americas, Europe, and Africa and suggested that they had once been joined.[114] Others before the twentieth century also posited similar ideas.[115]

But Alfred Wegener (1880–1930) generally gets credited for postulating continental drift in 1912. He observed that various continents shared fossil species that could not have traversed water and that represented originally different climatic zones. The most reasonable theory was to postulate that the continents themselves had moved. Stratigraphic sequences and structural elements of matching shorelines also suggested they once had comprised just one continent, which he named Pangaea ("all lands"). Moreover, matching ancient glacial changes from these continents seemed to confirm the theory.[116] Wegener's ideas, though widely accepted in Britain by 1925, were not fully accepted by American geologists until the 1960s.[117]

The revolution in plate tectonics that began in the 1960s was documented by the detailed mapping of the continents' locations from years past.[118] Providing the explanation for Wegener's continental drift, plate tectonics holds that the earth is covered by moving crustal plates driven by radioactive heat deep in the earth's mantle. For example, Great Britain has traveled great distances into different climate zones in the past due to plate tectonics.[119] The floors of the oceans thus continually regenerate themselves by spreading from the center and sinking at the edges. The revolution in geology produced by plate tectonics cannot be overstated.[120]

CONCLUSION

The earliest theories of the earth were mostly flood theories. But diluvialism struggled to account for the surprising geologic discoveries such as the lack of fossil mixing in the strata, different species such as extinct dinosaurs followed by new creatures, and more. Historians of geology agree that the rise of old earth geology involved much more than the acceptance of the

---

114. Leddra, *Time Matters*, 214.

115. Ibid., 215–16; Ellenberger, *History*, 2:310.

116. Bowler, *The Earth Encompassed*, 399; Ellenberger, *History*, 2:34; Leddra, *Time Matters*, 223–25.

117. Gohau, *History*, 187–200; Leddra, *Time Matters*, 230.

118. Bowler, *The Earth Encompassed*, 412; Leddra, *Time Matters*, 133.

119. Leddra, *Time Matters*, 149.

120. David B. Kitts, *The Structure of Geology* (Dallas: Southern Methodist University Press, 1977), 126.

theories of Hutton or Lyell. The vast majority were creationists opposed to evolutionary ideas as well as uniformitarianism.[121] Most geological pioneers sought in varying degrees to correlate their understanding of the earth's past with the Bible. Many of the geologists working at the time were evangelicals and believed in the truth of the Bible.[122]

Similar to the Copernican controversy, Bible-believing Christians practiced the conservatism principle in the lead-up to modern geology. They reluctantly courted the possibility of an old earth and whether the flood could explain most or at least major parts of modern earth science. They proposed a large number of hybrid flood models, but none won the day even among flood theorists. Old earth evangelicals, whether day-age or gap theorists, also never wavered in their commitment to biblical inerrancy.

There was no major controversy about the age of the earth or the geologic column two hundred years ago. But, of course, there is today. The difference between now and then is that the fossil column can be interpreted three different ways: as flood column, creation column, or evolution column. Beyond the obvious scientific questions, a significant number of theological issues are related to each view as well. We will look at some of those in the next four chapters. Each of our three evangelical groups (YEC, EC, and OEC) faces difficult questions.

Because of the age of the earth controversy, of special interest is how YECs understand and interpret the relevant scientific evidence. As we will see in chapter 7, leading modern young earth creationists are sophisticated and have worked hard on questions facing them. Those questions include the following: Should the fossil column be trusted or rejected? How should we think about the rise of new species? How should one understand extinctions? But first we turn in the following chapter to a brief survey of the history of young earth creationism.

121. Young and Stearley, *Bible, Rocks, and Time*, 108, 111; Leddra, *Time Matters*, 80; Ellenberger, *History*, 2:316.

122. Roberts, "Adam Sedgwick," 166.

Chapter 6

YOUNG EARTH CREATIONISM:
Responding to Geology

> "There seems to be no possible way to avoid the conclusion that if the Bible and Christianity are true at all, the geological ages must be rejected altogether."[1]
>
> —Henry M. Morris, *Scientific Creationism*

In 1929, during the height of anti-evolution campaigns in America, two leading fundamentalists cordially debated the two most popular creation theories before a large church audience. William Bell Riley (1861–1947), sometimes referred to as the "grand old man of fundamentalism," had founded the World Christian Fundamentals Association. An ardent anti-evolutionist, Riley defended the old earth day-age view. The day-age theory had been circulating among British geologists since about the time Newton published his *Principia*. As a way to harmonize Genesis with the growing awareness of the strata and fossils, the creation days were understood to represent geologic ages. Correlating the Bible's creation order with fossil sequences was deemed part of God-glorifying apologetics.[2]

The extremely popular Harry Rimmer (1890–1952), also ardently anti-evolutionist with a largely self-trained scientific apologetics ministry, argued for the old earth gap theory.[3] The "chaos-restitution" gap model

---

1. Henry M. Morris, *Scientific Creationism* (Green Forest, AR: Master Books, 1985), 255.

2. François Ellenberger, *History of Geology*, vol. 2, *The Great Awakening and Its First Fruits—1600–1810*, ed. Marguerite Carozzi (Rotterdam: A. A. Balkema, 1999), 341.

3. William Vance Trollinger, *Creationism in Twentieth-Century America: The Antievo-

121

also had been used by Christians in various versions for a couple of centuries and remained very popular with evangelicals until the 1960s.[4] The theory teaches that most fossilized strata were formed during a long period of chaos in the "gap" between the Bible's first two verses.

Neither debater could have dreamed their views would later be considered by a leading young earth creationist to have "allowed the evolutionary establishment to take over the nation's school systems, news media, and most other important institutions of our society."[5] The reason they felt right at home with their views is simple. For a century those views had dominated the evangelical and later the fundamentalist world. Rimmer's gap theory was popularized in the venerable *Scofield Reference Bible*. And the day-age theory had been advocated by the great anti-Darwinian theologian Charles Hodge. Riley graduated in 1888 from the Southern Baptist Theological Seminary, which favorably taught the day-age view. And just five years before the Riley-Rimmer debate, William Jennings Bryan presented the day-age view on behalf of the anti-evolution prosecution in the Scopes trial.[6]

In the 1920s, anti-evolutionists, generally their term of self-reference rather than "creationists," agreed on the dangers of Darwinism but not the correct interpretation of Genesis. Most fundamentalists held to the gap theory, some to the day-age theory, and only a small minority of mostly Seventh-day Adventists held to recent creation in six literal days. All three groups thought of themselves as biblical literalists, and primarily only the

lution Pamphlets of William Bell Riley (New York: Routledge, 1995), ix, xiii. Rimmer also advocated for a geographically local flood. J. David Pleins, *When the Great Abyss Opened: Classic and Contemporary Readings of Noah's Flood* (New York: Oxford University Press, 2003), 47. See also Ronald Numbers, *The Creationists: The Evolution of Scientific Creationism* (Berkeley, CA: University of California Press, 1992), 99.

4. John M. Lynch, "Introduction," in *Creationism and Scriptural Geology, 1817–1857*, 7 vols., ed. and intro. John M. Lynch (Bristol, England: Thoemmes Press, 2002), 1:x; and Rodney L. Stiling, "Scriptural Geology in America," in *Evangelicals and Science in Historical Perspective*, ed. David N. Livingston, D. G. Hart, and Mark A. Noll (New York: Oxford University Press, 1990), 178.

5. Henry M. Morris, *The Genesis Record: A Scientific and Devotional Commentary on the Book of Beginnings* (Grand Rapids: Baker, 1976), 46.

6. Ronald L. Numbers, *Darwinism Comes to America* (Cambridge, MA: Harvard University Press, 1998), 81; Thomas J. Nettles, *James Pettigru Boyce: A Southern Baptist Statesman* (Phillipsburg, NJ: P & R, 2009), 346–47.

Adventists regarded the earth's age or differing views of Genesis as particularly important in the contemporary battle of ideas.[7]

THE SCRIPTURAL GEOLOGISTS

Prior to the nineteenth century, Christians had not been doctrinally dogmatic about recent creation.[8] Until about 1815, few writers holding to a young earth attacked geological time, but the rise of so-called scriptural geology in Great Britain changed that for half a century.[9] The movement, perceiving modern geology a threat to Scripture, united behind two dominant themes: (1) the earth was only thousands of years old, and (2) geological formations resulted from the waters at creation, processes at work between creation and the flood, or the cataclysmic effects of the flood. Gap or day-age theories became viewed as a danger to the faith.[10] In 1833, George Fairholme (1788–1846) voiced the movement's complaint, that geologists had stopped relying on biblical testimony and instead sought to determine "the age of particular formations, from the nature of the fossils which they may be found to contain."[11] One scriptural geologist even

---

7. Numbers, *Darwinism*, 52–53, 80–81. In the middle of the nineteenth century, the term "creationists" referred to those who believed God specially created every human soul at conception rather than its having been inherited from parents (traducianism). During anti-evolutionism's heyday, the term probably languished due to so many versions of creationism. Ronald L. Numbers, "Creating Creationism: Meanings and Uses since the Age of Agassiz," in *Evangelicals and Science in Historical Perspective*, ed. David N. Livingstone, D. G. Hart, and Mark A. Noll (New York: Oxford University Press, 1990), 235.

8. Lynch, "Introduction," 1:x.

9. Michael Roberts, "Adam Sedgwick (1785–1873): Geologist and Evangelical," in *Geology and Religion: A History of Harmony and Hostility*, ed. Martina Kölbl Ebert (London: The Geological Society, 2009), 161–62. See also Stiling, "Scriptural Geology," 177–92.

10. Stiling, "Scriptural Geology," 179.

11. George Fairholme, *A General View of the Geology of Scripture* (London: James Ridgway, 1833), 222, vol. 4 in *Creationism and Scriptural Geology, 1817–1857*, 7 vols., ed. and intro. John M. Lynch (Bristol, England: Thoemmes Press, 2002). See also John Murray, *A Portrait of Geology* (London: Relfe and Fletcher, 1838), 3, vol. 5 in *Creationism and Scriptural Geology, 1817–1857*, 7 vols., ed. and intro. John M. Lynch (Bristol, England: Thoemmes Press, 2002).

suggested God could have simply created the earth with strata like these without any intermediary processes.[12]

Terry Mortenson of Answers in Genesis has written about the scriptural geologists in *The Great Turning Point: The Church's Catastrophic Mistake on Geology—Before Darwin*. His title acknowledges that old earth creationism (OEC) predated Darwinism. Mortenson also agrees with historians of geology that no direct lineage exists between today's young earth creationists (YEC) and the scriptural geologists.[13] But he expresses great appreciation for them because today's YECs' "interpretations of the geological and biblical records regarding creation, the Flood, and the age of the earth are essentially identical on the main points (though much expanded in detail) with those of the scriptural geologists."[14]

Granville Penn (1761–1844), one of the earliest scriptural geologists, commanded great respect within the movement. Another scriptural geologist described Penn as "enlightened," deserving to "be called the first great advocate for the Mosaic geology, amongst the men of science of our day."[15] Penn referred to Genesis as "Mosaical geology" and to the consensus about an old earth as "mineral geology." As the older term used before "geology" became standard, "mineralogy" was being abandoned even before Penn's day due to emphasis on fieldwork, which he lacked. Mortenson, contra other historians, claims Penn was competent to address geological issues due to reading relevant literature as well as "apparently" having "made some geological field observations on the continent."[16]

---

12. J. Mellor Brown, *Reflections on Geology* (Edinburgh: The Edinburgh Printing and Publishing Co, 1838), 17–19, vol. 1 in *Creationism and Scriptural Geology, 1817–1857*, 7 vols., ed. and intro. John M. Lynch (Bristol, England: Thoemmes Press, 2002).

13. Roberts, "Adam Sedgwick, 166.

14. Terry Mortenson, *The Great Turning Point: The Church's Catastrophic Mistake on Geology—Before Darwin* (Green Forest, AR: Master Books, 2004), 202–203.

15. Fairholme, *General View*, 74. Penn was the grandson of Quaker founder of the Commonwealth of Pennsylvania, William Penn.

16. Mortenson, *Turning Point*, 75. Mortenson goes to some lengths arguing against historical consensus, not to mention the view of other Christian geologists at the time, that some of the scriptural geologists deserve to be considered elite for their day. Ibid., 45–54. But on Penn and the others in the movement, see Martin Rudwick, "Minerals, Strata and Fossils," in *Cultures of Natural History*, ed. N. Jardine, J. A. Secord, and E. C. Spary (New York: Cambridge University Press, 1996), 266, 285; Stiling, "Scriptural Geology," 186; Lynch, "Introduction," 1:xiii; and Roberts, "Adam Sedgwick," 163. Fortunately, this issue is not pertinent to my analysis of their positions.

Assuming recent creation as the biblical view, Penn addressed concerns that might undermine interpreting the creation days as twenty-four hours long. Because he accepted modern astronomy, Penn understood twenty-four-hour days to result from the earth's axial rotation while orbiting the sun.[17] Yet Genesis 1:14–19 states God created the sun and moon to mark times, including days and years, on day four, not day one. So Penn translated Genesis 1:2 as "and the earth was invisible," arguing that God intentionally hid the earth. Penn claimed that the original readers certainly understood the sun *not* to be created on day four since it is the source of day one's light. Day four then represents a *revelation* of the source of day one's light. The sun was only "optically non-existent" before day four, thus creation days from the very first can be considered twenty-four hours long.[18] Scriptural geologist George Fairholme regarded Penn's arguments for a day one creation of the sun as "unanswerable."[19]

But Penn then charged OECs with "compromise and concession" because they "compel" God's language "to bend and conform to their speculations" for allowing creation days to signify an indeterminate length of time.[20] Mortenson describes Penn's having the sun created on day one as "rather arbitrary in his literal interpretation."[21] One might argue Penn was practicing the conservatism principle by never doubting the truth of the Bible. Because he accepted modern astronomy, and because the text could appear contradictory on its surface, Penn developed a hybrid interpretation of Genesis 1. Perhaps Penn could be questioned why, when making analogous interpretive moves, he understood OECs to be compromising and bending Scripture to their speculations.

Penn argued that the Bible only allows two "revolutions" to have shaped the earth. The first took place on creation day two when the earth's crust fractured, allowing much of the original water covering its surface to flow into its interior. But in discussing his second revolution, the flood, Penn

---

17. Granville Penn, *A Comparative Estimate of the Mineral and Mosaical Geologies*, 2 vols. (London: James Duncan, 1825), 1:182–89, 229, and especially 239, vol. 2 in *Creationism and Scriptural Geology, 1817–1857*, 7 vols., ed. and intro. John M. Lynch (Bristol, England: Thoemmes Press, 2002).

18. Ibid., 1:165, 170, 173.

19. Fairholme, *General View*, 45. See also ibid., 55, 58, 63.

20. Penn, *Comparative Estimate*, 1:186–87.

21. Mortenson, *Turning Point*, 71.

solved the old problem of accounting for enough water to cover the earth without utilizing that interior water. Instead, his flood did not necessarily cover the entire planet with water all at the same time. He argued that the Bible ("historical geology") clearly teaches that pre-flood continents and seas gradually traded places so the ark would not be destroyed in a whirl-pool. Mountains, then, are just massive erosion effects from the flood. But another scriptural geologist, George Bugg (1769–1851), believed Penn's flood theory unbiblical. Because "the Bible says the Flood covered all the mountains, he concluded that the Flood covered the 28,000-foot-high Himalayas."[22] Differences of scriptural geologists' opinions aside, Penn was confident the real problem was with modern geology's imaginary and confused conclusion based on fossil observations. His own "close and Assiduous examination" revealed that believing anything other than that his two biblical "revolutions" shaped the earth's geologic features "is the offspring of defective investigation, unregulated fancy, and a determined disrespect of authenticated testimony."[23]

Penn stressed that modern geologists had misinterpreted the fossils because they were not putting the Bible first. He accepted old earth creationist William Buckland's recent hyena, elephant, and hippopotamus fossil identifications in Kirkdale Cave. But Penn strongly reacted to Buckland changing his original view from believing the flood had swept the animals there from great distance to believing the animals actually lived there before dying in the flood.[24] Because Penn could find no mention in the Bible that northern latitudes had ever been tropical, those organisms could never have lived there. Penn, therefore, referred to the great Buckland's conclusion as a "manifest perversion of all logic, and in exclusion of the true and obvious explication of the phenomenon."[25] Fairholme also referred to Buckland's ideas as "wild and unreasonable theories." The "difficulties vanish" by believing Penn's view, that the Bible teaches our

---

22. Ibid., 89 n. 85.

23. Penn, *Comparative Estimate*, 2:244. See also ibid., 1:216–22; 2:24–37, 49, 61–64, and ibid., 2:273.

24. Peter J. Bowler, *The Earth Encompassed: A History of the Environmental Sciences* (London: Norton: 1992), 238–39; Martin Rudwick, *Worlds Before Adam: The Reconstruction of Geohistory in the Age of Reform* (Chicago: University of Chicago Press, 2008), 73–88; Michael Leddra, *Time Matters: Geology's Legacy to Scientific Thought* (Hoboken, NJ: Wiley-Blackwell, 2010), 110–11.

25. Penn, *Comparative Estimate*, 2:81–82. See also ibid., 2:83–97.

present continents were once antediluvian ocean floors. Current fossil locations, therefore, tell us nothing about where those organisms lived.[26] Despite Penn's claim that his view alone was biblically faithful, scriptural geologist George Young (1777–1848) believed the same evidence indicated a former universally temperate climate. In support of his "universal summer" hypothesis he cited none other than the frequently despised Charles Lyell.[27]

Penn sternly criticized geologists for taking the absence of human fossils in lower strata containing species such as dinosaurs to mean people did not live at those earlier times. Deeply convinced of his flood geology model that the original continents were now under the oceans, Penn argued no one should expect to find human fossils anywhere.[28] He did not explain why so many animal fossils from those same pre-flood continents are found.

The problem of extinctions, however, actually presented Penn a partial solution to another old problem: How could the ark have contained all the enormous numbers of land animals revealed in the fossils? Penn and later Fairholme went to great lengths to argue, in spite of the universal language in Genesis 6:17 and 7:21–23, that Noah was not literally commanded to take all the land animals on the ark. Those representative species not taken on board became extinct in the flood.[29] Young creatively handled the extinction problem similarly by geographically localizing this aspect of the flood. He argued that universal descriptions regarding the animals were not literal but "restricted to all those animals that were within his reach, all that were in that part of the world where he lived, or, all that God thought necessary for supplying the new world. Such orders might be given, and punctually executed, although many species, and even genera, were suffered to perish."[30] If the question was raised why fossils of extinct species are found only in lower strata, Penn again answered they lived in

---

26. Fairholme, *General View*, 244, 247, 268–69. See also Leddra, *Time Matters*, 112.

27. George Young, *Scriptural Geology* (London: Simpkin, Marshall and Co., 1840), 31–33, vol. 5 in *Creationism and Scriptural Geology, 1817–1857*, 7 vols., ed. and intro. John M. Lynch (Bristol, England: Thoemmes Press, 2002).

28. Penn, *Comparative Estimate*, 2:124–33.

29. Ibid., 2:134–44; Fairholme, *General View*, 164–65.

30. Young, *Scriptural Geology*, 71–72.

different places, not times.[31] Mortenson observes that Penn's extinction approach displayed "some inconsistency in arguing for the literal interpretation of Genesis."[32]

Interpreting the Genesis flood chapters non-literally might solve correlating animals on the ark with the great number of land animals revealed in the fossil record. But the sheer number of land animals alive today being descended from those on the ark still seemed a problem to the scriptural geologists. Beginning in the middle of the eighteenth century, this issue had been the first major flood problem discussed by many, including Linnaeus.[33] Some of the scriptural geologists employed the same non-literal approach to biblical language seeming to imply the flood destroyed all land animals not on the ark. Young suggested not only insects but also reptiles (and their eggs) might have survived the flood by floating on trees and vegetation.[34]

Penn solved the problem by adapting a theory from the geologists he opposed. For more than a century old earth creationists interpreted the fossil evidence to teach God had created new species at various times, especially following extinctions. Some scriptural geologists, however, found progressive creation onerous and unbiblical, described by James Mellor Brown as most "offensive to the plain reader of the Scriptures."[35] Yet Penn, consistent with his flood model, argued that since post-flood continents were former seabeds, plant life had to be created de novo just like the first creation week. Similarly, he suggested God likely created new post-flood animal species analogous to the creation week. Penn reasoned not all of today's land animals could have descended from those on the ark due to its limited space. God's moral purpose only required all humans descend from the first pair, but not all animals need descend from the creation week. Penn admitted he concluded this not from the Bible but from animals unique only to some continents today separated by water.[36] On the

---

31. Penn, *Comparative Estimate*, 2:134–44.

32. Mortenson, *Turning Point*, 75.

33. Janet Browne, *The Secular Ark: Studies in the History of Biogeography* (New Haven, CT: Yale University Press, 1983), 19. See also ibid., 221–25.

34. George Young, *Appendix* (London: Simpkin, Marshall and Co., 1840) vol. 5 in *Creationism and Scriptural Geology, 1817–1857*, 7 vols., ed. and intro. John M. Lynch (Bristol, England: Thoemmes Press, 2002), 16.

35. Brown, *Reflections*, 27.

36. Penn, *Comparative Estimate*, 2:209–29.

other hand, Young, who non-literally interpreted the universal biblical language regarding animals either taken on the ark or killed by the flood, could not abide even a one-time creation to replenish the post-diluvian earth.[37] Several other scriptural geologists also adopted a version of limited progressive creation after the flood.[38] Mortenson alludes to but offers no criticism of Penn's limited progressive creationist hybrid.[39]

In light of his stress on biblical fidelity, the most surprising move Penn made was to delete Genesis verses not amenable to his hybrid flood model. Penn's "Mosaical" (biblical) geology held that the Garden of Eden now lies on the ocean floor. But Genesis 2:10–14 presented him a problem because it associates four rivers with the Garden, two of which are recognizable today (the Tigris and Euphrates). Earlier flood theorists such as old earth creationist Jean-André Deluc (1727–1817) surmised pre-flood river names could be used post-flood to denote different rivers. Penn, on the other hand, argued at great length that Moses could not have written verses referring to a pre-flood Tigris and Euphrates. Therefore, Penn declared they should be removed from the Bible, though no manuscript evidence suggested they were not original. He avowed they must be later scribal marginal glosses. Therefore, "it is unquestionably the office and the duty of sound and scrupulous criticism, to demonstrate the invalidity" of the verses so "the important testimony" of the Mosaical geology *"may stand unimpaired."*[40] Fairholme also followed Penn's deletion of these verses, describing them as the result of "the ignorance of a subsequent transcriber."[41]

Some years later old earth creationist Hugh Miller described Penn's deletion of biblical verses as taking "strange liberties with a book which he professes to respect."[42] Deleting biblical verses because they commit an assumed geographical error is called conjectural emendation. Biblical

---

37. Young, *Appendix*, 16.

38. I am aware of George Fairholme in *General View*, 62–63, and the American scriptural geologists David Lord and Andrew Ure. See Thane Hutcherson Ury, *The Evolving Face of God as Creator: Early Nineteenth-Century Traditionalist and Accommodationist Theodical Responses in British Religious Thought to Paleonatural Evil in the Fossil Record* (Ph.D. diss., Andrews University, Seventh-day Adventist Theological Seminary, 2001), 251 n. 1.

39. Mortenson, *Turning Point*, 75.

40. Penn, *Comparative Estimate*, 2:230–43. Penn's quote is on 243. Emphasis his.

41. Fairholme, *General View*, 432. See also ibid., 432–39.

42. Miller, *Testimony*, 406.

conservatives have long avoided at all costs conjecturally adding or deleting verses well-established in the manuscript tradition, often chiding theological liberals for making similar moves.[43] Mortenson's appraisal of Penn
in this regard, therefore, is surprising: "While [Penn's] argument was not
convincing to some of his sympathetic readers, it was based on sound principles of textual criticism and, in methodology, did not represent a cavalier
approach to Scripture (which he considered to be the sacred Word of God),
as was charged by some of his critics. He was simply trying to solve the
apparent contradiction in Scripture."[44]

CONCERNS REGARDING THE SCRIPTURAL GEOLOGISTS

Mortenson affirms Penn for using "his skills in biblical and literary criticism to build his case for a literal six-day creation about 6,000 years ago."[45]
And Penn frequently rebuked OECs for supposedly compromising the
Bible to appease scientific speculation. But Penn practiced the same kind
of interpretive moves in "concession" to the new discoveries. He reinterpreted universal biblical language pertaining to the extent of land animals
on the ark so as to accommodate fossil evidence for extinctions. He used
the notion of a one-time progressive creation due to perceived problems
with the size of the ark and the scientific problem of unique post-flood
animals on water-surrounded lands.

The problem is not that Penn cautiously courted geological evidence
as did OECs in his day, though his excision of Scripture was completely
unacceptable. The problem was his inconsistency in harshly criticizing
OECs for doing what he did, while claiming they compromised the Bible
with science. Mortenson's concluding assessment praising Penn, therefore, is disconcerting: "Clearly it was his convictions about the truth and
authority of Scripture and his genuine interest in philosophically sound
argumentation that compelled him to pick up his pen against the theories
of the mineral geologists."[46]

---

43. On the importance of avoiding the subjectivity of conjectural emendations, see
Emmanuel Tov, *Textual Criticism of the Hebrew Bible* (Minneapolis: Fortress, 2011), 356.

44. Mortenson, *Turning Point*, 75.

45. Ibid.

46. Ibid., 76.

The scriptural geologists in general raise similar concerns. What distinguished them from other evangelical creationists in their day was their agreement that the earth was recently created and the fossil column should be understood primarily as a flood column, not a creation column. But their disagreements were extremely significant. They clashed over whether the flood waters geographically covered the earth and its mountains all at the same time. They disagreed whether it was biblically permissible to accept a pre-flood "universal summer" theory. They differed on how to interpret biblical universal language about animals taken aboard the ark or else destroyed in the flood. Some disdained while others accepted a limited version of progressive creation. Some even ended up with hybrid models consisting of a global flood combined with gap or day-age theories.[47] When Mortenson writes that "the scriptural geologists differed in their interpretation of some of the minor details of the scriptural account and of the geological evidence,"[48] one may wonder what counts as major.

The biggest concern is how scriptural geologists viewed themselves and some YECs today view them in relation to OECs. Mortenson claims the movement arose because "after several centuries of close ties between geology and Scripture, the study of the rocks and fossils was being divorced from the study of the Bible, resulting in a departure from the dominant, traditional interpretation of the early chapters of Genesis."[49] But two things should be noted in response. First, Christian geologists who believed geological evidence pointed to an old earth no more "divorced" their study from the Bible than the scriptural geologists. They did develop hybrid models such as gap or day-age, but the scriptural geologists also developed hybrid models. Second, there had been no "dominant, traditional interpretation" of Genesis at the time because old earth biblical interpretations had been quite common for more than a century. No Christian groups during that time, or in the past, had suggested the age of the earth was

47. Ury, *Evolving Face*, 251 n. 1. Ury's point, no doubt, is that such hybridized scriptural geologists continued to contend for a flood rather than a creation column. But if a scriptural geologist accepted any part of an old earth view such as gap or day-age, retaining only a geographical flood and flood column makes calling such an individual a scriptural geologist debatable.

48. Mortenson, *Turning Point*, 197.

49. Ibid., 55.

an essential Christian doctrine. Moreover, many aspects of the scriptural geologists' interpretations of Genesis were hardly traditional.

But it is fair to say that the scriptural geologists saw themselves as standing for something critically important, the recent creation of the earth and interpreting the geologic column as a flood column. Therefore, they believed it only right to rebuke OECs for forgetting "the words of Jesus that anyone ashamed of His words now will experience His being ashamed of them when He comes."[50] Thus Mortenson grimly writes: "All the scriptural geologists agreed about the grave importance of the controversy. Ultimately, they saw this as a part of a cosmic spiritual conflict between Satan and God, and those who rejected the plain teaching of Scripture (which, in their thinking, included the literal historical interpretation of Genesis 1–11) were unwitting enemies of the truth and of God."[51] In agreement, Mortenson writes of the scriptural geologists' sense of apocalyptic implications: "They believed that with the rejection of the plain teaching of Genesis, the proper interpretation and authority of the rest of Scripture would be undermined so that faith in other important biblical doctrines, including the origin of evil, the gospel, and the second coming of Christ, would slowly be eroded. These erosions of faith in turn would have a devastating effect on the life of the Church, the social and moral condition of the nation, and the spread of the gospel at home and abroad."[52]

Within just a few decades of its inception the scriptural geology movement was over. It had never attracted a large following or wielded much influence. Conservative Christians did not view the age of the earth as an essential doctrine, and old earth creationism became the standard in American Bible dictionaries, commentaries, and apologetics texts into the twentieth century.[53] Shortly after the demise of the scriptural geology movement, Darwinism provoked a truly major battle over the fossil column. For the following one hundred years, old earth evangelicals led the opposition to evolution, worrying what might come of "the life of the Church, the social and moral condition of the nation, and the spread of the gospel at home and abroad" if Darwinism were embraced. No doubt

---

50. Brown, *Reflections*, 38.
51. Mortenson, *Turning Point*, 214.
52. Ibid., 215.
53. Stiling, "Scriptural Geology," 181, 185, 187.

William Bell Riley and Harry Rimmer would have been shocked to hear that their own views, not Darwinism, were the problem.

THE ADVENT OF MODERN FLOOD GEOLOGY: THE SEVENTH-DAY ADVENTISTS

The scriptural geologists developed their views before the dawn of Darwinism. But the foundations of modern YEC "flood geology" arose in the early twentieth century specifically to combat Darwinism. Instead of combating, however, the mechanisms proposed for the transmutation of species, modern flood geology initially sought to undermine the time scales necessary for transmutation to occur, "In a sense, it was the advent of Darwinian evolution that revived the fortunes of the old nineteenth-century scriptural geology, by giving it a new practical purpose, a new name, and a new set of advocates."[54]

In a strange twist, something of scriptural geology's mantle fell to Seventh-day Adventists whose orthodoxy evangelicals have long debated. Doctrines often cited as problematic are: (1) a required Sabbatarian observance of Saturdays; (2) the Sanctuary Doctrine; and (3) veneration of the prophetic ministry of Ellen G. White (1827–1915), believed to have had as many as two thousand visions.[55] Emphasizing Saturday worship as necessary to fulfill the fourth commandment, the prophetess opposed all views undermining literal twenty-four-hour days of creation. In 1864, she published details of her out-of-body vision in which God confirmed that the creation week's length was just like any other. Her vision detailed that after the flood, God sent a mighty wind to cover the rotting corpses with trees, stone, and earth. The buried forests were transformed into combustible coal and oil as the cause of volcanoes and earthquakes. The wind also sheared off the tops of some mountains, reshaping parts of the earth's surface. With a prophetic rebuke, she charged that interpreting the creation days as long periods undermined the seventh-day Sabbath and constituted an "infidel supposition."[56]

---

54. Ibid., 188.

55. William Fagal, "How Many Dreams and Visions Did Ellen G. White Have?" http://ellenwhite.org/content/file/how-many-dreams-and-visions-did-ellen-g-white-have#document.

56. Numbers, *Darwinism*, 97. See also idem, *Creationists*, 74.

George McCready Price (1870–1963) brought together White's prophetic voice with the authority of science, or at least his own geological
ideas. In his early years he sold White's books door to door. Having only
formal scientific training required to teach elementary school, he never
did develop facility in identifying fossils in the field.[57] But he read geology books widely and eventually taught science in Adventist schools.
Price wrote prodigiously for decades, primarily opposing modern geology.
Though he never gained serious attention from geologists, his views eventually gained wide circulation in anti-evolutionist circles.

He initially accepted the order of the fossilized strata as had virtually
all geologists for more than one hundred years, including the scriptural
geologists. The great issue of the day for anti-evolutionists was whether the
fossils revealed universal common descent or God's special creation. But in
defense of Adventism's young earth position and to undermine Darwinian
time scales, Price eventually concluded that a terrible error in modern geology itself made Darwinism possible in the first place. The standard order
of the geologic column must be wrong.

In 1923, during the heyday of the anti-evolutionist movement, his magnum opus *New Geology* confidently argued for this central theme now
dominating his thinking.[58] At more than seven hundred pages, the book
was his most comprehensive and, compared to other anti-evolution books
at the time, was quite impressive. He even began gaining influence outside
Adventist circles.[59]

Price trumpeted his innovative anti-evolution discovery, rejection of
the standard fossil column itself, as "the most important law ever for-
mulated with reference to the order in which the strata occur."[60] His

---

57. Ronald Numbers, "Introduction," in *The Early Writings of Harold W. Clark and
Frank Lewis Marsh* vol. 8 in *Creationism in America: A Ten Volume Anthology of Documents,
1903–1961,* series ed. Ronald L. Numbers (New York: Garland Publishing, 1995), ix,
8–23; idem, *Creationists,* 75–76, 90.

58. George McCready Price, *New Geology: A Textbook for Colleges, Normal Schools,
and Training Schools; and for the General Reader* (Mountain View, CA: Pacific Press
Publishing Association, 1923).

59. Numbers, *Creationists,* 73; Stiling, "Scriptural Geology," 187. By the mid-1920s,
Price was recognized as the chief scientific authority for fundamentalists by the editor of
the journal *Science.* Quite a number of non-Adventist religious periodicals were seeking
his contributions. Numbers, *Darwinism,* 102.

60. Price, *New Geology,* 637.

"great law of conformable stratigraphic sequence" flew in the face of the long-standing understanding of the fossil record shared by evolutionists and anti-evolutionists, old earth creationists and the scriptural geologists. That traditional view held that the strata were laid down sequentially.

But in a section of *New Geology* titled "In Every Possible Relative Order," Price announced that his investigations had revealed that no natural order whatsoever could be found in the fossil record. His "great law" could be summarized as follows: "Any kind of fossiliferous beds whatever, 'young' or 'old,' may be found occurring conformably on any other fossiliferous beds, 'older' or 'younger.'"[61] Earlier geologists, he claimed, had been misled by "preconceived prejudices about 'extinct species' and catastrophism which we know warped their investigations in actual life."[62] These prejudices produced the conjecture of a worldwide order in an idealized fossil column that simply didn't exist. Had these earlier investigations not been so "warped," they would have seen that the lack of a natural order to the strata is better attributed to one cataclysm such as the flood.

Price's discovery, if true, could have destroyed both Darwinism and old earth creationism in one fell swoop. *New Geology* should have rocked the geological world, at least if anyone was listening and not blinded by "preconceived prejudices." But the enormous hurdle he faced was to convince others he had discovered a disorganized column earlier generations of flood-believing geologists had missed. Geologists, including Christians, remained unconvinced. Before long Price's influence even in Adventist circles began to wane.[63]

One of his students, Harold W. Clark (1891–1986), the first Adventist to earn a master's degree in geology, succeeded Price as professor of geology at the Adventists' Pacific Union College. Clark dedicated his *Back to Creationism* to Price, and initiated a trend championing creationism instead of anti-evolutionism. Like his teacher, Clark viewed Darwinism as "the crowning deception of the arch-enemy of souls foisted upon the race in his attempt to lead man away from the Saviour."[64] But whereas Price

---

61. Ibid., 638.
62. Ibid., 668.
63. Numbers, *Darwinism*, 103.
64. Harold W. Clark, *Back to Creationism* (Angwin, CA: Pacific Union College Press, 1929), 139, in *The Early Writings of Harold W. Clark and Frank Lewis Marsh*, vol. 8 in *Creationism in America: A Ten Volume Anthology of Documents, 1903–1961*, series ed.

had also attributed glaciation theory to the devil, Clark's field trips convinced him that post-flood North America may have been ice-covered for more than 1,500 years. Clark also rejected Price's idea that species had not changed since creation, instead believing hybridization had created many new species from the originals.

Though most contemporary old earth creationists might have balked at the latter idea as a kind of limited evolution, Price adjusted to his student's new ideas enthusiastically.[65] But Clark, having spent time in Oklahoma and Texas oil fields, also became convinced the standard geologic column was not fictional as Price taught. Though Clark gently broached the subject with his former teacher, Price became furious and in 1941 charged Clark with heresy before the Adventist West Coast governing body. The specific heresy was Clark's acceptance of the geologic column's order. Yet Clark still believed in a literal six-day recent creation and universal flood, ascribing the strata's order to pre-flood ecological zones successively destroyed by the rising flood waters. And though Price linked him with theories of satanic origin Ellen White had specifically denounced, the assembled ministers refused to condemn Clark. They urged Price and Clark to work out their differences to little effect. Price could not be reconciled with his former student.[66]

Price now recanted his earlier endorsement of Clark's limited acceptance of natural selection. Price expressed shame for having "conceded too much to the evolutionists."[67] But when Clark published *Genes and Genesis*, defending "limited Darwinian natural selection—within genera, families, and even orders—against the 'extreme creationism' of those who insisted that God had created every species,"[68] Price minced no words. Such shocking acceptance of broad speciation meant Clark was now a "semi-evolutionist," "an appeaser for the evolution theory," and "an intellectual Quisling."[69] And taking one more shot at Clark, Price later

Ronald L. Numbers (New York: Garland Publishing, 1995).

65. Numbers, "Introduction," x; idem, *Darwinism*, 105.

66. Numbers, *Darwinism*, 104; idem, "Introduction," xi; Young and Stearley, *Bible*, 238–39.

67. Numbers, "Introduction," xiv.

68. Ibid., xiii.

69. Personal letter of G. M. Price to D. J. Whitney, June 23, 1943, in Numbers, "Introduction," xiv.

published *Theories of Satanic Origin*, taking dead aim at "the theory of the long geological 'ages,' marked off by the differential dating of the fossils."[70]

But by then another Price protégé, Frank Lewis Marsh (1899–1992), the first Adventist to earn a Ph.D. in biology, also accepted extensive speciation. Believing Adam could not have named all the land species in one day as per Genesis 2, he held that equating modern species with the originally created kinds of Genesis 1 is to confuse taxonomic categories. Instead, coining a term from the Hebrew words for "created" and "kind," he suggested "baramin" as a biblical classification unit. Scientific research should determine the boundaries of this limited evolution, not assumptions based on a particular unit in modern taxonomy.[71]

At first Price believed Marsh had fallen for evolutionary propaganda, but eventually accepted Marsh's view. Yet Walter Lammerts (1904–1996), first president of the Creation Research Society and a central early figure in modern young earth creationism, could not disagree more. He believed accepting such large-scale speciation amounted to granting "everything that evolutionists ask for" but "to boil it down to just about five thousand years, on a scale that they don't even dream of in hundreds of thousands, or even millions, of years."[72] And though prominent evolutionist Theodosius Dobzhansky understood that Marsh rejected full-blown Darwinism, he stated Marsh's position still amounted to biological change at a speed even evolutionists could not imagine.[73]

Flood geology had come a long way since the scriptural geologists. The Adventists, like the scriptural geologists, agreed on the necessity of recent creation. But they now lived at a time when they also had to battle with Darwinism, even while increasingly accepting significant aspects of Darwinism itself. Especially problematic was their disagreement about the observable nature of the geologic column itself. Nevertheless, the ideas of the Seventh-day Adventists would profoundly affect Henry M. Morris, widely known as the father of modern young earth creationism.

---

70. George McCready Price, *Theories of Satanic Origin* (Loma Linda, CA: Author, n.d.), 3.

71. Numbers, *Darwinism*, 105.

72. Walter Lammerts et al., "Review of 'Creation, Evolution, and Science,'" November 18, 1944, Couperus Papers, in Numbers, "Introduction," xvi.

73. Ibid., xvii.

HENRY M. MORRIS: THE FATHER OF
MODERN YOUNG EARTH CREATIONISM

The Adventist flood geology movement did not win over the greater evangelical world. Evangelical anti-evolutionism remained largely committed to old earth gap or day-age theories. But Henry M. Morris vividly described an evangelical revolution that changed all that: "One of the most surprising phenomena of the second half of the twentieth century has been the resurgence of creationism—not a compromising amalgamation of evolutionary thought with theistic overtones, but a clear-cut, Bible-centered, literalistic, young-earth special creationism."[74] One may challenge his description of earlier evangelical creationists, but no one can deny that the now well-known young earth revival often conceives of itself in the way Morris describes.

The widely recognized trigger for this young earth-flood geology revolution was *The Genesis Flood*, published by Henry M. Morris and John Whitcomb in 1961.[75] By the time Morris described the young earth awakening, his books had been translated into at least ten languages. His and other like-minded flood theorists' approach to Genesis and science had "co-opted the generic creationist label . . . which only a half-century earlier had languished on the margins of American fundamentalism. People who called themselves creationists during the last quarter of the twentieth century typically assumed that most listeners would identify them as believers in a young Earth."[76]

In spite of the language Morris used in reference to earlier creationists, he certainly admired and was influenced by them. Morris acknowledged that the majority in the early twentieth century fought evolution and liberal theology, and that William Bell Riley was "one of the most outspoken fundamentalists and creationists of this period."[77] Morris also applauded

---

74. Henry M. Morris, *A History of Modern Creationism* (San Diego: Master Books, 1984), 13.

75. John C. Whitcomb and Henry M. Morris, *The Genesis Flood: The Biblical Record and Its Scientific Implications* (Phillipsburg, NJ: P & R, 1961). See Mortenson, *Turning Point*, 236 n. 203, and Numbers, *Creationists*, 187.

76. Numbers, *Darwinism*, 6. See also Christopher Rios, *After the Monkey Trial: Evangelical Scientists and a New Creationism* (New York: Fordham University Press, 2014), 115.

77. Morris, *History*, 58. See also ibid., 61.

the books of Harry Rimmer, "undoubtedly the most influential of the 'fundamentalist' creationists before the Darwin Centennial," for turning him away from theistic evolution in the early 1940s.[78] Morris also recognized old earth views "almost universally characterized the creationist testimony of the period,"[79] with old earth works like the *Scofield Reference Bible* having a tremendous impact on fundamentalism.

But in the end, Morris reproved them all, including Rimmer, for having "compromised on the vital issue of the age of the earth and flood geology."[80] Morris regarded the fundamentalists as "either so unconcerned with these basic scientific issues or so enamored with their schemes of evolutionary compromise that they had nothing significant to contribute"[81] to the pressing issue of creation and the flood. Though they had been anti-evolutionists, they had committed "evolutionary compromise." Thus "the vital Biblical doctrines of genuine creationism and Noachian catastrophism had to be upheld almost exclusively during the quarter century after the Scopes trial embarrassment by a denominational group which most of them considered to be a cult."[82] This "denominational group" was, of course, the Seventh-day Adventists. And though Morris disagreed with them on eschatology, revelation, and soteriology, he did not believe they were a "cult."[83] Instead they stood as the unlikely source for "the only serious *geological* defense of the Biblical view" and served as a rebuke and "sad commentary on the state of the orthodox denominations—as well as the supposedly 'fundamental' inter-denominational organizations—of the time."[84]

Morris regarded George McCready Price as the "most important creationist"[85] of the first half of the twentieth century. Morris described how Price made a "profound impression" on him with "his tremendous

---

78. Ibid., 89. See also ibid., 90. Morris admits he had been a theistic evolutionist in his undergraduate days at Rice University (95).

79. Ibid., 58.

80. Ibid., 92. See also ibid., 59.

81. Ibid., 119.

82. Ibid., 120.

83. Ibid., 80, 122. Morris wrote of his respect for their strong view of the Bible and many other basic Christian doctrines, and of his personally enjoying genuine Christian fellowship with some.

84. Ibid., 60, 120. Emphasis his.

85. Ibid., 79.

breadth of knowledge in science and Scripture, his careful logic, and his beautiful writing."[86] Price's lack of formal geology education rendered him an independent thinker scientifically and biblically, "constrained only by Scripture rather than the evolutionist party line of the schools and text-books. . . . [and made him] certainly far better educated, in the true sense, than 90% of the Ph.D.'s and Th.D.'s cranked out by the assembly lines of the educational establishment."[87] Morris acquired and read most of Price's twenty-five books and corresponded with him for a period of fifteen years until his death.[88] Ideas from Price and other Adventists are evident in *The Genesis Flood* and other books by Morris.[89]

The Genesis Flood: The Constitution of Modern Young Earth Creationism

George McCready Price, but not his disciples, attacked both Darwinism and old earth geology by rejecting the standard order of the fossil col-umn. Henry Morris followed Price in this move, and in *The Genesis Flood* applauded him as the authority who validated it. Morris somewhat gen-erously claimed that Price made "extensive study" of the strata and found them out of order "around the world." But if, as Morris claimed, Price's evidence was "very impressive and well documented," why did geologists not admit Price had rightly exposed modern geology's grand error? The rea-son was "ostensibly because of his largely self-made geologic education."[90] Morris presented an even more troubling reason geologists rejected Price's revolutionary discovery: "We feel that Price was *really* ignored because of his strong case against uniformitarianism, a case more easily ridiculed or

---

86. Ibid., 80.
87. Ibid., 81.
88. Ibid., 80.
89. Numbers, *Darwinism,* 109. Answers in Genesis, however, claims that it is "simply incorrect" that Morris "drew significant inspiration" from Price. See Mark Looy and Georgia Purdom, "Exposing *The Anointed*," October 4, 2011, Answers in Genesis, https://answersingenesis.org/reviews/books/exposing-the-anointed/. See also Andrew A. Snelling and Todd Wood, "Looking Back and Moving Forward," October 1, 2008, Answers in Genesis, https://answersingenesis.org/hermeneutics/looking-back-and-moving-forward/. Morris, however, was explicit about his admiration for Price and the Adventists.
90. Whitcomb and Morris, *Genesis Flood,* 184.

ignored than refuted."[91] Morris suggested geologists also refused to face the fact of an often disordered fossil record because their evolutionary scheme prevented any other interpretation: "This neatly packaged system of geologic interpretation has the effect of making it practically impossible ever to dislodge it by any amount of contrary evidence."[92] Morris elsewhere in the book alluded to Price's having uncovered the grand error of modern geology, and returned to the theme of a disordered column numerous times.[93]

Why did Morris so stress Price's "great law," that the strata can be found in every possible relative order? He explains in a personal reflection elsewhere the trauma he faced in his college days when realizing that not only the trained geologists but also the anti-evolution fundamentalists accepted the standard geologic column. But he felt careful study revealed the Bible can only be interpreted to support recent creation. Therefore, the standard fossil column cannot be true because it demonstrates the earth is old.[94] And he reasoned just as had Price: "If the geological ages were nonexistent, then evolution is impossible, and all the deadly philosophies based on it have no foundation. Therefore, why in the Name of Him who is absolute truth and holiness, should any Christian continue to compromise with such a system as this?"[95]

Yet Morris admitted that geology had revealed a "superficial appearance of 'evolution' of similar organisms in successively higher strata" leading to "the complexity of such 'index fossils' increasing with increasing elevation in the column, in at least a general way."[96] But even this "superficial appearance" is best understood to result from the flood's sorting mechanisms, animal mobility, and the increasing elevation of the organisms at the time the flood destroyed them. Morris listed the general order one would expect to find in the column as a result of the flood: marine vertebrates, amphibians, reptiles, birds, and then mammals. And this semblance of order is what the column reveals: "exactly what is to be expected

---

91. Ibid., 184 n. 3. Emphasis his.
92. Ibid., 136.
93. Ibid., 189. See also ibid., 135, 170–72, 180–200, 207–11, 271–72.
94. Morris, *History*, 96–97.
95. Ibid., 331.
96. Whitcomb and Morris, *Genesis Flood*, 274.

in light of the Flood account."[97] So Morris was arguing that the "superficial appearance of evolution" found in the column was just what a flood model of geology predicts. Thus, fossil beds statistically averaged "would tend to be deposited in just the order that has been ascribed to them in terms of the standard geologic column."[98]

Evangelicals reading Morris could be forgiven for struggling to hold these ideas about the geologic column's order in tension. In the first place, the anti-evolutionism they had been taught was most likely some version of old earth creationism, generally either gap or day-age. The fossil order, therefore, constituted positive evidence for creation, that is, the column was a creation column. After Darwin the paucity of transitional fossils in the same column also provided OECs an apologetics tool to counter evolution. So the Price-Morris contention that the standard column apparently supported Darwinism hardly fit with the traditional OEC apologetics arsenal.

If the alleged order of the column was fabricated as an artificial construct to support evolution, then a century and a half of evangelical apologetics had been egregiously wrong. The only biblically faithful option was to reject the purported order of the column. At the same time, Morris presented a kind of positive apologetic utilizing the broad order of the column, signaling a return to viewing it as a flood column. If the unwavering order of the fossils was spurious, the general order was not.

Most evangelicals reading *The Genesis Flood* did not have the scientific expertise to follow the many technical explanations found throughout its pages. Therefore, few could blame them if they struggled to know when to emphasize the disorder or the order of the fossils in this seemingly new approach. But here was an anti-evolutionist champion with real scientific credentials stepping forward at a time when many other evangelicals were capitulating to evolution.

Arguably the most exciting and understandable feature of *The Genesis Flood* also seemed to remove all doubt about the lie of evolution and an old earth. Darwin's only visual, the tree of life diagram, in *The Origin of Species* powerfully struck a chord in readers even when many continued to resist natural selection. Likewise, whether most readers could follow the details or not, several dramatic pictures in *The Genesis Flood* seemed to validate its

97. Ibid., 276.
98. Ibid.

message: human footprints and dinosaur tracks discovered side by side in the very same strata.

In a section in which Morris presents "misplaced fossils" according to the traditional geologic column, he drops a bombshell: "For example, there is the case of the human footprints that have frequently been found in supposedly very ancient strata."[99] If true, young earth creationists would have discovered the holy grail of fossil discoveries, disproving the entire foundation of modern geology. Morris states that these "frequently" found fossilized footprints would be accepted at face value if they didn't contradict evolutionary theory. Those who reject them "illustrate the methods by which the uniformitarians can negate even the most plain and powerful evidence in opposition to their philosophy. Nevertheless, it is obvious that it is only the philosophy, and not the objective scientific evidence, that would prevent one from accepting these prints as of true human origin."[100] The book displays dramatic and now infamous pictures from the Paluxy River Bed, describing them as "contemporaneous footprints of Man and Dinosaur," "plainly disproving the evolutionist's contention that the dinosaurs were extinct some 70 million years before man 'evolved.'"[101] One especially dramatic picture is labeled "Giant Human Footprints in Cretaceous Strata" and captioned with the reminder that Genesis 6:4 mentions "giants in the earth in those days."[102] Readers are informed similar giant human footprints have been found elsewhere, thus "dinosaurs and giant humans must have lived at the same time."[103]

Other creationists studied the Paluxy River prints and cast serious doubts on their validity. By the third edition of *The Genesis Flood* the pictures and text were removed. The story behind the prints and what called them into question is fascinating, and not all young earth creationists agree about the tracks still.[104] But Morris and Whitcomb are to be credited for removing what had been by far their most persuasive evidence for the

---

99. Ibid., 172.

100. Ibid., 173.

101. Ibid., 174.

102. Ibid., 175.

103. Ibid. Cf. the picture of ancient strata on p. 167 displaying "what appear to be human footprints!"

104. Morris recounts how he first learned of the tracks in *History*, 83. Numbers, *Creationists*, 202–203, 265–67, provides details of the revealing correspondence about the tracks behind the scenes between Morris, Whitcomb, and other creationists. For the

general reader. Yet this mattered little; by that time the young earth creationist revolution was well under way.

Though *The Genesis Flood* argued that the flood narrative "demands a
literal interpretation of the universal terms,"[105] it appeared to use the scriptural geologists' strategy that universal language did not apply to extinct
animals. Morris suggested that if dinosaurs were taken onto the ark, they
likely became extinct due to post-flood climate changes.[106] But he thought
it "more likely . . . that animals of this sort were not taken on the Ark at
all, for the very reason of their intended extinction."[107]

Morris urgently stressed that the young age of the earth and the flood
column idea were critical for biblical fidelity. But if here he tightened what
counted as creationist orthodoxy, he also broadened that orthodoxy elsewhere. Anti-evolutionist evangelicals had long regarded species as God's
created biological units. Morris introduced his readers to the baraminology
approach of Adventist Frank Marsh, easily solving the number of animals
on the ark problem.[108] Morris also suggested exotic possibilities for biblical
interpretation based on continental drift, and discussed a post-flood ice

---

perspective of a non-Christian scientist who worked to expose the error the tracks as
evidence for human and dinosaur co-existence, see Ronnie J. Hastings, "The Rise and
Fall of the Paluxy Mantracks," American Scientific Affiliation, http://www.asa3.org/
ASA/PSCF/1988/PSCF9-88Hastings.html. John Morris, "The Paluxy River Mystery,"
Institute for Creation Research, http://www.icr.org/article/paluxy-river-mystery/, provides
his version of the story. Unfortunately, ICR has not removed from its website other articles
still promoting the tracks. For the view of Answers in Genesis, see Elizabeth Mitchell,
"Paluxy River Tracks in Spotlight," Answers in Genesis, https://answersingenesis.org/
dinosaurs/footprints/paluxy-river-tracks-in-texas-spotlight/, who gently distances AiG
from "provocative" young earth promoters of the tracks like Carl Baugh who are not part
of "the mainstream of the creation movement."

105. Whitcomb and Morris, *Genesis Flood*, 86.

106. Ibid., 280 n. 2.

107. Ibid., 69 n. 3. Apparently the exemption also applied to worms and many insects
that could have survived outside the ark. Ibid. Morris also cites Frank Lewis Marsh for the
idea that most vegetation survived outside the ark. Ibid., 66–70.

108. Ibid. Applying this idea in his commentary on Genesis, Morris suggests that
this could explain how Adam named "every" beast of the field and "every" bird of the
air, although the text doesn't say "kinds" were brought before the first man. Morris also
suggests the possibility that in spite of the universal language, God would not have brought
"wild animals living at considerable distance from man and his cultivated fields." Morris,
Genesis Record, 97. Since this was pre-fall, and because God brought "wild" animals to the
ark, and because Genesis 2:19 states that God created them out of the ground and brought
them to Adam, the interpretive options Morris struggled with here are surprising.

age with perhaps continent-sized ice sheets thousands of feet thick.[109] And though he believed evolutionary bias tainted radiometric dating, he admitted something had caused "apparently higher proportions of radiogenic materials in the 'older' strata, that is, those which were usually deposited earlier and deeper than the others."[110]

Henry M. Morris: The Tone of Young Earth Creationism

Just as with the scriptural geologists and George McCready Price, Morris continued the tradition of declaring that the issue of the age of the earth and the flood are of supreme importance. In *The Long War Against God*, Morris argued that modern old-earth geology itself was part of the long war against God because it destroyed flood geology and opened the door for evolution.[111] Any evangelical believing in an old earth obviously was part of the problem. But even a biblical inerrantist not accepting that "a worldwide cataclysmic deluge would have completely reworked and redeposited all the geologic strata" qualified one as part of the "compromise" with evolution.[112] Morris had redrawn the boundary for essential Christianity with young earth creationism and belief in the flood column constituting the line. And he proclaimed the stakes could hardly be higher. "The fact is . . . that the failure of Bible-believing Christian churches and schools to aggressively defend and promote true biblical creationism is a major cause of the takeover by evolutionary humanism of our entire society—its schools, news media, courts, and all other aspects thereof."[113]

CONCLUSION

In many ways *The Genesis Flood* has become like a constitution for modern YEC. As a founding document, it provides its essential system of beliefs and

---

109. Morris suggested continental drift as an interpretive option for Genesis 10:25: "for in his days the earth was divided." See Morris, *Genesis Record*, 261. On the ice age, see Whitcomb and Morris, *Genesis Flood*

110. Whitcomb and Morris, *Genesis Flood,* 366.

111. Henry M. Morris, *The Long War Against God: History and Impact of the Creation/ Evolution Conflict* (Green Forest, AR: Master Books, 1989), 102.

112. Ibid., 101–102.

113. Ibid., 105.

laws. But because it is not considered perfect, it is amendable. As we will see in the following chapter, amendments have been made or attempted by contemporary YECs. But the core of the system seems quite fixed.

What lies at its core? The recent creation of the earth is non-negotiable. So also is viewing the geologic column as a flood column. As a subset of the flood column is the less strict geographically universal flood. The notion is less strict because certain flexibility among YECs has been allowed without censure. For example, some have not interpreted the universal language of Genesis literally regarding the land animals in relation to the ark. In light of the scientific evidence for extinctions, the scriptural geologists and Henry Morris felt free to understand certain animals like dinosaurs might have been intentionally left off the ark. And some scriptural geologists who did not believe the flood waters covered the earth all at the same time receive no reprimand. Flexibility is allowed in understanding the *how* of the flood or even some of its "universal" details. But the general notion of a worldwide fossil-causing flood is critical.

In spite of its importance, however, some debate remains among young earth creationists about the flood column. Henry Morris in adopting the central notion of Price about the geologic column has left open the door for difficulties. On the one hand, the column should be understood as not nearly as orderly as modern geology teaches. This move removes evidence for evolution (and an old earth). On the other hand, the column does display a significant amount of orderliness that must be turned to the defense of the flood. As we will see in the following chapter, holding the two notions in tension can be the source for in-house YEC debate.

Similarly, Morris did not nail the door shut on radiometric dating by declaring it completely untrustworthy. By acknowledging some correlation with its dates and the order of the strata, room for debate remains, not to mention confusion among rank-and-file YECs. And against the traditional anti-evolutionist resistance to speciation, Morris adopted the baraminology approach of Adventist Frank Marsh. The move solves problems in some YEC models, but as we will see in the next two chapters, it raises questions regarding acceptable YEC limits on speciation. When does the degree and rate of YEC speciation become evolutionary itself? And should speciation limits be determined in advance or by scientific investigation? Without doubt, the employment of broad speciation in the service of anti-evolutionary YEC models is counterintuitive even to non-specialist

YECs. At times some YEC attacks on evolutionary biology seem to take a back seat to their assaults on old earth geology.

Finally, the tone Morris set may be the hardest part of his legacy to amend. By all accounts he was a godly and kind man. But because he believed his viewpoint so important, he felt it imperative to thunder like a prophet to God's people. Some of his sternest reproaches were directed toward those who shared his deepest concerns (anti-evolution, defense of inerrancy, etc.) if they "compromised" with OEC geology. But if the issue separates those on either the side of God or Satan as Price, Morris, and Mortenson have written, then even fellow conservative evangelicals warrant such rebukes as unwitting enemies of God and truth.

Chapter 7

DO YOUNG EARTH CREATIONISTS PRACTICE EVOLUTIONARY SCIENCE?

Christians' faith is not built by wedding atheistic theories of history with the Bible.[1]

—Ken Ham and Terry Mortenson, "Special Feature: Hugh Ross Exposé"

I had presented a meager case that the age of the earth should not function as an evangelical essential. But that unfinished paper I read at the 2001 annual meeting of the Evangelical Theological Society (ETS) was a thing of the past. My entire focus in 2002 was living a day at a time with the effects of ongoing chemotherapy. That changed when I got word that my new friend Terry Mortenson of Answers in Genesis (AiG) was going to present a paper the following year with the words "A Response to Ted Cabal's 2001 ETS Paper" in the title. Frankly, I was shocked anyone thought my opinion important enough to merit a response. And I especially thought my central point, that the earth's age is not an essential evangelical doctrine, should not be especially controversial.[2]

---

1. Terry Mortenson and Ken Ham, "Special Feature: Hugh Ross Exposé," Answers in Genesis, August 23, 2002, https://answersingenesis.org/creationism/old-earth/special-feature-hugh-ross-expose/. "Atheist" theories refer to old earth theories in general and the big bang theory in particular.

2. See the preface for more on how Terry's and my papers ultimately led to this book.

But Mortenson disagreed, stating that "the age of the earth is abso-lutely foundational to the Christian faith."[3] And in spite of my chemo-therapy, his response energized me to dig into this subject even deeper. His inferences made it personal, casting aspersions on the integrity of anti-evolutionary old earth creationists (OECs), claiming they hold their views "because of a fundamental refusal to be subject to the authority of God's Word"[4] and that most OECs for the past two centuries have done so "trying to maintain an intellectual respectability"[5] while "trembling at the words of scientists."[6] OECs, including ETS members, need "to resubmit to the authority of the inspired, inerrant Word of God, that we claim to believe."[7] Though he cited no one reporting such motives, Mortenson was rebuking the alleged dishonorable intentions of past and present biblical inerrantists who disagreed with him on the earth's age.

As we've seen, these past OECs carried the fight to evolutionists, but Mortenson presented his metric for diagnosing them as "evolutionists." Other than young earth creationists (YECs), which he termed "biblical creationists,"[8] all other evangelicals are evolutionists because they submit the Bible to "atheistic" or naturalistic science, "which says that nature is all that exists and therefore we must explain everything by time plus chance plus the laws of nature working on matter."[9] He then defined this natu-ralistic evolution as composed of three strands. The first is astronomical evolution, specifically an atheistic version of the big bang. The second is geological evolution, an atheistic version of modern geology. The third is an atheistic version of evolutionary biology.

---

3. Terry Mortenson, "'Evangelicalism and Young-Earth Creationism: Necessary Bedfellows?' A Response to Ted Cabal's 2001 ETS Paper," unpublished paper presented at the annual meeting of the Evangelical Theological Society, Toronto, Canada, November 20, 2002, 2.

4. Ibid., 26.

5. Ibid., 22.

6. Ibid., 23.

7. Ibid., 22. AiG describes the annual sessions as attended by "those scholars and leaders at ETS who don't stand on the authority of Scripture (the majority of attendees)" who need to be challenged to reconsider their views and to take God at His Word from the very first verse." Ken Ham, "AiG Reaches Out to Bible Scholars," Answers in Genesis, November 23, 2013, https://answersingenesis.org/blogs/ken-ham/2013/11/23/aig-reaches-out-to-bible-scholars/.

8. Mortenson, "Response," 4.

9. Ibid., 3.

So by Mortenson's definition of the three strands, young earth (or "biblical") creationists graded out as "0/3" evolutionary. OECs were "2/3 evolutionist" because they "accept astronomical and geological evolution" (i.e., an old universe and earth).[10] Theistic evolutionists are "3/3 evolutionists." Perhaps realizing by virtue of his earlier definitions he has just equated theistic evolutionists with atheism, Mortenson then softened their diagnosis to "(or 99%, if we count 1% for believing that God is behind evolution)."[11]

Mortenson never cited evangelicals who professed belief that "nature is all that exists" and "time plus chance plus nature's laws" explain everything. But whatever the reasoning for his evangelical "evolutionary" metric, the rest of the paper essentially argued that everyone but YECs submit the Bible to the authority of science. "It is only because science has supposedly proven the age of the Earth and universe to be billions of years old. That evolutionary science, rather than the text of Scripture, is what is driving the various reinterpretations of Genesis 1–11 has been admitted by many."[12] Whether I was ready or not, Mortenson's inference that I was an "evolutionist" with ungodly motives compelled me to undertake my investigation into the age of the earth controversy.

EARTH'S CATASTROPHIC PAST: A TEST CASE

It seemed fair to me, with tongue planted in cheek, to look into the most authoritative contemporary YEC science and see if any of it qualifies as "evolutionary." So we will make the assessment using Mortenson's metric in geology, astronomy, and biology. Moreover, we will also examine whether leading YECs submit biblical interpretation to science.

Late in his life, Henry Morris personally requested geologist Andrew Snelling to write an "updated and revised version" of *The Genesis Flood*. At the time Snelling served at the Institute for Creation Research (ICR)

---

10. Mortenson's geology strand also erred in claiming old earth geology "in the early 19th century" was based on "deistic and atheistic geologists" who found "no geological evidence of a global Flood at the time of Noah." Ibid., 7. But, as we've seen, leading old earth geologists at the time defended the Bible in light of geology while continuing to believe in a global flood responsible for the earth's surface features.

11. Ibid., 4. Mortenson defined the strands on p. 3.

12. Ibid., 8.

but since has become director of research at AiG.[13] Arguably Snelling's two-volume *Earth's Catastrophic Past: Geology, Creation, and the Flood* serves as the most comprehensive systematic treatment of young earth creationism today. Snelling is generally more measured than some YECs in the way he describes those who disagree with him. He also commendably recognizes that "extreme care must be taken not to either force scientific details from the Scriptures or to manipulate the geological data to achieve agreement between the geologic and biblical records."[14] And he also rightly notes "that due care must be exercised in the levels of certainty and dogmatism attached to our understandings of the scientific information and implications that we might derive from the Scriptures."[15]

YOUNG EARTH CREATIONISM AND MODERN GEOLOGY

The Fossil Column

We saw in chapter 6 that Henry Morris rejected the notion of a standard order to the fossil column. He believed George McCready Price had thoroughly exposed its evolutionary bias. Morris often described the standard geologic column as the basis for evolution and the great age of the earth, therefore making it something that must be staunchly resisted in the name of biblical faithfulness.

But Snelling has reversed course by generally accepting the standard geologic column. Of course believing in recent creation, Snelling nevertheless believes the fossilized strata are consistently sequenced, thus "the geologic column itself is not an imaginary construct—not an abstract representation of interpretation built upon unprovable assumptions about timescale and geological processes in the past—but instead is based on the empirical data of field observations and careful geologic mapping."[16]

Over and again Snelling stresses the importance of recognizing "that the order of occurrence of fossils in the rock record is based on real and verifiable observational field data and does not depend in any way on the

---

13. Andrew A. Snelling, *Earth's Catastrophic Past: Geology, Creation, and the Flood*, 2 vols. (Green Forest, AR: Master Books, 2009), 1:xiv.

14. Ibid., 2:467.

15. Ibid.

16. Ibid., 1:312. Cf. ibid., 1:329.

evolutionary interpretation which the conventional geological community imposes on the fossil record."[17] This trustworthy order of the fossilized strata includes the noteworthy pattern "that there is the ever-increasing percentage of extinct groups as one goes further back in the fossil record."[18] Thus "the overall 'big picture' of the global sequences of rock strata and their relationship to one another as expressed in the standard geologic column is a physical reality that is a reliable record of the earth's geologic history."[19] Snelling honestly admits that once one recognizes the reliable strata sequences, "then the sheer magnitude of the apparent long and complex geological history for the earth might seem to lend strong support to the uniformitarian interpretation of a billions-of-years geological timescale."[20]

So, because of the "essential consensus on the empirical data that needs to be explained in any geologic model of earth history,"[21] Snelling interprets the Bible accordingly. For instance, his biblical beliefs lead him to hold that humans and dinosaurs must have lived at the same time.[22] But because the two are considerably separated in the geologic strata, he interprets the biblical scenario to mean "they didn't live spatially together in the pre-Flood world."[23] The dinosaurs likely lived at a lower elevation than the Garden of Eden "in distinct and geographically separated biological communities or biomes."[24] Snelling even entertains the possibility that dinosaurs and humans lived on separate island continents in the pre-flood world.[25] Snelling holds this understanding of the biblical picture because of "the spatial separation of the fossil remains of these biomes in the geologic record."[26]

Snelling's scientifically informed biblical model differs considerably from the biblical model displayed at the Answers in Genesis Creation Museum. Replete with sculpted and animatronic dinosaurs, the museum

---

17. Ibid., 1:347.
18. Ibid., 1:354. See also ibid., 1:356–59, for Snelling's discussion of the eight mass extinctions as understood by conventional geologists.
19. Ibid., 1:327. Cf. ibid.,1:347.
20. Ibid., 1:331.
21. Ibid., 1:335.
22. Ibid., 2:677.
23. Ibid., 2:731.
24. Ibid., 2:678. See also ibid., 2:677.
25. Ibid., 2:730.
26. Ibid.

advertises that it "brings the pages of the Bible to life, casting its charac-
ters and animals in dynamic form and placing them in familiar settings.
Adam and Eve live in the Garden of Eden. Children play and dinosaurs
roam near Eden's Rivers."[27] Snelling has distanced himself from the view
of Morris, which portrayed the order of the geologic column as a fiction
based on evolutionary bias. But Snelling has maintained commitment to
a young earth based on biblical conviction. Because of his view of the
geologic column, he does not expect evidence like the Paluxy River Bed
tracks to confirm that humans and dinosaurs crossed paths. The Answers
in Genesis Creation Museum, however, conveys the impression that the
Bible teaches human and dinosaurs lived together in Eden.

In this regard, one with Snelling's more careful approach would not be
compelled to look for dinosaurs in the Bible. And whatever one's views on
the age of the earth, instances of interpreting biblical passages as references
to dinosaurs clearly comes from "submitting" the Bible to modern science.
Why? Because the church never interpreted those passages that way prior to
the discovery of dinosaurs in the modern era. In other words, such biblical
interpretations could never have occurred until modern paleontology first
revealed the alleged correlations. Books and articles abound from a YEC
perspective with dramatic biblical allusions to dinosaurs.[28] But the problem is not that scientific theories inform YEC biblical interpretation. YEC
theories like the vapor canopy can come and can go when either biblical
or scientific problems are identified.[29] I've already argued that historically

---

27. From AiG's website, http://creationmuseum.org/.

28. For examples of confident interpretations that the Bible alludes to specific dinosaurs,
see Ken Ham, *The Great Dinosaur Mystery: Solved!*, fifth printing (Green Forest, AR: Master
Books, 2005), 43–47, 69–73, and Tim Chaffey and Jason Lisle, *Old-Earth Creationism
on Trial: The Verdict Is In* (Green Forest, AR: Master Books, 2008), 175–76. For similar
treatments, see Bodie Hodge and Laura Welch, *Dragons: Legends and Lore of Dinosaurs*
(Green Forest, AR: Master Books, 2011), and Mike Liston, John Whitmore, and Buddy
Davis, *The Great Alaskan Dinosaur Adventure* (Green Forest, AR: Master Books, 1998).
Regarding ancient Christian interpretation of the especially popular "dinosaur" texts in
Job 40:15 and 41:34, see Manlio Simonetti and Marco Conti, eds., *The Ancient Christian
Commentary on Scripture: Job* (Downers Grove, IL: InterVarsity Press, 2006), 208–17.
Ancient commentators were as divided as moderns regarding interpretive details of
behemoth and leviathan, but indicated no understanding of them as extinct animals.

29. Though predating him, Henry Morris popularized the view, interpreting
Genesis 1:6–7 to refer to a protective water vapor barrier over the earth permitting the
gigantism of plants and animals revealed by modern paleontology. The canopy theory

conservative Christians have cautiously courted scientific theories as part of the conservatism principle. The point is that YECs interpret the Bible in light of modern "evolutionary" science just as do OECs. Morris tried to present evidence of humans and dinosaurs in the same strata because he believed the geologic column an "evolutionary" fiction. But Snelling accepts that column order, and holds that humans and dinosaurs lived in separate biomes because their fossils are not found in the same strata. In Snelling's case, and the same would be true of many other leading YECs today, the very same "evolutionary" geology used by OECs is believed and applied to biblical understanding, but compressed to fit within a recent creation model.

---

explained Genesis 2:5–6 to mean rain never fell on the earth before the flood. And the water canopy answered the old question of the flood's water source (Gen. 7:11) and protected the earth from the sun's harmful radiation, explaining the longevity of antediluvian human life. Henry Morris, *The Genesis Record: A Scientific and Devotional Commentary on the Book of Beginnings*, fifth printing (Grand Rapids: Baker, 1980), 59–61, 191, 194. On the theory's background, see Ronald L. Numbers, *The Creationists: The Evolution of Scientific Creationism* (Berkeley, CA: University of California Press, 1992), 401 n. 47. Vapor canopy defenses include John C. Dillow, *The Waters Above* (Chicago: Moody Press, 1981), and David E. Rush and Larry Vardiman, "Pre-Flood Vapor Canopy Radiative Temperature Profiles," paper presented at the Second International Conference on Creationism, Pittsburgh, Pennsylvania, July 30–August 4, 1990, and published in *Proceedings of the Second International Conference on Creationism*, ed. R. E. Walsh and C. L. Brooks (Pittsburgh: Creation Science Fellowship, Inc., 1990), 231–40. See also Larry Vardiman, "Temperature Profiles for an Optimized Water Vapor Canopy," 'http://www. icr.org/i/pdf/research/ Canopy.pdf, and John MacArthur, *The Battle for the Beginning: Creation, Evolution, and the Bible* (Nashville: W Publishing Group, 2001), 90–91. But the canopy theory eventually fell on hard times. YEC Russell Humphreys wrote in 1994 that "the idea of a canopy atop the atmosphere did not come down from Sinai with Moses, engraved by the finger of God on the back side of the stone tablets. Instead, it was a human interpretation of scripture which was, for a time, the best understanding we could come up with. I think that time has passed. In spite of the large emotional investment some of us may have put into the canopy model, I suggest that now is a good time to re-evaluate the model, to see if it is worth any further effort." Russell Humphreys, *Starlight and Time* (Green Forest, AR: Master Books, 1994), 63. Snelling rejects interpreting Genesis 2:5 to mean no rain ever fell before the flood, and rejects the vapor canopy theory based on its scientific problems. Snelling, *Catastrophic Past*, 1:195; 2:472, 698. Numerous surveys of my seminary students reveal that many have been taught the theory as integral to YEC, yet are unaware that it has been largely abandoned by most of the movement's leaders. Younger students who can articulate the canopy theory rarely are aware of the many differing views embraced by YEC over the past two centuries, much less that anti-evolutionist OEC ruled conservative evangelicalism until about fifty years ago.

Radiometric Dating

To his credit, Snelling admirably admits that his flood geology model does not resolve all problems. "Without doubt, the most important and serious of these perceived problems is the question of time. There are, of course, many lines of geological evidence that appear to strongly imply that the earth and its various rock strata are millions, and even billions, of years old, immensely older than the straightforward biblical interpretation."[30] In this regard, Snelling especially cites radiometric dating. Morris himself had admitted that something had caused "apparently higher proportions of radiogenic materials in the 'older' strata, that is, those which were usually deposited earlier and deeper than the others."[31]

As a standard YEC response to the vast agreement in various radiometric dating methods, Snelling observes that no one can "determine the original numbers of atoms of the daughter isotopes. Nor were human observers present throughout the histories of most rocks . . . to determine whether the rocks and minerals have remained closed to loss or gain of parent and/or daughter isotopes, and if the rates of radioactive decay of the parent isotopes have not changed."[32] But again to his credit, Snelling admits the first two of these questions is not significant enough to undercut the good scientific reasons to trust the data derived from radiometric dating. Therefore, Snelling candidly acknowledges that at today's rates of decay "it must be concluded that hundreds of millions of years worth of radioactive and nuclear decay must have occurred during the accumulation of the geologic record."[33] And again, "the inescapable conclusion is that the radioisotope ratios in many rock units have resulted from hundreds of millions of years, and even billions of years, of radioactive decay (at today's measured rates)," and "radioactive decay has been the dominant producer of the measured daughter isotopes alongside their parent radioisotopes."[34] Though he rejects the dates derived thereby, Snelling notes that "radioisotopic ratios are empirical data in the same way as other

30. Snelling, *Catastrophic Past*, 2:798.

31. John C. Whitcomb and Henry M. Morris, *The Genesis Flood: The Biblical Record and Its Scientific Implications* (Phillipsburg, NJ: P & R, 1961), 366.

32. Snelling, *Catastrophic Past*, 2:800.

33. Ibid., 2:837.

34. Ibid.

geochemical analyses for major and trace elements in the rocks. Thus, the use of radioisotopic ratios in correlating Precambrian rock units should not automatically be scorned and disregarded simply because vast 'ages' are commonly derived from them."[35] Radiometric "dating," then, is accurate "as a correlation tool."[36]

Snelling obviously does not endorse everything about radiometric dating, noting that different radiometric dating methods can sometimes yield conflicting dates. He regards this fact as a conclusive demonstration of "the unreliability of the radioisotope methods for 'dating' rocks."[37] But Snelling has already conceded that these "hundreds of millions of years worth of radioactive and nuclear decay must have occurred during the accumulation of the geologic record."[38] So conflicting dates between radiometric methods actually serve as a clue to "the possibility that accelerated radioisotope decay occurred during some event or events in the past."[39]

The idea of accelerated radioisotope decay enables Snelling to accept the overall reliability of radiometric dating. Dramatic acceleration of the normal rates is consistent with Snelling's general theory that during the flood "many other geologic processes were occurring at catastrophic rates."[40] Indeed, the heat thus generated would have been adequate "to drive the catastrophic geologic processes during the Flood event,"[41] but not so excessive as "to melt minerals and rocks."[42] But instead of during the flood, most of the accelerated radioisotope decay, "several billion years worth (at today's measured rates)," occurred "most likely during the first two and a half days of the Creation Week, from the initial creation of earth through the formation of dry land."[43] By placing most of the accelerated radioisotope decay during the first few days of the creation week, Snelling avoids the problem recognized by YECs that the "amount of heat produced by a decay rate of a million times faster than normal during the year

35. Ibid., 1:326.
36. Ibid.
37. Ibid., 2:843.
38. Ibid., 2:837.
39. Ibid., 2:846.
40. Ibid., 2:847.
41. Ibid.
42. Ibid.
43. Ibid., 2:848.

of the Flood could potentially vaporize the earth's oceans, melt the crust, and obliterate the surface of the earth."[44] On the other hand, some YECs are concerned that placing the rapid decay rate during the creation week "would introduce the concept of 'decay' during this period that was stated by God to be 'very good.' This issue probably merits further study, but could easily be resolved if the term 'decay' were understood as 'process.'"[45] The bottom line is that Snelling accepts the science that Mortenson would deem "evolutionary" or "atheistic" if Snelling also accepted its old earth implications.

CONTINENTAL DRIFT AND PLATE TECTONICS

Plate tectonics is perhaps the most important theory in modern geology. The earth's crust is divided into major "plates" that move and collide, forming mountains and mid-ocean ridges and causing volcanoes and earthquakes. Entire continents and ocean basins have been reconfigured by the movements of these plates. Indeed, our current continents formed by the breaking up of a supercontinent as over time its mass separated and rode apart on top of different plates. These recent but foundational ideas in modern geology are accepted by a number of leading YECs today, including Andrew Snelling.[46]

Snelling admirably notes that YECs need to account for this old earth evidence, that is, the "astonishing" and "amazing agreement between the rates of past plate motion inferred from radioisotope dating, combined with the plate displacements implied by plate tectonics theory, and the rates of plate motion actually measured for the earth today."[47] He concedes that old earth plate tectonics provides such a unifying conceptual framework for many past and present geologic features that were it not for "the eyewitness revelation of the catastrophic events in earth history given us in the Scriptures, this assumption is not unreasonable, particularly as there is also a biblical basis for continuity in the operation of

---

44. Larry Vardiman, "RATE in Review: Unresolved Problems," *Acts & Facts* 36, no. 12 (2007): 6.

45. Ibid.

46. Snelling lays out the basic case in *Catastrophic Past*, 1:365–78.

47. Ibid., 1:380.

natural processes that the Creator set in operation after He had created the earth."[48]

Because Snelling finds the geological evidence compelling, he bases his flood theory on *"catastrophic plate tectonics,* with the gradual motions of crustal plates today being merely residual effects of the cataclysm."[49] He uses the model to explain many of the flood descriptions in Genesis such as the forty days and nights of rain resulting not from clouds (or a vapor canopy) but from earth's cleaving open and releasing heated jets of water shooting high into the atmosphere that condensed into rain.[50] Snelling contends that the geologic laws operating today may have been the same "during the Flood except they operated on larger and more rapid scales."[51] These "larger and more rapid scales," as described in the title of one YEC article, imply that during the flood the "Continents Didn't Drift, They Raced."[52] Again, the key difference between the geological processes of Snelling and OEC is their very rapid speed.

Snelling then interprets the Bible in light of this science, suggesting that Genesis 1:9–10 should be read as implying the earth was originally created with "one interconnected supercontinental landmass."[53] Morris himself had even suggested plate tectonics caused rapid continental separation as late as the event of Genesis 10:25, thus splitting up the human race geographically.[54] Again, biblical interpretation influenced by science is not new, but when OECs do it, some YECs accuse them of submitting the Bible to "evolutionary" science.

---

48. Ibid., 1:389.

49. Ibid., 2:684–85. Emphasis his. Snelling's source for the concept derives from his teamwork in S. A. Austin, J. R. Baumgardner, D. R. Humphreys, A. A. Snelling, L. Vardiman, and K. P. Wise, "Catastrophic Plate Tectonics: A Global Flood Model of Earth History," in *Proceedings of the Third International Conference on Creationism*, ed. R. E. Walsh (Pittsburgh: Creation Science Fellowship, 1994), 609–21.

50. Snelling, *Catastrophic Past*, 2:471–73.

51. Ibid., 2:688.

52. Brian Thomas, "Continents Didn't Drift, They Raced," August 23, 2012, Institute for Creation Research, http://www.icr.org/article/5588/.

53. Snelling, *Catastrophic Past*, 2:469. See also ibid., 1:194.

54. Morris, *Genesis Record*, 260–61, Morris concluded the more likely interpretation was the supernatural confusion of languages at Babel. Wise, *Faith, Form, and Time*, 181–95, gently distances himself from the novel Genesis 10:25 plate tectonics interpretation by Morris.

YOUNG EARTH CREATIONISM AND MODERN ASTRONOMY

Henry Morris rejected the notion of "stellar and galactic evolution" claiming that "no one has ever *seen* a star or galaxy evolve, or change at all."[55] But YEC astronomer Danny Faulkner doesn't care for using the term "evolution" in this context, noting that Morris had argued "that the birth of new stars would be tantamount to the appearance of a new kind of animal, something that the creation model does not allow. But is the birth of new stars more like the creation of new creatures, or is it more like the replacement of dead ones? We know that animals die and so must be replaced, so perhaps this is the proper analog to stellar birth."[56] This smaller issue in YEC astronomy relates to one much bigger.

The immense distances starlight travels to reach earth would take as much as billions of years at the speed of light, implying an old universe. Faulkner notes that though not the majority, some members of the preeminent young earth scholarly society, the Creation Research Society, hold the view that though "the earth and all that is on it were created a few thousand years ago, most of the universe was created in the distant past of 'in the beginning' of Genesis 1:1. A careful reading of the statement of belief of the CRS reveals that this belief is compatible with that statement."[57] Nonetheless, most YECs like Snelling hold to a recent creation of the universe too.

A traditional YEC solution is to understand that God instantaneously created the starlight without it having to travel immense distances. But if starlight was created in transit, Faulkner notes this means supernovae observations are illusions rather than the explosive deaths of stars. And if none of the events observed in the heavens really happened, the situation is analogous to believing God had created the fossils in rocks without the creatures ever having existed.[58] Snelling proffers two solutions, one being that perhaps light traveled at a speed near infinity at the time of creation, an explanation that carries its own problems.[59]

---

55. Morris, *Genesis Record*, 67.

56. Danny Faulkner, "The Current State of Creation Astronomy," paper presented at the Fourth International Conference on Creationism, Pittsburgh, Pennsylvania, August 1998, 12.

57. Ibid., 1.

58. Ibid., 14.

59. Snelling, *Catastrophic Past*, 1:223. But see Faulkner, "Current State," 13–14, for

Snelling's second solution for the starlight problem is the most interesting because it uses big bang evidence. He clearly rejects anything resembling an old universe version of big bang cosmology as "purely evolutionary and naturalistic,"[60] much in the same way Mortenson dubbed such astronomy "1/3 evolution." Actually the so-called big bang theory has historically been seen to support a finite universe, that is, one with a beginning. Naturalists have rejected this implication, seen by Christians and non-Christians alike as potentially supporting something like a biblical creation. As Nobel laureate and NASA astrophysicist George Smoot commented, "There is no doubt that a parallel exists between the big bang as an event and the Christian notion of creation from nothing."[61] Little surprise, then, that naturalists seek to find ways to reinterpret the evidence to dismiss its theistic or creation implications. And some YECs seek to use the same evidence in support of their creation models.

Snelling's second starlight solution seems quite close to big bang theory. He notes numerous times that the Bible alludes to God's stretching out the firmament, which was created on the second day. So he offers as scientific explanation YEC physicist Russell Humphrey's white hole cosmology in which the universe was originally created small but then stretched out, including the light.[62] Snelling doesn't get into the scientific details, but Humphreys adapts big bang science to a young earth model.[63] The expansion of the universe from the earth's perspective would have taken place by about the fourth Genesis creation day. But an earth day could be equivalent to "billions of years worth of physical processes"[64] taking place elsewhere in the universe. Humphreys notes how his theory lines up with

---

problems regarding the structure of matter itself entailed by imagining a different speed of light, a fundamental constant.

60. Ibid., 2:655.

61. George Smoot quoted in Fred Heeren, *Show Me God: What the Message from Space Is Telling Us about God*, Wonders vol. 1, rev. ed. (Wheeling, IL: Day Star Publications, 1997), 139. Smoot headed NASA's important COBE project, which measured the anisotropy of the background microwave radiation of the big bang.

62. Snelling, *Earth's Catastrophic Past*, 1:223.

63. D. Russell Humphreys, *Starlight and Time: Solving the Puzzle of Distant Starlight in a Young Universe* (Green Forest, AR: Master Books, 1997). Ken Ham wrote the foreword.

64. Humphreys, *Starlight*, 37.

the Bible's time frame: "Scripture says, and my theory agrees, that the universe is young *as measured by clocks on earth*."[65]

Again the problem is not that a YEC thinker is convinced of the evidences in support of the big bang. Prominent YEC Kurt Wise, who rejects big bang theory, admits it "is well-evidenced."[66] Nor is the difficulty even the modified big bang interpretation of Genesis. The real problem is that what counts as "evolutionary" or "atheistic" science for OECs doesn't appear to apply to YECs. The Humphreys model can use billions of years of cosmic processes, just so long as "only a few thousand years . . . elapsed since the beginning of creation in the reference frame of the earth."[67]

YOUNG EARTH CREATIONISM AND MODERN BIOLOGY

We saw in chapter 4 that until Darwin, most thinkers rejected the notion of a shared evolutionary history for living things. Evolution was more often than not associated with naturalism, and fixed species were generally considered a given. After Darwin, most evangelicals dug in their heels on the issue, with conservatives eventually becoming the anti-evolutionists of the early twentieth century.

Following the lead of the Adventists, however, speciation began to be more accepted among conservatives. Baraminology arose, the notion that biblically created kinds were not identical to any humanly conceived taxonomic units, and could be broader than species, genus, or even the family.

---

65. D. Russell Humphreys, "Seven Years of Starlight and Time," http://www.icr.org/starlightandtime/starlightandtime.html; Institute for Creation Research. Emphasis his.

66. Wise, *Faith, Form, and Time*, 89.

67. Faulkner, "Current State," 14–15. Opponents of Humphrey's model Samuel R. Conner and Don N. Page, "Starlight and Time Is the Big Bang," *Creation Ex Nihilo Technical Journal* 12, no. 2, (1998): 174–94, argue that "this model is actually a trivial variant of the standard Big Bang model, with its attendant implications for the age of the Universe and the Earth time required for light to travel from distant galaxies to the Earth" (174). And even a sympathetic popular understanding of Humphrey's book views it as relying "on presuppositions or starting assumptions from the Big Bang." But, perhaps due to the model's retaining a young earth (if not young cosmos), "it is purely biblical in nature which is vital to provide for a model based on creationism" ("White Hole Cosmology," Creation Wiki: Encyclopedia of Creation Science). Faulkner himself has proposed a more recent YEC starlight solution: Danny R. Faulkner, "A Proposal for a New Solution to the Light Travel Time Problem," *Answers Research Journal* 6 (2013): 279–84, www.answersingenesis.org/contents/379/arj/v6/light_travel_time_problem.pdf.

The baramin concept provided solutions for a variety of centuries-old problems involving enormous numbers of species such as Adam's naming the animals in one day and getting all the land animals on the ark.[68] By the time of the revolution under Henry Morris, speciation increasingly was accepted in YEC circles without being considered evolutionist. "Micro-evolution" and "macro-evolution" became commonly used terms in YEC circles to distinguish "good" from "bad" evolution.

Snelling credits modern biology, specifically the past "hundred and fifty years of investigations in zoology and genetics," for revealing "the amazing potentialities for diversification with which the Creator endowed the Genesis kinds."[69] So not every species of land-dwelling animal needed be taken on the ark, otherwise the age-old problem of fitting them all on board arises. As AiG states, "The Bible does not say God brought every individual or every species to Noah, since *species* is a modern concept."[70] Though enormous speciation had occurred since creation, God needed only to select one species from among the "diversification" of each "Genesis kind" to put on the ark. Thus after the flood, Snelling argues these surviving Genesis kinds experienced extremely "rapid post-Flood speciation,"[71] with most of the "genetic 'shuffling' taking place in the first thousand years or so" after the flood.[72] The resultant "rapid intrabaraminic (within created kinds) diversification" produced "many new varieties of animals and plants that split into sub-populations to establish and fill all the different new ecological niches in the post-Flood world."[73] Many YEC laypeople, as my student surveys have revealed, often are unaware of the large-scale speciation involved in these concepts. Consequently, AiG, in relation to this widespread misunderstanding of the ark's animal makeup,

---

68. This concern and solution were seen even by the father of modern taxonomy, Linnaeus. Kurt P. Wise, "Mammal Kinds: How Many Were on the Ark?" in *Genesis Kinds: Creationism and the Origin of Species*, Center for Origins Research, Issues in Creation Journal, no. 5, ed. Todd Charles Wood and Paul A. Garner (Eugene: OR: Wipf & Stock, 2009), 130.

69. Snelling, *Catastrophic Past*, 1:132.

70. Marcus Ross, "No Kind Left Behind: Recounting the Animals on the Ark," *Answers Magazine,* Answers in Genesis, January 1, 2013, https://answersingenesis.org/noahs-ark/no-kind-left-behind/. Emphasis his.

71. Snelling, *Earth's Catastrophic Past*, 1:129. See also ibid., 1:164.

72. Ibid., 1:164. See also ibid., 1:175–76.

73. Ibid., 2:791.

notes that the truth "is sure to surprise us . . . and to remind us that there's much more to the Ark than we ever imagined."[74]

The broad limits of speciation accepted by many leading YECs are indeed surprising. Just a few decades ago Henry Morris suggested biblical kinds most often referred to species, occasionally genus, and only once in a while the family level.[75] Today's YECs more often see the reverse, with the biblical kind more likely "at the level of conventional families, subfamilies, or small uniform orders."[76] YECs still debate speciation's limits, with "conservative creationists" viewing baramins composed of only several species and more "liberal creationists" accepting "a great deal of speciation and many species per baramin."[77] Thus even within YEC circles, the "more liberal" who believe that some baramins encompass more than one genus can legitimately be described as embracing macro-evolution or megaevolution, the terms used by evolutionists to refer to broad-scale changes resulting in new genera, families, and beyond. The

---

74. Ross, "No Kind." Emphasis his. Leading YECs differ in their estimates of the baramins on the ark, but they are always considerably lower than the number of living and extinct species. For example, Whitcomb and Morris, *Genesis Flood*, 69, estimated conservatively on the outside that "35,000 individual vertebrate animals" were on the ark. On the low side Snelling, *Catastrophic Past*, 1:136–37, believes "the preponderance of the evidence shows, the 'created kind' or *baramin* was possibly equivalent in most instances to the family," therefore, "there would have only been about 2,000 animals on the Ark."

75. Morris, *Genesis Record*, 63.

76. Creation Biology Society, "About Us: Consensus Positions on Various Origins Topics," http://www.creationbiology.org/content.aspx?page_id=22&club_id=201240&module_id=37893. The Creation Biology Society is specifically dedicated to developing a YEC model of biological origins, and its executive council includes Tim Brophy from Liberty University (treasurer), Joe Francis from The Master's College (secretary), and Georgia Purdom from Answers in Genesis.

77. Todd Charles Wood and Paul A. Garner, "The Real Debate over Creationism and Species," in *Genesis Kinds: Creationism and the Origin of Species*, Center for Origins Research, Issues in Creation Journal, no. 5, ed. Todd Charles Wood and Paul A. Garner (Eugene: OR: Wipf & Stock, 2009), 3. Cf.: "Many creationists seem to accept species fixity with no speciation at all, while other creationists uncritically accept neodarwinian mechanisms, so long as the changes stay within the perceived 'boundaries' of the baramin. Still others apply the imperfection principle of degeneration to the question of speciation, insisting that all evolution necessarily results in the degradation of the 'perfect,' created population." Todd Charles Wood and Megan J. Murray, *Understanding the Pattern of Life: Origins and Organization of the Species*, gen. ed. Kurt P. Wise (Nashville: B&H, 2003), 169.

preferred term, however, is "intrabaraminic diversification."[78] A former YEC describes the situation this way: "There are still species fixists within the radical creationist camp—especially in that fraction which is mostly innocent of both orthodox and creationist biological theory—but for the most part, radical creationists are quite comfortable with the fact of evolution. In fact, some believe in the power of evolution to an extent that would make Richard Dawkins blush. . . . Radical creationists have entertained every taxonomic level short of the kingdom as marking the approximate limits of evolveability for the various 'kinds' of organisms."[79]

One example of such surprising YEC acceptance of broad intrabaraminic diversification is seen in the work of Kurt Wise, one of the undisputed leaders in baraminology. For some time Wise has argued that "creationists not divert resources or concern in the direction of 'transitional form' arguments."[80] The reason is, as Darwin expected, intermediates have been discovered such "as the mammal-like reptile groups between the reptiles and the mammals."[81] "Creationists therefore need to accept this fact. It certainly CANNOT be said that traditional creation theory expected (predicted) any of these fossil finds."[82]

Wise accepts evidence secular evolutionists commonly cite in support of whale evolution: "At this point in time, the largest challenge from the

---

78. Wood and Murray, *Pattern of Life*, 170.

79. R. A. Peters, "Theodocic Creationism: Its Membership and Motivations," in *Geology and Religion: A History of Harmony and Hostility*, ed. Martina Kölbl-Ebert, Geological Society Special Publication no. 310 (London: The Geological Society, 2009), 321.

80. Kurt Wise, "Towards a Creationist Understanding of Transitional Forms," *Creation Ex Nihilo Technical Journal* 9, no. 22 (1995): 216.

81. Ibid., 218.

82. Ibid., 219. Emphasis his. Cf.: "Mammal-like reptiles stand between reptiles and mammals, both in the position of their fossils and in the structure of their bones. The reptiles, and the phenacodontids, stand between the horses and their claimed ancestors. In like manner, some fossil genera are stratomorphic intermediates in the group in which they are classified. They are the oldest fossils known in the group and most similar to the group from which they are supposedly descendent. Examples include Pikaia among the chordates, Archaeopteryx among the birds, Baragwanathia among lycopods, Ichthyostega among the amphibians, Purgatorius among the primates, Pakicetus among the whales and Proconsul among the hominoids." Kurt P. Wise, "The Origin of Life's Major Groups," in *The Creation Hypothesis*, ed. J. P. Moreland (Downers Grove, IL: InterVarsity Press, 1994), 227.

stratomorphic intermediate record appears to this author to come from the fossil record of the whales."[83] He argues that "some of the animals which are aquatic or marine today may not have been aquatic at the time of the Flood," and "whales might turn out to be another example. Only when including the legged archaeocetus (and/or possibly the terrestrial suborder Acreodi) do the whales have fossil record continuous with the Flood. Vestigial legs and hips in modern whales confirm legged ancestors of the whales existed only a short time ago. It is possible that the purely marine cetaceans of the present were derived from semi-aquatic or even terrestrial ancestors on the ark."[84]

To be sure, Wise rejects universal common descent. And he certainly passes the test of having his large-scale "intrabaraminic diversification," including that of whales, accomplished within a recent creation, even if it means that on average the mammal kinds on the ark have generated 100 to 250 species each just since the flood.[85] Interestingly, some YECs emphasizing rapid intrabaraminic changes are looking for mechanisms in addition to Neo-Darwinian natural selection and mutation to account for such extremely rapid speciation.[86]

---

83. Wise, "Transitional Forms," 219.

84. Wise, "Mammal Kinds," "143. Cf.: "During the development of some sperm whales the fetus develops portions of hind limb and pelvic bones and subsequently resorbs them. Other modern cetaceans have other bones in embryology and sometimes adulthood which suggest hind limb vestiges. This suggests that modern cetaceans have latent genetic information for the development of small hind limbs. Could this mean that *Basilosaurus*, for example (which has hind limbs and pelvis), is actually an early post-Flood representative of some cetacean baramin and that modern cetaceans of that baramin are actually descendant from it — or something similar to it?" Wise, "Transitional Forms," 219." Readers unfamiliar with the dramatic structural bodily changes involved in Wise's proposal may easily search the Internet for articles on whale evolution and the terms he used such as "archaeocetus," "Acreodi," and "Basilosaurus."

85. Wise, "Mammal Kinds," 145. Cf. idem, "Transitional Forms," 219: "The earth's biota exploded with intrabaraminic diversification (10 to 100-fold in mammal species and 1,000-fold in insect species), and organisms spread across the earth and developed make-shift communities."

86. For example, Wood and Murray, *Pattern of Life*, 178, note that "we can now see that diversification is far too fast, specific, and permanent to be generated by neodarwinism." Cf. Joseph Francis of The Master's University: "Natural selection and mutation, although woven into the fabric of creation, would not have enough time based on our current understanding of evolutionary mechanisms to produce the rapid speciation events required by these new theories in young creationism." Joseph Francis, "Symbiosis, Relationship and the Origin of Species," in *Genesis Kinds: Creationism and the Origin of*

Curiously, AiG frequently refers to those who believe whales descended from land animals as "evolutionists."[87] Yet AiG does not refer to Kurt Wise as an evolutionist who holds the same view, albeit the evolutionary changes occurred extremely rapidly. Indeed, Snelling cites Wise's work in baraminology approvingly, and AiG features a number of Wise's articles.[88] But OECs such as Hugh Ross and Fazale Rana who reject whale evolution are frequently described as evolutionists by AiG despite their clear and specific rejection of theistic evolution.[89]

Snelling uses the baraminology approach to solve an old problem. Genesis 2:19 states: "Out of the ground the LORD God formed every beast of the field and every bird of the sky, and brought them to the man to see what he would call them; and whatever the man called a living creature, that was its name." Snelling sees no need to take the verse literally, instead restricting the animals only to those in the Garden and not an "exhaustive" list.[90] Perhaps there were only three thousand animal and bird kinds in the Garden, and at the rate of naming just ten kinds per hour, all would have been named in five hours. Yet Snelling notes the importance of interpreting Genesis in an "entirely literal" way.[91]

Species, Center for Origins Research, Issues in Creation Journal, no. 5, ed. Todd Charles Wood and Paul A. Garner (Eugene: OR: Wipf & Stock, 2009), 164.

87. See "Whale Evolution," Answers in Genesis, https://answersingenesis.org/kids/sea-animals/whale-evolution/; Terry Mortenson, "Fossil Evidence of Whale Evolution?: Answering Evolutionist Professors in the UK," March 25, 2014, https://answersingenesis.org/aquatic-animals/fossil-evidence-of-whale-evolution/; and Elizabeth Mitchell, "Whale Skull Equipped for Sonar Shows Echolocation Appears Abruptly in the Fossil Record," Answers in Genesis, March 22, 2014, https://answersingenesis.org/extinct-animals/whale-skull-equipped-for-sonar-shows-echolocation-appears-abruptly-in-the-fossil-record/. The above are just some of the AiG articles which construe the notion that whales descended from land animals as "evolutionary."

88. For example, Snelling, *Catastrophic Past*, 1:134, n. 17, and "Latest Articles by Kurt Wise," Answers in Genesis, https://answersingenesis.org/bios/kurt-wise/.

89. "Theistic Evolution," February 2012, Reasons to Believe, http://www.reasons.org/rtb-101/theisticevolution; Hugh Ross, "Whale Ankles—No Support for Neodarwinism," April 1, 2000, Reasons to Believe, http://www.reasons.org/articles/whale-ankles—no-support-for-neodarwinism; Fazale Rana, "Is the Whale Pelvis a Vestige of Evolution?" Reasons to Believe, November 17, 2014, http://www.reasons.org/articles/is-the-whale-pelvis-a-vestige-of-evolution.

90. Snelling, *Earth's Catastrophic Past*, 1:236.

91. Ibid., 1:242.

INTERNAL YEC CONTROVERSY

YECs themselves have internal controversies, including whether to accept aspects of Snelling's book. One ongoing YEC controversy pertains to deciding which geologic evidence points to the flood or instead to events since then.[92] Another concerns whether plate tectonics is even a proper ground for an acceptable YEC flood geology model.[93] Still another has to do with whether the geologic column itself should be accepted (like Snelling), rejected (like Price), or a bit of both.[94] And ever since the scriptural geologists, YECs have disagreed as to just what part of the fossil column should be attributed to the flood.[95]

---

92. "Some would like to place the flood boundary much lower in the GC, making many strata post-flood, while others seem to doubt the reality of the GC itself. This is contrary to the position of Morris, who maintains that virtually no strata have been deposited in the post flood world." Faulkner, "Current State," 2.

93. In addition to the older hydraulic sorting model of Price and Morris, newer models in the United States include catastrophic plate tectonics and the Hydroplate Theory of Walter Brown. Ibid. Cf. Terry A. Hurlbut, "Hydroplate Theory V. Catastrophic Plate Tectonics," Conservative News and Views, December 14, 2011, http://www.conservativenewsandviews. com/2011/12/14/creation/hydroplate-theory-v-catastrophic-plate-tectonics/.

94. For an overview of YEC controversies pertaining to Snelling's book, see Michael J. Oard, "Excellent summary of scientific evidence for Creation and the Flood, but controversial in some areas: A review of Earth's Catastrophic Past: Geology, Creation and the Flood, volumes 1 and 2 by Andrew Snelling," Creation Ministries International, http://creation.com/review-snelling-earths-catastrophic-past. Oard rejects two "paradigms of uniformitarian geology" that Snelling presents: "I do not believe he has demonstrated that the geological column and plate tectonics need to be accepted by creationists. . . . So, many creationists are left with having to take it on faith that the geological column and plate tectonics are absolutes that creationists need to fit into biblical Earth history." Ibid. On the geologic column controversy, see also idem, "The geological column is a general Flood order with many exceptions," Creation Ministries International, http://creation.com/geologic-column-general-order: "There is a degree of controversy in creationist circles about the relationship between the evolutionary geological column and Flood geology. Some creationists hold that the geological column represents the exact sequence of deposition during the Flood as well as the post-Flood period. The only change needed is to shorten the uniformitarian timescale. Other creationists want to throw out the entire geological column. Still others believe that it is a general sequence with many exceptions."

95. See the excellent article in AiG's Answers Research Journal by Seventh Day Adventist Warren H. Johns, "Scriptural Geology, Then and Now," Answers in Genesis, November 30, 2016, https://answersingenesis.org/age-of-the-earth/scriptural-geology-then-and-now/.

Related to such controversies as these then is the "developing schism in Flood geology."[96] Snelling's philosophical approach, represented by popular groups like AiG and ICR, has been termed by some YECs as "the remodelled naturalistic approach" because it seeks "to adapt and modify existing concepts and ideas derived from naturalism (e.g., the standard geologic timescale, plate tectonic theory, and radiometric age-dating)."[97] This "naturalistic" approach "has become widely accepted among creationists and promoted by many of the young-earth creation organizations because it is consistent, except by time differences, with the popular plate tectonic theory taught in most public and private schools."[98]

Some YEC leaders believe the Snelling-AiG-ICR approach has other very serious problems in addition to and because of its acceptance of "naturalistic" science. One "seemingly indefensible and irrational" example results from its attempts "to set the pre-Flood/Flood and Flood/post-Flood boundary at specific contacts along the compressed timescale" of the geologic column. Another concerns "its acceptance of excessively old age dates that are believed to be the result of accelerated nuclear decay which occurred predominately during Creation Week and the Flood." Yet accepting the relative accuracy of radiometric dating as well as accelerated plate tectonic theory creates "serious heat issues that individually and separately generate sufficient heat to melt the entire earth during the global Flood." Thus "adaptation of the Remodelled approach creates new issues separate from its naturalistic source, many of which appear to require miracles for their resolution. Is this how creation science should advance?"[99]

The "diametrically opposed" YEC view, termed the "reconstructed Bible-based approach," seeks to be faithful to the vision of Henry Morris in *The Genesis Flood*, which refused to be "defined from the naturalistically based standard geologic timescale."[100] This less popular approach seeks a "reconstructed geologic history based solely on an outline derived from the Bible."[101] Proposed independently by Tasman Walker and Carl Froede

---

96. Carl R. Froede Jr. and A. Jerry Akridge, "Developing Schism in Flood Geology," Creation Ministries International, http://creation.com/flood-geology-schism.
97. Ibid.
98. Ibid.
99. Ibid.
100. Ibid.
101. Ibid.

Jr., this "framework is a ground-up approach to defining earth's biblical geologic history based on the divisions of time outlined in Scripture." And opposed to the Snelling-AiG-ICR model, this version "liberates Bible history from the conflicting philosophical assumptions inherent in remodelling naturalistic geologic history (e.g., standard geologic timescale, lithostratigraphy, biostratigraphy, and radiometric age-dating)."[102] Therefore, the "mutually exclusive constructs of a Remodelled versus Reconstructed framework of biblical geologic history will ultimately result in disunity between the camps defending Flood geology."[103]

CONCLUSION

This brief survey of contemporary recent creationists' interaction with modern science could be taken to mean they deserve a failing grade on the "evolutionary" or "atheistic" science scale. But that is hardly the point. The work that Snelling has done deserves to be complimented for its sophistication, honesty, and desire to honor God and his Word. The point, however, is that some YECs who rebuke others for their relations to modern science should take pause. Calling OEC science "naturalistic" doesn't make it so, especially if the same ministry accepts the same science reinterpreted to fit a recent time frame. How can a reduced time scale cleanse scientific theory of naturalism or atheism? Indeed, some leading YEC ministries are now being criticized by other recent creationists for being too "naturalistic" in their scientific approaches.

Similar observations can be made about the oft-repeated accusation by some YECs that OECs undermine biblical authority in deference to modern science. But as we've seen, all conservative evangelicals have intuitively practiced the conservatism principle in relating science and theology. YECs themselves practice the very same approach by correlating their biblical interpretations in light of science they believe true. But condemning others for doing the same is hardly consistent or considerate.

---

102. Ibid.
103. Ibid.

Chapter 8

BIBLICAL INERRANCY AND THE AGE OF THE EARTH:
Three Evangelical Approaches

The Chicago Statements on Biblical Inerrancy and Hermeneutics "opened the door to false ideas in the church."[1]
—Terry Mortenson, "Affirmations and Denials Essential to a Consistent Christian (Biblical) Worldview"

"In our day . . . it is clear that inerrancy is an intellectual disaster."[2]
—Kenton Sparks, "After Inerrancy: Evangelicals and the Bible in a Postmodern Age"

I tried to focus, nonetheless I was awestruck. As a relatively new seminary professor I had the honor of the most influential living evangelical theologian visiting one of my classes. Carl F. H. Henry was still extremely sharp even though he was now well into his eighties. After a very long pause in response to a student's question, he displayed his contagious sense

---

1. "Affirmations and Denials Essential to a Consistent Christian (Biblical) Worldview," Answers in Genesis, https://answersingenesis.org/answers/affirmations-denials-christian-worldview/. The material is also one of the appendixes of Terry Mortenson and Thane H. Ury, eds., *Coming to Grips with Genesis: Biblical Authority and the Age of the Earth* (Green Forest, AR: Master Books, 2008), 453–58.

2. Kenton Sparks, "After Inerrancy: Evangelicals and the Bible in a Postmodern Age," The BioLogos Foundation, https://biologos.org/uploads/static-content/sparks_scholarly_essay.pdf.

of humor: "All the files are still there; they just take longer to find." Henry had patiently listened as I delivered a portion of my scheduled lecture on the age of the earth and evolution. When given the lectern, he kindly affirmed my point that the age of the earth was not the critical issue that evangelicals should stress.

Henry knew well even then that the revival of evangelical scholarship that he helped inaugurate continued to wrestle with evangelical-defining disputes. Almost from the outset that mid-twentieth-century revival had seemed to lose its way. The American Scientific Affiliation, of which Henry was an early member, made an early about-face on universal common descent. Conservative reaction made ready the way for *The Genesis Flood* and the launching of modern young earth creationism (YEC).[3]

Conservative evangelicals were especially dismayed when their new flagship institution, Fuller Theological Seminary, soon abandoned confessional biblical inerrancy.[4] Having been one of the four founding faculty members, Henry knew firsthand the trend in evangelical scholarship to reject inerrancy. Therefore, as part of a movement to defend and clarify biblical inerrancy, he gathered with several hundred evangelical leaders in 1978 to produce the Chicago Statement on Biblical Inerrancy (CSBI). In addition to Henry, some of the other CSBI signers included D. A. Carson, Norman Geisler, Walter Kaiser, J. I. Packer, and R. C. Sproul.[5]

---

3. See chapter 4.

4. For the intriguing story, see George M. Marsden, *Reforming Fundamentalism: Fuller Seminary and the New Evangelicalism* (Grand Rapids: Eerdmans, 1988).

5. For a full list of the signatories, see "List of Signers of the Chicago Statement on Biblical Inerrancy," Dallas Theological Seminary, http://library.dts.edu/Pages/TL/Special/ICBI_1_typed.pdf. Three major summits were held over time, each producing its own statement. Summit II held in 1982 to discuss biblical interpretive principles, produced the Chicago Statement on Biblical Hermeneutics. The final summit in 1986 created the Chicago Statement on Biblical Application. See "Records of the International Council on Biblical Inerrancy," Dallas Theological Seminary, http://library.dts.edu/Pages/TL/Special/ICBI.shtml. "One of the last actions of the ICBI was to transfer records of the organization to the archives at Dallas Theological Seminary to preserve them for future research. The ICBI files date from about 1978 to 1989 and fill sixty-nine linear feet. The records include correspondence, files regarding publications, documents about seminars and lay congresses, financial records, and copies of the statements adopted at the three conferences. The collection also has some scrapbooks and preservation copies of books published by the ICBI." Ibid.

A year later Henry would pen volume 4 of his magnum opus *God, Revelation, and Authority* in which he not only provided a potent examination and defense of the doctrine of inerrancy, but also reproduced the CSBI in full.[6] Henry expressed the view of conservative evangelicals and the CSBI: "Verbal inerrancy implies that truth attaches not only to the theological and ethical teaching of the Bible, but also to historical and scientific matters insofar as they are part of the express message of the inspired writings."[7]

INERRANCY AND THE CHICAGO STATEMENTS

The CSBI has been described as "probably the first systematically comprehensive, broadly based, scholarly, creed-like statement on the inspiration and authority of Scripture in the history of the church."[8] A thorough explication of the CSBI is beyond the purview of this book. But this sophisticated document, even when rejected, serves as the starting point for discussion among evangelicals concerning biblical inspiration and inerrancy.[9] A follow up statement was produced which is also especially important for clarifying scriptural inerrancy, the Chicago Statement on Biblical Hermeneutics (CSBH).

The CSBI and CSBH are particularly relevant to the debate about creation and the age of the earth. They address the relationship of science and theology which evangelicals had been debating for more than a century. Article XII of the CSBI specifically denies "that Biblical infallibility and inerrancy are limited to spiritual, religious, or redemptive themes, exclusive of assertions in the fields of history and science. We further deny that scientific hypotheses about earth history may properly be used to overturn the teaching of Scripture on creation and the flood."[10]

---

6. Carl F. H. Henry, *God, Revelation and Authority*, vol. 4, *God Who Speaks and Shows: Fifteen Theses, Part Three*, 6 vols. (Waco, TX: Word Books, 1979), 4:211–19.

7. Ibid., 4:205.

8. "Records of the Council on Inerrancy."

9. For example see James R. A. Merrick and Stephen M. Garrett, eds., *Five Views on Biblical Inerrancy*, Counterpoints: Bible and Theology (Grand Rapids: Zondervan, 2013). In this volume, only R. Albert Mohler Jr., "When the Bible Speaks, God Speaks: The Classic Doctrine of Biblical Inerrancy," 29–58, defends the CSBI unreservedly.

10. "The Chicago Statement on Biblical Inerrancy," Dallas Theological Seminary, http://library.dts.edu/Pages/TL/Special/ICBI_1.pdf. See also Article XIII, which denies

Indeed, the Chicago Statements' position on science-theology debates mirrors that of Galileo discussed in chapter 2. Galileo and the CSBI share a fundamental assumption: the Bible is inerrant because it is divinely inspired. Article IX of the CSBI affirms that divine inspiration ensured the biblical authors wrote truthfully on everything they "were moved to speak and write." Their "finitude or fallenness," therefore, did not introduce "distortion or falsehood into God's Word." Article XI denies the possibility for "the Bible to be at the same time infallible and errant in its assertions. Infallibility and inerrancy may be distinguished, but not separated."[11]

Galileo's proposal also assumed that the inerrant Bible cannot conflict with scientific truth. Article XX of the CSBH agrees "that since God is the author of all truth, all truths, biblical and extrabiblical, are consistent and cohere, and that the Bible speaks truth when it touches on matters pertaining to nature, history, or anything else." Article XXI of the CSBH affirms "the harmony of special with general revelation and therefore of biblical teaching with the facts of nature. We deny that any genuine scientific facts are inconsistent with the true meaning of any passage of Scripture." The exposition section of the CSBH states: "Since all facts cohere, the truth about them must be coherent also; and since God, the author of all Scripture, is also the Lord of all facts, there can in principle be no contradiction between a right understanding of what Scripture says and a right account of any reality or event in the created order."[12]

Galileo also proposed two interpretive steps for dealing with apparent science-theology conflicts with which the Chicago Statements agree. Galileo contended that no unproven conflicting scientific theory should ever be granted authority over the Bible. Article XX of the CSBH denies "that extra-biblical views ever disprove the teaching of Scripture or hold priority over it." And Article XXII affirms "that Genesis 1–11 is factual, as is the rest of the book. We deny that the teachings of Genesis 1–11 are mythical and that scientific hypotheses about earth history or the origin

---

the propriety of evaluating Scripture "according to standards of truth and error that are alien to its usage or purpose." Thus in relation to the subject at hand, inerrancy is not negated by "a lack of modern technical precision" or "observational descriptions of nature."

11. Ibid.

12. "The Chicago Statement on Biblical Hermeneutics," Dallas Theological Seminary, http://library.dts.edu/Pages/TL/Special/ICBI_2.pdf.

of humanity may be invoked to overthrow what Scripture teaches about creation."[13]

Galileo's final methodological step, however, allows for the possibility that a scientific theory might be proven true as opposed to a traditional biblical interpretation. In such cases, one should assume the interpretation is in error. Article XX of the CSBH carefully but essentially states the same, affirming "that in some cases extra-biblical data have value for clarifying what Scripture teaches, and for prompting correction of faulty interpretations." Its exposition section further spells out this interpretive step: "Any appearance of contradiction here would argue misunderstanding or inadequate knowledge, either of what Scripture really affirms or of what the extra-biblical facts really are. Thus it would be a summons to reassessment and further scholarly inquiry."[14]

THE EVANGELICAL THEOLOGICAL SOCIETY AND INERRANCY

In the first chapter we looked at the leading evangelical creationist ministries today representing three approaches to creation and the age of the earth. Each organization also holds three very different understandings of biblical inerrancy and the Chicago Statements. Reasons to Believe (RTB) is the most influential old earth creationist (OEC) group. RTB is the only group of the three affirming the CSBI without reservation. "We at Reasons to Believe are so impressed with the outstanding achievement of the ICBI [International Council on Biblical Inerrancy] in carefully defining what biblical inerrancy is and what it is not that we have every member of our staff scholar team commit to its articles of affirmations and denials."[15]

But due to its size and influence, the most significant evangelical group affirming biblical inerrancy is the Evangelical Theological Society (ETS). As the world's largest group of evangelical scholars, ETS requires for membership a commitment to biblical inerrancy as expressed in its doctrinal basis. Due to controversies and questions, the society adopted the CSBI

---

13. Ibid.
14. Ibid.
15. Hugh Ross, "If We Allow Science to Correct the Bible, Doesn't That Make Science God?" Reasons to Believe, August 3, 2016, http://www.reasons.org/blogs/todays-new-reason-to-believe/if-we-allow-science-to-correct-the-bible-doesnt-that-make-science-god.

to advise "members regarding the intent and meaning of the reference to biblical inerrancy in the ETS Doctrinal Basis."[16] Thus the CSBI remains, at least officially, the benchmark for understanding the doctrine of biblical inerrancy for the scholarly society. ETS requires no expressed commitment to a particular creation view.

Answers in Genesis (AiG) regards YEC to be a minority viewpoint in the ETS. Ken Ham describes "most" members as having "compromised on Genesis with views like theistic evolution, the gap theory, the day-age view, the cosmic temple view, and so on."[17] BioLogos leaders seem to regard their view, evolutionary creationism (EC), to be in the minority among ETS members, too.[18] Both AiG and BioLogos are likely correct that ETS members more often than not are OECs rather than YECs or ECs.

ANSWERS IN GENESIS AND INERRANCY

Some YECs today have a love-hate relationship with the Chicago Statements. Henry Morris and John Whitcomb, authors of *The Genesis Flood*, both signed the CSBI at the first summit in 1978. But they could not sign in good conscience the CSBH produced at the second summit in 1982. Morris recounted the reason: the CSBH "finally adopted by the Council was so innocuous on the subject of origins that it would not even exclude evolution as an acceptable interpretation."[19]

In chapter 6 I compared *The Genesis Flood* to a kind of YEC constitution. Amendments can and have been made to a great many details of modern YEC. But the teachings of a young earth and the flood column are essentially non-negotiable. These indispensable doctrines affect the way AiG approaches biblical inerrancy. On one hand, AiG praises the CSBI and CSBH as "two wonderful documents affirming the inerrancy of the Scriptures."[20] But on the other, though the Statements were helpful "for

---

16. "Bylaws," Evangelical Theology Society, http://www.etsjets.org/about/bylaws.

17. Ken Ham, "AiG Reaches Out to Bible Scholars," Answers in Genesis, November 23, 2013, https://answersingenesis.org/blogs/ken-ham/2013/11/23/aig-reaches-out-to-bible-scholars/.

18. Brad Kramer, "5 Common Objections to Evolutionary Creationism," BioLogos, November 30, 2015, http://biologos.org/blogs/brad-kramer-the-evolving-evangelical/5-common-objections-to-evolutionary-creationism.

19. Henry M. Morris, "The Days Do Matter," *Acts & Facts* 33, no. 10 (2004).

20. Ken Ham, "Do Bible Inerrancy and Millions of Years Go Together?" Answers

the church's understanding of Scripture," the portions "related to creation, evolution, and the age of the earth were inadequate and opened the door to false ideas in the church."[21] Even the creators or signers of the Statements, if they deny a recent creation, "have compromised with man's ideas in Genesis."[22] Though signers of the Statements may claim the Bible inerrant in history and science, "they deny this belief by their inconsistent treatment of Genesis. They plainly show that they do not accept millions of years, astronomical, geological, or, at times, biological evolution because the biblical text demands it but, rather, because of the supposed scientific data. It's a clear compromise of God's Word that undermines biblical inerrancy."[23]

In chapter 7 we detailed how some leading YECs, including those at AiG, practice as much "astronomical, geological, or, at times, biological evolution" as OECs. These YECs also reinterpret parts of Genesis "because of the supposed scientific data." It is thus not easy to see how such YECs by their own definition are also not guilty of undermining biblical inerrancy.

Nevertheless, understanding inerrancy as necessarily including YEC explains AiG's rather low view of ETS. Ken Ham describes ETS annual meetings as attended by scholars and leaders "who don't stand on the authority of Scripture (the majority of attendees)" and need to be challenged to reconsider their views and to take God at His Word from the very first verse."[24] Terry Mortenson claims that since most ETS members affirm both inerrancy and OEC, they must "believe the scientific majority is telling the truth."[25] And because these members "haven't read Genesis carefully or creationist literature," they "compromise with anti-biblical naturalistic myths about origins."[26] Thus most inerrantists today "are

---

in Genesis, July 29, 2015, https://answersingenesis.org/blogs/ken-ham/2015/07/29/do-bible-inerrancy-and-millions-years-go-together/.

21. "Affirmations and Denials."

22. Ham, "Inerrancy and Millions."

23. Ibid.

24. Ken Ham, "AiG Reaches Out to Bible Scholars," Answers in Genesis, November 23, 2013, https://answersingenesis.org/blogs/ken-ham/2013/11/23/aig-reaches-out-to-bible-scholars/.

25. Terry Mortenson *"Inerrancy and the Undermining of Biblical Authority,"* video, Creation Library Series, Answers in Genesis, 2015.

26. Ibid.

trembling at the words of men called scientists rather than trembling at the Word of God."[27]

So because the inadequacy of the Chicago Statements "opened the door to false ideas in the church,"[28] AiG proposes supplementing the Statements with their own "Affirmations and Denials Essential to a Consistent Christian (Biblical) Worldview (ADCW)."[29] AiG's supplementation of the Chicago Statements in actuality is a reformulation. Article VI excludes as inerrantists anyone who doesn't believe Genesis teaches that the creation occurred "between about 6,000–10,000 years ago." One also cannot be an inerrantist who believes that "scientific 'evidence' used to 'prove' millions of years is objective fact and not heavily influenced by naturalistic presuppositions (Article 4)." Inerrantists must believe the flood "produced most (but not all) of the geological record of thousands of meters of strata and fossils that we see on the earth's surface today," and inerrantists must deny that "the thousands of meters of sedimentary rock formations with their fossilized remains were largely produced after or before the Flood or even before Adam" (Article XI)." Article VIII stipulates that inerrancy denies "there has ever been any evolutionary change from one of the original created kinds into a different kind (e.g., fish to amphibian, reptile to mammal, reptile to bird, ape to man, or land mammal to whale, etc.)."[30]

This sweeping reformulation of biblical inerrancy is justified as reflecting "the almost universal consensus of the church throughout history, until the early 19th century."[31] Yet this explanation is remarkably puzzling. The church could not have enjoyed near universal consensus throughout history regarding the strata and fossils because they were neither discovered nor understood until modern times. How could the church have agreed before the 19th century to reject scientific "evidence" for millions of years as objective fact or attribute it to naturalistic presuppositions when most of it was discovered in the last two hundred years (such as radiometric dating, expansion of the universe, and plate tectonics)?

AiG's emending the Chicago Statements creates new problems in light of our examination of YEC science in the previous chapter. We saw that

27. Ibid.
28. "Affirmations and Denials."
29. Ibid.
30. Ibid.
31. Ibid.

some YECs accept speciation as broadly as "land mammal to whale." Even if they reject universal common descent and believe the "evolutionary change" occurred several thousand years ago, are they not by AiG's reformulation excluded as inerrantists? AiG's placing limits on baraminology is reminiscent of the reason Henry Morris rejected the CSBH, because it did not exclude evolution. But some contemporary YECs have broadened the limits of the baramins into far broader taxa than OECs have ever considered. Still, does not baraminology attempt "to classify fossil and living organisms into baramins" based on scientific criteria, "such as physical characteristics and DNA sequences?"[32] How can AiG limit the conclusions of baraminology before the science has been completed?

YECs are also in disagreement about how to interpret the impact of the flood on the geologic column. How can AiG define inerrancy in such a way that might exclude even other YECs? Why risk submitting the doctrine of inerrancy to the fluctuations of such scientific theories? Why not specifically reject the order of the column (as do some YECs) as based on "naturalistic presuppositions" before one can be an inerrantist? Why link belief in the geologic column and fossils to inerrancy in the first place since no one dreamed of the flood column until relatively modern times? Why must one be taught any modern science before being deemed a true inerrantist?

The CSBH seems to present a far more stable understanding of inerrancy in light of biblical interpretation. It contends that "What the Bible says about the facts of nature is as true and trustworthy as anything else it says." Because it does not present its truths in the language of modern science, "differences of opinion as to the correct scientific account to give of natural facts and events which Scripture celebrates can hardly be avoided."[33] And because the Bible does not use scientific language, its proper interpretation "does not require scientific knowledge about the internal processes of God's creation for the understanding of its essential message about God and ourselves."[34] The CSBH says it well: "It is not for scientific

---

32. Bodie Hodge and Georgia Purdom, "What Are 'Kinds' in Genesis?" Answers in Genesis, April 16, 2013, https://answersingenesis.org/creation-science/baraminology/what-are-kinds-in-genesis/.

33. "Chicago Statement on Hermeneutics."

34. Ibid.

theories to dictate what Scripture may and may not say,"[35] and this would include not only OEC and EC but also YEC theories.

AiG's desire to emend the Chicago Statements raises many unanswered questions. But no one can doubt the urgency with which they present the project. YECs with at least a master's degree in theology are pressed to submit their name to AiG in public support of this reformulation of inerrancy. They note that "Luther was willing make the effort to nail the 95 thesis [sic] on the door of the Wittenberg church, come what may, and millions of Christians before and since have been willing to stand for the truth of God's Word in spite of prison or even death. So, if you agree with this document, please take the relatively few minutes needed to stake your name on this document, which is taking a stand in the face of massive compromise with millions of years in the church worldwide, compromise that is undermining the authority and reliability of the Word of Almighty God."[36]

BIOLOGOS AND INERRANCY

Unlike AiG and ETS, BioLogos does not officially endorse biblical inerrancy, much less the CSBI. "We believe the Bible is the inspired and authoritative Word of God"[37] is how its "What We Believe" online page states it. BioLogos also states, "We do not think that evangelicals must relinquish inerrancy, believe that Paul was wrong about Adam, or believe that the fall was not historical in order to accept the BioLogos model. A careful reading of the BioLogos site should make it clear that these traditional evangelical views are also represented and defended."[38]

Yet, it seems fair to say that likely most of those closely affiliated with BioLogos would not hold to a conservative view of inerrancy along the lines of the CSBI. Of course BioLogos is under no compulsion to represent traditional conservative evangelical views equally, including inerrancy. As their mission statement declares, "BioLogos invites the church and the

---

35. Ibid.

36. Ibid. The most widely recognizable name of the original signatories is John MacArthur, D.D., Grace Community Church.

37. "What We Believe," BioLogos, http://biologos.org/about-us/our-mission/.

38. Darrel Falk, "The BioLogos Forum: A Place for Conversation," BioLogos, December 6, 2010, http://biologos.org/blogs/archive/the-biologos-forum-a-place-for-conversation.

world to see the harmony between science and biblical faith as we present an evolutionary understanding of God's creation." Its mission has to do with presenting evolutionary creation, not biblical inerrancy.

But conservative evangelicals will be troubled by prominently featured BioLogos articles arguing for errors in the Bible.[39] The articles, some of which are clearly not "traditional," are also "represented and defended" by BioLogos. One prominent article of this sort, "After Inerrancy," is especially provocative in claiming that "in our day . . . it is clear that inerrancy is an intellectual disaster."[40] Why is this clear? Kenton Sparks argues that "we've now crossed an evidential threshold that makes it intellectually unsuitable to defend some of the standard dogmas of the conservative Evangelical tradition," thus the church needs help to "get its bearings in a world without Biblicistic inerrancy."[41]

For Sparks, traditional ways of dealing with internal biblical tensions or with external evidence won't suffice.[42] Even more troubling are biblical texts treating ethical matters that "strike us as downright sinister or evil," that is, "the so-called 'dark side' of Scripture." In its treatment of women or Canaanites, "Scripture exhibits all of the telltale signs of having been written by finite, fallen human beings who erred in the ways that human beings usually err. If this is the case, in what sense can we say with a straight face that Scripture is God's Word?"[43]

Therefore, if we are wise, we must assume that Scripture, in a manner similar to the creation warped by the fall, "is both beautiful and broken. No less than the creation, Scripture's human authors, and the book that they wrote, stand in need of redemption."[44] But how can the Bible be redeemed? In precisely the same way humans are: "by the death, burial,

---

39. For example, Denis Lamoureux, "Was Adam a Real Person? Part 3," BioLogos, September 17, 2010, http://biologos.org/blogs/archive/was-adam-a-real-person-part-3.

40. Kenton Sparks, "After Inerrancy: Evangelicals and the Bible in a Postmodern Age," The BioLogos Foundation, https://biologos.org/uploads/static-content/sparks_scholarly_essay.pdf, 5. His ideas are more fully developed in the following: idem, *God's Word in Human Words: An Evangelical Appropriation of Critical Biblical Scholarship* (Grand Rapids: Baker Academic, 2008), idem, *Sacred Word, Broken Word: Biblical Authority and the Dark Side of Scripture* (Grand Rapids: Eerdmans, 2012).

41. Sparks, "After Inerrancy," 1.

42. Ibid., 3, 10.

43. Ibid., 4.

44. Ibid., 11.

resurrection, ascension and return of our Savior, Jesus Christ. Until that final day comes, we shall continue to struggle with the problems of pain and suffering, and with the problems in Scripture. These are our problems that Christ has graciously taken upon himself."[45]

In practice, this means the believer should ask questions of the Bible such as: "Is the author right or wrong? Wise or unwise? . . . Did this author get his history right?"[46] Sparks suggests this questioning leads to concluding that biblical discourses at times "are contradictory and, in extreme cases, on the verge of what we would in other situations call vice."[47] But even Scripture's "most broken elements, speak a word from God," so no one need exclude "parts of the Bible from the theological conversation."[48] Instead, believers should practice "a 'Christocentric' reading of Scripture" which "will naturally emphasize Jesus' programmatic statement that the whole law is summed up in the words, 'Love God, and love your neighbor.'"[49] If we practice this approach to Bible reading, Sparks contends that Christians will "not embrace as healthy those elements in the biblical text that do not conform to the litmus test of love. These dark elements attest instead to the brokenness of humanity and its need for love and redemption."[50]

Sparks proposes that this kind of Bible reading is being led by the Spirit of God. Even the "wind of culture," which includes critics of Christianity, might be used by the Spirit to help us understand the Bible's ethical problems better. "So we cannot easily say beforehand where (or how) the Spirit might lead us as it [sic] guides us in reading Scripture."[51] "In the end, I suspect that it is not really possible to say with much precision what the Spirit does, and how the Spirit works, as he assists us in our theological reflection."[52] But "we derive our theology from the broken voices of Scripture, tradition and cosmos, and with the mysterious help of the Spirit. Good theology pursues the truth by listening to and coherently ordering all of

---

45. Ibid., 13.
46. Ibid., 14.
47. Ibid.
48. Ibid.
49. Ibid., 15.
50. Ibid.
51. Ibid., 16.
52. Ibid., 18.

these important voices."[53] Sparks assures evangelicals that "this untidy situation is not as serious as it first appears," because it does not render the Bible "useless as a vehicle of grace" nor "impugn God's character by association."[54] God is not responsible for the "human error and vice" insinuated into the Bible, only that which is good and true.[55]

"Traditional" evangelicals, however, will ask: why believe such "readings" are of the Spirit? And how does one ascertain which biblical texts about Jesus provide "the litmus test of love" for rejecting other biblical texts? Jesus taught many things, such as the reality of hell, which could be deemed "dark." Indeed, Sparks suggests elsewhere that Jesus's teaching on hell "was largely the theology of a first-century Jew. And where that first-century theology was limited in its vision, so too was the theological vision of Jesus."[56] So Sparks claims that the teaching of Jesus on hell erred in not being "wholly compatible with a Christian theology of love and compassion."[57] The "'Christocentric' reading of Scripture" pits even the biblical Jesus at times against the biblical Jesus.

The traditional approach is to trust the biblical Jesus such that his "dark" sayings serve as loving warnings to escape God's true and coming righteous judgment. Some non-traditional theologians may feel free to "coherently order" all the "voices" to ascertain when the Bible is "dark" or not. But conservatives cannot bring themselves to assume that posture. Honest questions about difficulties need not be excluded in evangelical scholarship. But the historical tradition seeks answers grounded at the end of the day by assuming biblical truthfulness from the outset.

BioLogos encourages traditional evangelicals to consider that evolution and loving their Bible may go hand in hand. But this article hardly facilitates that consideration for the "traditional." Indeed, for them the conversation about evolution and the Bible can go nowhere so long as BioLogos uniformly defends the truth of evolution but is willing to "represent and defend" proposals suggesting the Bible contains unredeemed error and evil. Not only evangelicals, but Christians through the ages would be startled to hear that the Bible revealing their Savior needs his salvation, too.

---

53. Ibid.
54. Ibid.
55. Ibid.
56. Sparks, Sacred *Word*, 27.
57. Ibid., 26.

Not long before Carl Henry spoke in my classroom, he had written about what, in hindsight, he might have done differently in his life. He also addressed what he would not change, something which BioLogos is willing to change: "Those who contrast the authority of Christ with the authority of Scripture do so at high risk. Scripture gives us the authentic teaching of Jesus and Jesus exhorted his apostles to approach Scripture as divinely authoritative. There is no confident road into the future for any theological cause that provides a fragmented scriptural authority and—in consequence—an unstable Christology. Founded by the true and living Lord, and armed with the truthfulness of Scripture, the church of God is invincible. Whatever I might want to change in this pilgrim life, it would surely not be any of these high and holy commitments."[58]

Similarly, the CSBI closes by recognizing that evangelicals may set aside biblical inerrancy. But if they do, Henry's "fragmented scriptural authority" comes into play: "if for the time being basic evangelical doctrines are still held, persons denying the full truth of Scripture may claim an evangelical identity while methodologically they have moved away from the evangelical principle of knowledge to an unstable subjectivism, and will find it hard not to move further."[59]

CONCLUSION

The three evangelical perspectives surveyed above agree that one's understanding of biblical inspiration and interpretation is critically related to how one approaches science in general and the age of the earth and evolution in particular. No doubt, RTB desires to persuade evangelicals to adopt OEC and even the day-age theory which it advocates.[60] But its understanding of inerrancy is unaffected by its understanding of the Bible or scientific data.

AiG, while stressing an inerrant Bible, assumes its biblical interpretation of a young earth and a flood-shaped geologic column is also inerrant. In the end, AiG leadership conflates these interpretive issues with inspiration

---

58. D.A. Carson and John D. Woodbridge, eds., *God and Culture: Essays in Honor of Carl F. H. Henry* (Grand Rapids: Eerdmans, 1993), 392–93.

59. From the section "Inerrancy and Authority" in "Chicago Statement on Inerrancy."

60. "Days of Creation," Reasons to Believe, http://www.reasons.org/rtb-101/daysofcreation.

in their call to emend the Chicago Statements. But distinguishing inspiration and interpretation is both necessary and important. AiG leaders imply that their YEC is so clear and correct biblically that those who disagree do so because they "are trembling at the words of men called scientists rather than trembling at the Word of God."[61] But claiming to know the unexpressed motives of other inerrantists who differ over the age of the earth surely hurts the AiG cause. The Word of God alone judges "the thoughts and intentions of the heart" (Heb. 4:12).

The BioLogos article reviewed above rejects biblical inerrancy to avoid alleged interpretive and intellectual disaster. But the article's position makes it impossible to interpret the Bible correctly precisely because it fundamentally errs on Scripture's nature. Because the piece advocates the interpreter sit as judge to determine alleged errors and evils in the Bible, classical theological liberalism lurks more closely than its evangelical language might indicate. But why one should have confidence those remaining evangelical doctrines will not eventually devolve in heterodox directions remains unclear. We will briefly review in the next chapter some concerns about the compatibility of Darwinism and biblical orthodoxy. But so long as BioLogos defends the acceptability of proposals about the Bible such as the one above, concerned evangelicals will find little hope for constructive dialogue.[62]

---

61. Mortenson. "Inerrancy and Undermining." Cf. "Chicago Statement on Hermeneutics," Article XXIII: "We affirm the clarity of Scripture and specifically of its message about salvation from sin. We deny that all passages of Scripture are equally clear or have equal bearing on the message of redemption."

62. On evangelicalism's identity in connection with inerrancy, see John D. Woodbridge, "Evangelical Self-Identity and the Doctrine of Biblical Inerrancy," in *Understanding the Times: New Testament Studies in the Twenty-First Century: Essays in Honor of D. A. Carson on the Occasion of His 65th Birthday*, ed. Andreas J. Köstenberger and Robert W. Yarbrough (Wheaton, IL: Crossway, 2011), 104–40.

Chapter 9

THEOLOGICAL TRIAGE:
Drawing Doctrinal Boundaries

> Liberals have never met a doctrine worth fighting for; fundamen-
> talists have never met a doctrine not worth fighting for.
>
> —Anonymous

Sixteenth-century Lutherans certainly had a robust sense of heresy. They were willing to imprison even the son-in-law of Martin Luther's great collaborator Philipp Melanchthon. Caspar Peucer married Magdalena, Melanchthon's daughter, and taught Copernican astronomy at Wittenberg. But Peucer's twelve-year imprisonment was not for crypto-Copernican-ism: he had taught the new science openly even if cautiously. Instead, he was incarcerated for crypto-Calvinism.[1] Even the great Kepler would later be expelled from the Lutheran congregation in Linz in 1612. Holding a Calvinist view of communion (Christ is spiritually present), he couldn't sign in good conscience the Lutheran Formula of Concord (Christ is sub-stantially present in the sacramental union of bread and wine with the body and blood of Christ). But this had nothing to do with his enthusiastic advancement of Copernicanism.[2]

Boundaries are an inevitable fact of life. No boundaries are more import-ant for humans than worldview boundaries. We decide how to live and die

---

1. Robert S. Westman, *The Melanchthon Circle, Rheticus, and the Wittenberg Interpretation of the Copernican Theory* (Cambridge, MA: Society for Comparative Study of Society and History, 1975), 181.
2. Max Caspar, *Kepler* (Mineola, NY: Dover Publications, 1993), 211–20.

based on them. Christians have always believed theological boundaries are essential for identifying, nurturing, and protecting the faith. But knowing where, when, and how to draw Christian doctrinal boundaries is not necessarily easy.

Creationist ministries necessarily must draw boundaries for their teams of co-workers. For Answers in Genesis (AiG), the boundaries include recent creation, a geographically universal flood, speciation limits, and biblical inerrancy. Reasons to Believe (RTB) draws lines around an ancient earth, narrow speciation, and inerrancy. BioLogos defines its ministry around evolution (and modern science); biblical inspiration and authority (not inerrancy); and the incarnation, death, and resurrection of Jesus Christ.[3] More things, of course, could be listed distinguishing these three leading evangelical creationist ministries. But as we saw in the previous chapter, even their different understandings of the nature of biblical inspiration set them apart.

Non-specialist evangelicals presented with the differences between these three organizations must sort through complex biblical, theological, philosophical, scientific, and historical information. Enormous resources are expended in presenting, defending, and criticizing each other, so deciding which to believe (if any) presents a daunting challenge. With extremely serious theological charges sometimes leveled, careful thinking is crucial in deciding where to draw lines. And, of course, it's possible to get the boundaries right, but to go about setting them in wrong ways.

THEOLOGICAL TRIAGE

R. Albert Mohler Jr. helpfully suggests a way to reflect on "which Christian doctrines and theological issues are to be given highest priority in terms of our contemporary context."[4] He uses the notion of triage, the process used in settings like emergency rooms in which patients are sorted according to the urgency of their medical need. Though recognizing the task is not

---

3. BioLogos notes that its members may accept biblical inerrancy, but it has no commitment to it. See "About BioLogos," BioLogos, http://biologos.org/about-us/.

4. R. Albert Mohler Jr., "A Call for Theological Triage and Christian Maturity," July 12, 2005, http://www.albertmohler.com/2005/07/12/a-call-for-theological-triage-and-christian-maturity/. Any applications of Mohler's theological triage concept are strictly mine.

easy, Mohler proposes Christians use a theological triage of three levels to ascertain theological urgencies.

First-level doctrines are essential to Christianity, and include "doctrines such as the Trinity, the full deity and humanity of Jesus Christ, justification by faith, and the authority of Scripture."[5] Mohler notes that Christ's death, burial, and bodily resurrection are such that those who reject them are "by definition, not Christians."[6] Similar things can be said about the Trinity and justification by faith. He notes that the authority of Scripture is a first-order doctrine because otherwise the church is left "without any adequate authority for distinguishing truth from error," leading to "an eventual denial of Christianity itself."[7]

Second-order doctrines are those that do not define Christianity, but Christian disagreements "will create significant boundaries"[8] such as those that separate congregations and denominations. Examples include the meaning and mode of baptism and whether women can serve as pastors. "Many of the most heated disagreements among serious believers take place at the second-order level, for these issues frame our understanding of the church and its ordering by the Word of God."[9]

Finally, third-level doctrines are those "over which Christians may disagree and remain in close fellowship, even within local congregations."[10] Christians affirming the bodily and historical return of Christ may debate a variety of other eschatological matters yet remain closely united in ministry and mission. Prioritizing doctrines in this way does not imply Christians should consider any biblical truths insignificant. But Mohler rightly spells out the extremes: "The mark of true liberalism is the refusal to admit that first-order theological issues even exist. Liberals treat first-order doctrines as if they were merely third-order in importance, and doctrinal ambiguity is the inevitable result. Fundamentalism, on the other hand, tends toward the opposite error. The misjudgment of true fundamentalism is the belief that all disagreements concern first-order doctrines. Thus,

---

5. Ibid.
6. Ibid.
7. Ibid.
8. Ibid.
9. Ibid.
10. Ibid.

third-order issues are raised to a first-order importance, and Christians are wrongly and harmfully divided."[11]

DARING TO APPLY THEOLOGICAL TRIAGE TO THREE EVANGELICAL CREATIONIST MINISTRIES

Without question, what follows in this chapter is the hardest portion of this book to write. The temptation is to recommend that readers apply the principles of theological triage as they see fit to the issues already raised. Of course, I hope the previous chapters made a thoughtful contribution for doing just that. Yet I know my students appreciate when I teach not only the issues but also state my position. My bias is rooted in my conservative evangelicalism. I think the earth is likely old but am not dogmatic about it. I firmly reject universal common descent. I hold with conviction to the Chicago Statement on Biblical Inerrancy. And I am consciously motivated by a desire to remain faithful above all to biblical orthodoxy such as the kinds of things Mohler lists as examples of first-level doctrines. But I am also very aware of the complexity of these matters as well as my short-sightedness and fallibility. What follows then are just my opinions, but I hope they serve as starting points for more fruitful conversations between evangelicals. With an open Bible, I pray our hearts and minds will also be open to listen to those who disagree.

One more word before applying the principles of theological triage to the three most influential evangelical creationist organizations. These groups, like any of us, can draw the lines in the wrong places by either being too inclusive or too restrictive. So we will look only briefly at those issues I think most important which are inside or outside those lines. Unfortunately, space limitations preclude my highlighting the good things I really could say about each.

BioLogos

BioLogos desires conversation with evangelicals about evolution. And they seek to do that thoughtfully and respectfully. But in light of the views the group entertains, I believe their boundaries are too broad. The problem

---

11. Ibid.

is not what any particular BioLogos leader might believe, for I have met some who are not only delightful Christians but also biblically serious. The problem is the group's openness to an array of problematic ideas that it thereby recommends the church consider adopting. What the group regards as evangelically permissible inevitably becomes central to their message to the church too. Conservative evangelicals will find most troubling that BioLogos teaches (1) universal common descent should be entertained, and (2) the rejection of inerrancy can be entertained. In defense of (1), BioLogos notes that evangelicals have embraced universal common descent in the past without becoming theological liberals or worse. Their primary example is B. B. Warfield.

The writings of Benjamin B. Warfield (1851–1921) remain extremely influential with conservative evangelicals for his extensive articulation and defense of biblical inerrancy. Often he is presented as a conservative evangelical who could take both the Bible and evolution seriously. For instance, BioLogos reports that Warfield, "the ablest modern defender of the theologically conservative doctrine of the inerrancy of the Bible, was also an evolutionist."[12] Yet Warfield's views were quite different from some of those BioLogos presents.

We reviewed in the previous chapter the BioLogos-featured article, "After Inerrancy" by Kenton Sparks that lays out the case to reject "dark" texts in the Bible. Warfield would have radically opposed offering such a proposal to the church. He lamented that some theologians in his day understood biblical inspiration to be "less of the truth of God and more of the error of man."[13] In this view portions of biblical teaching may be "safely neglected or openly repudiated."[14] Warfield noted such theories of inspiration agreed less on knowing just how to discern where the Bible could be trusted than "their common destructive attitude toward some higher view of the inspiration of the Bible."[15] He contended that these faulty conceptions of biblical inspiration and authority were of two kinds.

---

12. BioLogos Editorial Team, "Evolution and Our Theological Traditions: Calvinism, Part 10," BioLogos, April 26, 2011, http://biologos.org/blogs/archive/evolution-and-our-theological-traditions-calvinism-part-10.

13. B.B. Warfield, *The Inspiration and Authority of the Bible*, ed. Samuel G. Craig (Phillipsburg, NJ: P & R, 1948), 105.

14. Ibid.

15. Ibid.

The "rationalistic" view understands not words, but only biblical concepts addressing faith and practice to be inspired. The "mystical" approach presents Christian experience as trustworthy to lead believers to accept just those parts of Scripture that speak to them.[16]

In opposition to such theories, Warfield offered the "church doctrine of inspiration," which "is not the invention nor the property of an individual, but the settled faith of the universal church of God; from the first planting of the church until today."[17] The church doctrine doesn't shift its affirmations to fit changing human thoughts, "but from the beginning has been the church's constant and abiding conviction as to the divinity of the Scriptures committed to her keeping."[18] The church doctrine views the Bible "as the Word of God in such a sense that whatever it says God says—not a book, then, in which one may, by searching, find some Word of God, but a book which may be frankly appealed to at any point with the assurance that whatever it may be found to say, that is the Word of God."[19] Warfield acknowledged difficulties in the doctrine of plenary inspiration, but believing virtually anything has its problems. In the end, he felt the difficulties faded when one asks whether "the whole church of God from the beginning has been deceived in her estimate of the Scriptures committed to her charge."[20] Warfield would never have countenanced offering proposals to the church such as "After Inerrancy."

BioLogos also reminds readers that Warfield was an evolutionist. Take, for instance, the BioLogos article, "How Have Christians Responded to Darwin's 'Origin of Species'?"[21] The article states that for Warfield "a high view of biblical authority was fully compatible with a divinely guided process of evolution."[22] But in the context of such a title, the uninformed reader would not realize the level of Warfield's concern about Darwinism. As historians Mark Noll and David Livingstone write: "Of key importance in Warfield's thinking was his willingness throughout a long career to

---

16. Ibid., 112–13.
17. Ibid., 106.
18. Ibid.
19. Ibid.
20. Ibid., 128.
21. "How Have Christians Responded to Darwin's 'Origin of Species'?" BioLogos, updated July 10, 2012, http://biologos.org/common-questions/christianity-and-science/christian-response-to-darwin.
22. Ibid.

accept the possibility (at times, the probability) of evolution, while always denying Darwinism strictly defined."[23]

One BioLogos article excerpted from a Mark Noll book hints at Warfield's criticisms of Darwinism, noting that he "consistently rejected materialist or dysteleological explanations for natural phenomena (explanations that he usually associated with 'Darwinism')," and that Warfield excluded all explanations such as "Darwin's rejection of divine agency."[24] These things and more need be unpacked before Warfield be considered as "just one example" of a "conservative Christian theologian" among "many church leaders in the late 19th century [who] actually embraced Darwin's theory as insight to the means by which God created the world."[25]

In the first place, Warfield recognized Darwin's personal turn toward agnosticism not only represented his view of the Bible but also his view of the world. He noted that Darwin's drift "from faith in a divine order in the world" was divided into two distinct periods. The first period ended with Darwin no longer believing "that God had ever spoken to men in his Word; at the end of the second he more than doubted whether the faintest whisper of his voice could be distinguished in his works. He was never prepared dogmatically to deny his existence; but search as he might he could not find him, and he could only say that if he existed he was, verily, a God that hides himself."[26] With this view of the world, "the doctrine of Evolution, which was given scientific standing by Darwin's *Origin of Species* (1859), became almost at once the prime support and stay of the atheistic propaganda. In every department of thought 'evolution' is

---

23. Mark A. Noll and David N. Livingstone, "Introduction: B. B. Warfield as Conservative Evolutionist," in B. B. Warfield, *Evolution, Scripture, and Science: Selected Writings*, ed. and intro. Mark A. Noll and David N. Livingstone (Grand Rapids: Baker, 2000), 13.

24. Mark Noll, "B. B. Warfield, Biblical Inerrancy, and Evolution," BioLogos, August 22, 2011, http://biologos.org/blogs/archive/b-b-warfield-biblical-inerrancy-and-evolution/. This article was excerpted from chapter 3 of Noll's book *Jesus Christ and the Life of the Mind* (Grand Rapids: Eerdmans, 2011).

25. Francis Collins, "Evolution and the Imago Dei," BioLogos, May 11, 2009, http://biologos.org/blogs/archive/evolution-and-the-imago-dei.

26. B. B. Warfield, "Darwin's Arguments Against Christianity," *Homiletic Review* (January 1889): 9-16, in *Selected Shorter Writings,* ed. John E. Meeter, 2 vols. (Phillipsburg, NJ: P & R, 1971–1973), 2:133. On Warfield's further reflections on Darwin's agnosticism, see ibid., 2:140–41.

supposed to account for everything, while itself needing no accounting for."[27]

As opposed to Darwinism, Warfield believed not only must God have created the original "stuff," but he must also have been involved in each stage of development.[28] Theories that speak of evolution as God's method of mediate creation but reject God's providential guidance of the development cannot properly be called creation. The intrinsic powers of nature itself cannot produce something new, otherwise the process is not creation at all.[29] For Warfield "the creation narrative in Genesis "cannot be satisfied by any evolution pure and simple, that is, by any providentially led process of development, but requires the assumption of a direct intervention of power from on high productive of something that is specifically new. . . . The difference between the modern speculator and the Biblicist cannot be conciliated at this point until and unless the speculator is willing to allow the intrusion into the course of evolution—if it be deemed actual in this case—of a purely supernatural act productive of something absolutely new which enters into the composite effect as a new feature."[30] Without these

27. B. B. Warfield, "Atheism," in the *New Schaff-Herzog Encyclopedia,* reprint (Grand Rapids: Baker, 1977 [1908]), 1:346–47 in B. B. Warfield, *Selected Shorter Writings,* ed. John E. Meeter, 2 vols. (Phillipsburg, NJ: P & R, 1971–1973), 1:40. Warfield chided evolutionists elsewhere for not making clear to non-scientists that evolution cannot ultimately be proven. See B. B. Warfield, "Review of A. A. W. Hubrecht, *The Descent of the Primates: Lectures Delivered on the Occasion of the Sesquicentennial Celebration of Princeton University* (New York: Scribner, 1897), *Presbyterian and Reformed Review* (October 1898), in B. B. Warfield, *Evolution, Scripture, and Science: Selected Writings,* ed. and intro. Mark A. Noll and David N. Livingstone (Grand Rapids: Baker, 2000), 183–87.

28. B. B. Warfield, "Review of William Elder, *Ideas from Nature: Talks with Students* (Philadelphia: American Baptist Publication Society, 1898), *Presbyterian and Reformed Review,* 10 (July 1899): 546–47, in B. B. Warfield, *Evolution, Scripture, and Science: Selected Writings,* ed. and intro. Mark A. Noll and David N. Livingstone (Grand Rapids: Baker, 2000), 188–90.

29. B. B. Warfield, "Creation, Evolution, and Mediate Creation," *The Bible Student,* n.s. 4, no. 1 (July 1901): 1–8, in B. B. Warfield, *Evolution, Scripture, and Science: Selected Writings,* ed. and intro. Mark A. Noll and David N. Livingstone (Grand Rapids: Baker, 2000), 197–210. For Warfield any evolutionary theory denying creation, that is, the divine volitional process, is unacceptable.

30. B. B. Warfield, *The Bible Student* n.s. 8 (November 1903): 5, in B. B. Warfield, *Evolution, Scripture, and Science: Selected Writings,* ed. and intro. Mark A. Noll and David N. Livingstone (Grand Rapids: Baker, 2000), 215–16.

supernatural or spiritual elements, Warfield viewed all such evolutionary schemes as essentially atheistic.[31]

God's stamp also must be seen in his work. Warfield thereby rejected all scientific theories like Darwinism that "oppose teleology and design."[32] He found the anti-teleological zeal of Darwinists to be "very depressing." He asked "why should they make their recognition or non-recognition of teleological factors the test of the acceptability of theories? This gives the disagreeable appearance to the trend of biological speculation . . . that it is dominated, in a word, by philosophical conceptions not derived from science, but imposed on science from without."[33]

As Noll and Livingstone note, Warfield was also adamant about the unity of the human race as a prerequisite for biblical soteriology.[34] Therefore he insisted that the human race must be absolutely restricted to the descendants of the originally created couple, Adam and Eve.[35] He wrote in 1911: "So far is it from being of no concern to theology, therefore, that it would be truer to say that the whole doctrinal structure of the Bible account of redemption is founded on its assumption that the race of man is one organic whole, and may be dealt with as such. It is because all are one in Adam that in the matter of sin there is no difference, but all have fallen short of the glory of God. . . . The unity of the old man in Adam is the postulate of the unity of the new man in Christ."[36]

---

31. B. B. Warfield, "Review of Herman Bavinck, *Schepping of Ontwikkeling* [*Creation or Development*] (Kampen: J. H. Kok, 1901), in *Presbyterian and Reformed Review* 12 (July 1901): 507, in B. B. Warfield, *Evolution, Scripture, and Science: Selected Writings*, ed. and intro. Mark A. Noll and David N. Livingstone (Grand Rapids: Baker, 2000), 195–96.

32. Noll and Livingstone, "Introduction," 40.

33. B. B. Warfield, "Review of Vernon L. Kellogg, *Darwinism Today: A Discussion of Present-Day Scientific Criticism of the Darwinian Selection Theories, Together with a Brief Account of the Principal and Other Proposed Auxiliary and Alternative Theories of Species-Forming* (New York: Henry Holt, 1097), in *Princeton Theological Review* (October 1908), in B. B. Warfield, *Evolution, Scripture, and Science: Selected Writings*, ed. and intro. Mark A. Noll and David N. Livingstone (Grand Rapids: Baker, 2000), 250.

34. Noll and Livingstone, "Introduction," 40.

35. B. B. Warfield, "On the Antiquity and the Unity of the Human Race (excerpts)," *Princeton Theological Review* 9 (January 1911): 1–25, in B. B. Warfield, *Evolution, Scripture, and Science: Selected Writings*, ed. and intro. Mark A. Noll and David N. Livingstone (Grand Rapids: Baker, 2000), 285.

36. Ibid., 287.

And finally, Warfield practiced the conservatism principle. He cautiously examined new scientific theories such as evolution, but clearly rejected the notion that science has authority over the Bible. In the first place, he argued, not only the Bible needs interpretation. Science itself is a human interpretation of facts, not the facts themselves. Thus even if biblical teachings required interpretation, Warfield noted that it is only reasonable that propositional statements ("word-statements") given by God in Scripture be preferred over those given by scientists.[37]

Warfield's openness to evolution may be an eye-opener to traditional evangelicals. But this brief survey of Warfield's views should reveal the considerable distance between them and those of BioLogos. In the end, his assessments "cannot, of course, pronounce definitively on theological-scientific questions at the start of the twenty-first century" for evolutionary creationists such as those at BioLogos.[38] But that is the point. His views ran counter to the mainstream views of BioLogos by his insistence on teleology and design in the natural world, supernatural intervention in biological creation, the descent of humanity from Adam, and an unswerving commitment to biblical inerrancy and its authority in relation to science.

Warfield seriously courted evolution, but he never married Darwinism. The conditions he stressed necessary for a relationship were impossibly anti-Darwinian. Many conservative evangelicals continue to share these concerns, if not Warfield's openness to evolution.

Answers in Genesis

I am grateful most young earth creationists do not believe the earth's age is worth dividing over. In my denomination, church, and school, I suspect young earth creationists (YECs) outnumber old earth creationists (OECs), but our skirmishes over the age of the earth have never led to division. In spite of deep commitments to either view, the age of the earth has been considered a level-three doctrine.

---

37. B. B. Warfield, "Review of Randolph S. Foster, *Creation: God in Time and Space* (New York: Hun & Eaton, 1895), in *Presbyterian and Reformed Review* 7 (July 1896): 561–62, in B. B. Warfield, *Evolution, Scripture, and Science: Selected Writings*, ed. and intro. Mark A. Noll and David N. Livingstone (Grand Rapids: Baker, 2000), 173–74.

38. Noll, "B. B. Warfield and Evolution."

As noted in the previous chapter, I believe Answers in Genesis has drawn boundaries for inerrancy too narrowly. Their view not only submits biblical inspiration to a particular view of the earth's age, but also to modern scientific theories such as specific views of the fossil column, details about taxonomy, and Neanderthals.[39] Moreover, AiG insists that rejection of YEC has led and will lead to the ruined condition of the church and the world. If their warnings are true, my church, denomination, and school will fall because we have not heeded them. Christians who "tremble" before scientists rather than God's Word have no place in Christian leadership.[40] But if AiG's alarms are false yet we acted on them, we would become divided in mission and fellowship for terribly wrong reasons. Note this sampling of the terrible effects AiG claims follows from embracing OEC: the downfall of Western culture and morals, the loss of Christians' personal faith, and the undermining of the gospel itself.

For example, in response to a blog arguing why a Christian might hold an old earth view, Terry Mortenson posted the following on AiG's website as part of his reasoning to reject OEC:

> Furthermore, historically, the church's widespread acceptance of millions of years over the past 200 years has contributed massively to a growing resistance to the gospel in nations that were in the past very influenced culturally by biblical Christianity and also in communist, Buddhist and Hindu nations. That acceptance also has been a very significant reason, among others, that many children raised in gospel preaching churches

---

39. "Affirmations and Denials Essential to a Consistent Christian (Biblical) Worldview," Answers in Genesis, https://answersingenesis.org/answers/affirmations-denials-christian-worldview/.

40. Ken Ham writes that OECs ignore the plain teaching of the Bible but "tremble at man's word instead (i.e., his dating methods and his fallible science). Until God's people clearly teach and demonstrate to the world that we all need to tremble at the Word of God, biblical authority will not be restored." Ken Ham, "Whose Word Do You Tremble At?" Answers in Genesis, December 27, 2001, https://answersingenesis.org/days-of-creation/whose-word-do-you-tremble-at/. See also Terry Mortenson, "Why Don't Many Christian Leaders and Scholars Believe Genesis?" Answers in Genesis, May 31, 2010, https://answersingenesis.org/genesis/why-dont-many-christian-leaders-and-scholars-believe-genesis/. Many more examples expressing the same idea, and often with similar "tremble" wording, can be found on the AiG website.

and Christian families have (since leaving home) departed from the church or even the faith they once professed. There has indeed been a "slippery slide" of the church into much apostasy. Denominations that were once orthodox 100 or 150 years ago are now liberal and deny the biblical gospel. Europe, Britain, and America, which once were so powerfully impacted by the gospel and were launching pads for missions to the world, are now post-Christian and increasingly anti-Christian. Who would have thought 30 years ago that professing evangelicals today would doubt or deny that Adam ever existed or would embrace or accept homosexual behavior? The undermining of the truth of Genesis 1–11 regarding the age of the earth and the Flood has unquestionably contributed to the undermining of the truth of Genesis 1–3 regarding Adam, marriage, and sexuality both in the church and in the culture."[41]

Certainly if these things are true, then my church, school, and denomination need to take action to remove OEC leaders sooner rather than later. On the other hand, if these dreadful accusations are false, they should be recanted. Space precludes a detailed response, but several things should be noted.

First, though these kinds of far-reaching claims are not uncommon, the careful historical work substantiating them is. Extremely serious but controversial accusations should first be carefully grounded on evidence. Which historians of Christian missions argue that OEC caused gospel resistance in communist, Buddhist, and Hindu nations? Do church historians document that OEC led to theological liberalism in once healthy denominations? Do cultural historians testify that OEC led Western nations to anti-Christian status?

Sweeping claims of these sorts are frightening to those who must trust the leaders making them. But claims are easier to make than justify. For instance, AiG would rightly be disturbed if, say, an extremely influential OEC ministry made a claim like the following:

---

41. Terry Mortenson, "A Response to a Gospel Coalition Blog on the Age of the Earth," Answers in Genesis, April 22, 2015, https://answersingenesis.org/age-of-the-earth/a-response-to-a-gospel-coalition-blog-on-the-age-of-the-earth/.

About the time of the rise of modern (old earth) geology, the modern missionary movement was born. As the earth's creation column was being revealed, William Carey took the gospel to Hindus and Adoniram Judson evangelized Buddhists. Braced by their convictions about the creation column, OECs also led the way in resisting Darwinism after publication of *The Origin of Species* in 1859. At the turn of the twentieth century, OEC fundamentalists stood in the gap against theological liberalism. And by the middle of the twentieth century, OEC dominance among evangelicals produced tremendous godly effects upon the United States. As Gallup reports, greater than "95% of Americans identified as Christian in the 1950s,"[42] the highest percentage of the twentieth century.

Tragically, the publication of *The Genesis Flood* in 1961 launched the modern YEC movement. That decade saw prayer thrown out of public schools and the rise of the drug and free sex culture. By the 1980s Henry Morris celebrated the proliferation of YEC ministries that led to 44% of Americans believing in YEC.[43] But that was the decade when hippies became yuppies (materialistic), MTV began to be piped into homes via cable TV, and AIDS was first observed among drug users and homosexual men in the United States. By 2008, the YEC revolution had fully come into its own: the creation column had become a flood column with 60% of Americans believing in a flood "within the past 10,000 years that covered all of the earth and was responsible for most of the rock layers and fossils that are seen across the world."[44]

---

42. Frank Newport, "Percentage of Christians in U.S. Drifting Down, but Still High," Gallup, December 24, 2015, http://www.gallup.com/poll/187955/percentage-christians-drifting-down-high.aspx.

43. Henry M. Morris, *A History of Modern Creationism* (San Diego: Master Books, 1984), 311.

44. "Americans' Scientific Knowledge and Beliefs about Human Evolution in the Year of Darwin," National Center for Science Education, https://ncse.com/library-resource/americans-scientific-knowledge-beliefs-human-evolution-year. The same polling data shows the utter confusion of Americans about creation-evolution issues. For example, 39% believe "God created the universe, the earth, the sun, moon, stars, plants, animals, and the first two people within the past 10 000 years." But only 18% claim to believe "The earth is less than 10,000 years old!"

During that decade the culture and church hit new moral and spiritual lows, with young people leaving the church in droves. The undermining of the truth of OEC interpretations of Genesis has unquestionably contributed to the undermining of both the church and the culture.

Of course, these two paragraphs above are nonsense, even though genuine polling data is cited. Any number of similarly alarming claims can be made using questionable cause fallacies. Or to turn Mortenson's reasoning on its head, one could claim that since now YEC has become so popular among creationists, we should soon expect a revival of the missions and morality so damaged by the once-dominant OEC.

As we saw in chapters 3 and 4, historians attribute the past cultural dethronement of evangelical influence to other causes. Biblical theology was displaced in the academy by the humanities.[45] Theological liberalism aided and abetted this move by making the inner life of humanity the rightful place to ground religious knowledge.[46] But by far the biggest factor was the widespread impact of Darwinism, with its attendant naturalistic influences.[47] Evangelical and fundamentalist leaders in the culture wars a century ago termed themselves "anti-evolutionists" for a reason.[48] Contesting evolution united them; agreement about the interpretive details of Genesis was considered largely unimportant.[49]

AiG faces its own critics who use the kinds of criticism AiG directs at OECs. A small but serious Christian movement today argues that the

---

45. Jon H. Roberts and James Turner, *The Sacred and the Secular University* (Princeton, NJ: 2000), 119. See also ibid. 14, 36.

46. Ibid., xi, 1–13, 28.

47. Jon H. Roberts, *Darwinism and the Divine in America: Protestant Intellectuals and Organic Evolution, 1859–1900* (Madison, WI: University of Wisconsin Press, 1988), xviii, 63, 233; John Hedley Brooke, "Darwin and Victorian Christianity," in *The Cambridge Companion to Darwin,* ed, Hodge and Radick, 216; and Paul K. Conkin, *When All the Gods Trembled: Darwinism, Scopes, and American Intellectuals* (Lanham, MD: Rowman & Littlefield, 1998), xi.

48. Ronald L. Numbers, *Darwinism Comes to America* (Cambridge, MA: Harvard University Press, 1998), 52, 80.

49. Numbers, *Darwinism,* 53. See also Ronald L. Numbers, "Creating Creationism: Meanings and Uses since the Age of Agassiz," in *Evangelicals and Science in Historical Perspective,* ed. David N. Livingstone, D. G. Hart, and Mark A. Noll (New York: Oxford University Press, 1990), 235.

real problem occurred long before the rise of modern geology. This group contends that the turn to heliocentrism defined the moment when biblical authority was surrendered to science. The chief proponent of this view, Gerardus Bouw, now retired professor at Baldwin-Wallace College in Berea, Ohio, holds a Ph.D. in astronomy from Case Western Reserve University.[50] He contends that any variance between the "readings" of astronomy and the Bible are always due to error in the readings of the "Book of Nature."[51] The earth "is not older than about six thousand years," and "the Bible teaches us of an earth that neither rotates daily nor revolves yearly about the sun; that it is at rest with respect to the throne of him who called it into existence; and that hence it is absolutely at rest in the universe."[52] Bouw contends: "If God cannot be taken literally when he writes of the 'rising of the sun,' then how can he be taken literally in writing of the 'rising of the Son?'"[53]

AiG featured astronomer, Danny Faulkner, believes Bouw's view is a problem for YECs: "Alas, there are recent creationists in the world today who are geocentrists. They teach that the rejection of God's Word did not begin with Darwin's theory of biological evolution or even with Hutton and Lyell's geological uniformitarianism. Instead, they argue that the scientific rebellion against God began much earlier with heliocentrism."[54] Faulkner goes on to present an extensive argument biblically and scientifically why geocentrism should be rejected.

Bouw rises to the challenge, claiming Faulkner's criticism "is very shallow and often misrepresents geocentricity, geocentrists, the history of the Copernican revolution, its evidences, and the authority of

---

50. "The Testimony of Gerardus Dingeman Bouw," Association for Biblical Astronomy, http://www.geocentricity.com/bibastron/bouw_bio.html.

51. "Credo of the Biblical Astronomer," Association for Biblical Astronomy, http://www.geocentricity.com/.

52. Ibid.

53. Gerardus D. Bouw, *A Geocentricity Primer: Introduction to Biblical Cosmology* (Cleveland: The Biblical Astronomer, 1999), 1.

54. Danny Faulkner, "Geocentrism and Creation," Answers in Genesis, August 1, 2001, https://answersingenesis.org/creationism/arguments-to-avoid/geocentrism-and-creation/. AiG features many of Faulkner's articles. See "Latest Articles by Dr. Danny R. Faulkner," Answers in Genesis, https://answersingenesis.org/bios/danny-faulkner/articles/.

Scripture."[55] Bouw concludes his response by charging Faulkner with rejecting the biblical teaching of a geocentric universe for no "reason other than his opinion. In effect, his view is founded on the assumption that the proper interpretation of the Bible in the realm of science may await future discoveries by science."[56] Faulkner's worries that geocentrism makes YEC an easy target for critics is "sheer nonsense" because knowledgeable antagonists can single out the hypocrisy of insisting the days of Genesis 1 are literal but the sun's rising and setting is not. Bouw contends that YECs like Faulkner who reject geocentrism do so "for the sole purpose of appearing intellectual and acceptable to the world, which desire is enmity with God (James 4:4). The creationist movement is fortunate that evolutionists don't understand these simple issues, for if they did, creationists would be shamed and held contemptible even more than they are now."[57]

Other Christian groups such as the Missouri Lutherans also defended geocentrism "well into the twentieth century."[58] But the point here is that Bouw's rejection of heliocentrism and Faulkner's defense of it remarkably parallel debates between OECs and YECs. In this case Faulkner and other YECs who reject geocentrism find themselves being accused of surrendering Scripture to science.

Especially troubling is the way AiG frequently makes the confusing and misleading claim that YEC is a gospel issue.[59] In an article titled, "Millions of Years—Are Souls at Stake? Biblical Authority," Ken Ham writes, "Well, it isn't a salvation issue—but it is!"[60] He argues that OECs interpret the Bible in light of science, which "means God's Word is not

---

55. Gerardus D. Bouw, "Geocentricity: A Fable for Educated Man?" Association for Biblical Astronomy, http://www.geocentricity.com/ba1/fresp/index.html.

56. Ibid.

57. Ibid.

58. Numbers, *Darwinism,* 7. For a well-respected twentieth-century Lutheran theologian defending geocentrism see Franz Pieper, *Christian Dogmatics,* 3 vols., trans. Theodore Engelder et al. (St. Louis: Concordia, 1950), 1:473: "It is unworthy of a Christian to interpret Scripture, which he knows to be God's own Word, according to human opinions (hypotheses), and that includes the Copernican cosmic system." Thanks to John W. Rasmussen for this citation.

59. A search on the AiG web site for "gospel issue" reveals the many articles on this theme.

60. Ken Ham, "Millions of Years—Are Souls at Stake? Biblical Authority," Answers in Genesis, January 1, 2014, https://answersingenesis.org/theory-of-evolution/millions-of-years/are-souls-at-stake/.

the final authority and is not without error. It also opens the door to others doing this with other historical claims of Scripture—such as the Resurrection and virgin birth."[61] This charge is especially irresponsible and self-defeating. As we have seen in chapters 6 and 7, YECs make the very same moves in relating theology and science, just with compressed time scales. Does this mean YECs' reading speciation and plate tectonics/continental drift into the Bible opens the door for others to reject the resurrection of Christ and virgin birth?

Ham considers especially problematic the OEC view that animals died before the fall of Adam. After making his biblical and scientific case, Ham argues that "it seems obvious that bloodshed, death of animals and man, disease, suffering, and thorns came after sin."[62] And because the Old Testament sacrificial system set the stage for Christ's sacrifice, "if there was death and bloodshed of animals before sin, then this undermines the atonement. Also, if there were death, disease, bloodshed, and suffering before sin, then such would be God's fault—not our fault! Why would God require death as a sacrifice for sin if He were the one responsible for death and bloodshed, having created the world with these bad things in place?"[63] Ham concludes: "So to believe in millions of years is a gospel issue. This belief ultimately impugns the character of the Creator and Savior and undermines the foundation of the soul-saving gospel."[64]

Ham's claim creates a sense of urgency for AiG's message, but is nonetheless theologically careless. Describing the age of the earth as a salvation issue would be shockingly heretical and is therefore trivial. But calling it a gospel issue that "undermines the foundation of the soul-saving gospel" is a seriously similar assertion certain to create a major boundary between believers over the age of the earth. Debating OECs over the issue of animal death before the fall is perfectly reasonable. But Ham's assurance that those who disagree can still be saved hardly ameliorates his accusation that OECs undermine the very mission of Jesus.

Ham's move is based on arguing from non-human effects of the fall. Questions about those effects have been raised for centuries. Did the fall

---

61. Ibid.
62. Ibid.
63. Ibid.
64. Ibid.

affect the heavens, too, or were heavenly bodies expected to be perfect (e.g., no craters on the moon)? Did certain animals develop carnivorous features after the fall (fangs, claws, and digestive systems)? Did any scientific laws change post-fall (e.g., second law of thermodynamics)? Debate over animal death before the fall is both interesting and important, but to refer to it as a gospel issue is reckless—precisely because the saving work of Christ has to with the fall's effects on human beings.

AiG's muddled theology can be seen in the way it discusses the gospel on its website. On the one hand, AiG's clearest gospel presentation, "The Gospel of Jesus Christ," has no mention of the age of the earth.[65] Someone might stumble upon that page and believe the gospel without having any conception about the age of the earth debate whatsoever. That person might have no idea either about AiG's position on YEC, much less AiG's making the age of the earth a gospel issue. The same would have been true during the heyday of OEC when response to the gospel preaching of Charles Spurgeon, the fundamentalists and Billy Graham fared quite well. They might have been wrong on the age issue, but it certainly did not undermine the gospel.

On the other hand, perhaps the least clear and most problematic AiG page regarding the gospel is titled, "Creation Evangelism—From A to Z."[66] The article begins with one sentence stating its purpose: "Creation evangelism—using the biblical account of creation to spread the gospel—is not just for pastors and evangelists; it's for everyone, old and young alike."[67] No evangelical should quibble with that general notion. The creation does point to the Creator from whom the human race is hopelessly separated by its sin. But an alphabetized list follows this opening sentence, ostensibly to help Christians use clues from the creation to present the gospel of Jesus Christ. Unfortunately, what follows is a lengthy list short on specifically presenting Christ and his salvation but long on promoting YEC and AiG. The strategies "to spread the gospel" that follow include AiG bumper stickers, dinosaur trading cards, and even placing "creation

---

65. "The Gospel of Jesus Christ," Answers in Genesis, https://answersingenesis.org/about/good-news/.

66. "Creation Evangelism—From A to Z," Answers in Genesis, September 19, 2006, https://answersingenesis.org/gospel/evangelism/creation-evangelism-from-a-to-z/.

67. Ibid.

booklets and tracts *in public restrooms, especially in stalls.*"[68] AiG has every right to promote its ministry via items like those in the list. But when the ministry offers items that do not promote the gospel of Jesus Christ, yet speaks of them in the context of spreading "the gospel," perhaps it should reconsider just what constitutes gospel issues.[69]

D. A. Carson notes that to describe something as a "gospel issue" can be just another way of categorizing the importance of doctrinal issues into either important or not. And because the gospel is supremely important, calling an issue a gospel issue then draws a boundary around it. But often the issue at hand is just a hot topic, albeit important, that defines our particular interests.[70] Prominent YEC Todd Wood agrees with Carson. Wood rightly emphasizes that the doctrine of creation and even how God created are important. But he finds the use of describing YEC as a gospel issue "alarming." He notes the gospel is "not about when God created the universe," but "is about Jesus and how we obtain life through Him. We ought

---

68. Ibid. Clicking on the link in the article, "Creation Booklets and Tracts," takes one to a page titled "Witnessing Tools" which offers various AiG products such as tracts, booklets and DVDs. But the topics are as much about the flood, carbon dating, the big bang, etc. as the gospel of salvation in Christ. See "Witnessing Tools," Answers in Genesis, https://answersingenesis.org/store/books/witnessing/.

69. Perhaps Ham's muddled thinking on gospel issues can be attributed to the way his ministry developed. He recounts how his creation ministry was transformed years ago. Early on he spoke in churches on topics such as the age of the earth, "but it certainly didn't seem to stir them with the passion I had for the creation/evolution topic." But his reading of *The Genesis Record* by Henry Morris caused him to appreciate once again "how foundational the book of Genesis was to the rest of the Bible." So he sought to understand better how his audience viewed Genesis and why they did not think it more important. In response, he developed his "Relevance Sermon. It was a 30-minute talk on why Christians should believe in a literal Genesis. I explained how Genesis was foundational to all doctrine and that Christians shouldn't add millions of years to God's Word—that this destroys the foundation of the gospel." Following that sermon, his listeners were stirred with passion for his creation message. AiG continues to stir its followers by constantly declaring that rejection of its YEC message undermines cultural morality, the church's faith, and the gospel itself. See Ken Ham, "Practical Creation Evangelism," Answers in Genesis, July 1, 2002, https://answersingenesis.org/gospel/evangelism/practical-creation-evangelism/. The material is taken from chapter 11 of Ham's book *Why Won't They Listen? The Power of Creation Evangelism* (Green Forest, AR: Master Books, 2002).

70. D. A. Carson, "What Are Gospel Issues?" *Themelios* 39.2 (2014): 215–19, http://tgc-documents.s3.amazonaws.com/themelios/Themelios39.2.pdf#page=.

not add to the gospel other things, important though they may be."[71] He also is bothered the way the "gospel issue" is "too often used as a weapon to beat up those who disagree with the person using it." And Wood is especially alarmed that "gospel issue" maneuvers "seem to be adding to the gospel. The gospel is not the story of Jesus' salvation + my favorite doctrine. Even if those doctrines are true (and important), we should not attach them directly to the gospel. The Bible has very strong words for people who try to place extra burdens on people in addition to the gospel. That makes a false gospel. Ironically, it seems to me that calling things 'gospel issues' is an actual gospel issue."[72]

Reasons to Believe

A fair critique of this book would be the lack of equal time spent criticizing Reasons to Believe (RTB). But the intention is not to give them a pass, but to argue that the age of the earth is the wrong place to draw lines. So of the three major creationist ministries, RTB stood out the least because it completely affirms the Chicago Statement on Biblical Inerrancy (CSBI). On the other hand, AiG desires to reformulate the CSBI in its image, and BioLogos promotes acceptance of dangerous anti-inerrancy viewpoints. RTB also does not accept universal common descent as does BioLogos.

However, Hugh Ross, president of RTB, does deserve criticism for some of the ways he has exacerbated the age of the earth controversy. He has been rightly criticized for seeking to solve perennial theological debates by use of the concept of extra-dimensionality. Perhaps this might have been less a concern if he just related the concept to something like God's relationship to creation. But Ross seeks to tackle Trinitarianism, Christology, divine sovereignty and human freedom, and more by use of at least eleven space-time dimensions. In response to the first edition of *Beyond the Cosmos*[73] containing these ideas, Ross met with a panel at a national meeting of the Evangelical Theological Society in 1997. Most noted their appreciation for

---

71. Todd Wood, "But Is It a Gospel Issue?" *Todd's Blog*, September 14, 2016, http://toddcwood.blogspot.com/2016/09/but-is-it-gospel-issue.html.

72. Ibid.

73. Hugh Ross, *Beyond the Cosmos: What Recent Discoveries in Astrophysics Reveal about the Glory and Love of God*, 3rd ed. (Orlando: Signalman Publishing, 2010).

his apologetics work. But his "extra-dimensionality" approach to theology was less warmly received. William Lane Craig criticized Ross: "I find his attempt to construe God as existing in hyper-dimensions of time and space and to interpret Christian doctrines in that light to be both philosophically and theologically unacceptable."[74] Craig went on to challenge Ross either to explain his positions better or "else to modify his views so as to avoid them."[75] Ross claimed his way of explaining things to laypeople had been misunderstood, that he unwaveringly holds to orthodox theology. Perhaps a common perception among evangelical theologians regarding his theological work applies also to other creationist ministries: scientists do better science and theologians do better theology.[76]

Ross has also been noted In calling for evangelical councils to bring resolution to the age of the earth controversy. Unfortunately, when calling for these councils early on, he referred to the current dispute as "analogous" to the problem at the Council of Jerusalem (Acts 15). The issue decided at that council, Ross notes, was that certain teachers were adding legalistic burdens to Gentiles, blocking them from saving faith in Christ. The immediate context of his analogy was his telling the story of a new believer attacked by radical YECs, making impossible demands on the young convert's faith.[77] The seeming analogy of YECs as legalists was hardly an auspicious way to call for a council with them. Eventually Ross claimed the council idea was not working, so he called for testing the competing age of the earth models. By means of testing their respective hypotheses, in a short time the issue should be settled as to which view was correct.[78]

Ross has gone on to publish several books touting the testability and success of his model relative to other competitors such as naturalistic evolution, theistic evolution, and young earth creationism. Not helping calm

74. William Lane Craig, "Hugh Ross' Extra-Dimensional Deity," in *Philosophia Christi: Journal of the Evangelical Philosophical Society* 21, no. 1 (Summer 1998): 31.

75. Ibid.

76. Ross to his credit not only handled the meeting humbly but has posted on the RTB website the entire journal on the issue. See "Philosophia Christi," Reasons to Believe, November 13, 1999, http://www.reasons.org/articles/philosophia-christi.

77. Hugh Ross, *Creation and Time: A Biblical and Scientific Perspective on the Creation-Date Controversy* (Colorado Springs, CO: NavPress, 1994), 159–61.

78. Hugh Ross, *A Matter of Days: Resolving a Creation Controversy* (Colorado Springs, CO: NavPress, 2004), 245–50.

the fray over the age debate, he wrote in 2009: "One serious critique of young-earth creationist attempts to explain the natural realm is that their explanations, typically rooted in religious dogma, have no flexibility to adapt and self-correct as knowledge increases."[79] But that is not true. As we saw in chapter 7, contemporary YEC models have adapted dramatically to the latest science over the decades. And YEC leaders have been willing to abandon ideas and models they believed were no longer viable (e.g., the vapor canopy). R. A. Peters, apparently no longer a creationist of any sort, argues that even secular science should not treat YECs as the church has sometimes handled heretics: demanding faith and persecuting infidels. He argues that young earth creationists are continuing to develop more sophisticated and self-critical traditions.[80]

BioLogos soon published an article noting that RTB had not been exactly correcting itself in responding to genetic data relative to human evolution. The article claimed RTB appeared to cherry-pick data "in an attempt to support a pre-determined position that humans and other apes do not share ancestry. As such this model is not a model that a believer can hold with scientific integrity. It may well be that RTB offers their model in good faith: if so, however, it demonstrates that they are not qualified to address these lines of evidence in a scientific manner."[81] The writer went on to reprimand RTB for compromising Christian witness to unbelieving scientists who know the science.[82] RTB responded via BioLogos that the books in question had been hurried out between two different publishers to meet the Darwin Day Celebration. "There was nothing done to be

---

79. Hugh Ross, *More than a Theory: Revealing a Testable Model for Creation* (Grand Rapids: Baker, 2009), 20.

80. Richard A. Peters, "Theodicic Creationism: Its Membership and Motivations," in *Geology and Religion: A History of Harmony and Hostility,* ed. Martina Kölbl Ebert (London: The Geological Society, 2009), 319–20. Examples of the most responsible, creative, and progressive of the creationist voices he cites include the Geoscience Research Institute (research and apologetics arm of the Seventh-day Adventists), the Creation Research Society, the Creation Science Fellowship, and the Baraminology Study Group.

81. Dennis Venema, "An Evangelical Geneticist's Critique of Reasons to Believe's Testable Creation Model, Pt. 2," BioLogos, November 18, 2010, http://biologos.org/blogs/dennis-venema-letters-to-the-duchess/an-evangelical-geneticists-critique-of-reasons-to-believes-testable-creation-model-pt-2.

82. Ibid.

deliberately deceptive regarding the failure to mention the work on the whole genome of the chimpanzee."[83]

Whatever was at work in this incident, RTB got a dose of its own medicine. No doubt RTB has borne the brunt of many a fiery YEC dart through the years. But contending that YECs should put their models to the test is tricky business because others can choose to set up tests of their own making for RTB.

GENERAL LESSONS LEARNED FROM THIS STUDY

Biblical Christians historically have practiced the conservatism principle in science-theology conflicts. The practice was founded on the assumption of biblical inerrancy, the coherence of biblical and natural facts, and a reluctance to adjust biblical interpretation unless proven science made clear the biblical interpretation had been wrong. Contrary to its stated position, even AiG practices this complex but necessary Galileo proposal. And in spite of differing positions on the age of the earth and other science-theology issues, AiG and RTB both have practiced the conservatism principle. BioLogos, on the other hand, not only maintains no commitment to biblical inerrancy but is willing to propose views far removed from anything like a traditional understanding of inspiration. Its apparent openness for a one way submission of the Bible to the terms of modern science distinctly rejects the Galileo proposal.

None of the three ministries are denominationally accountable, thus they are under no obligation to present robust theological systems. Their effects, however—theologically and emotionally—on churches are significant. Obviously very different doctrines of creation, humanity, and the fall of Adam are presented. And as mentioned, the three groups offer quite different approaches to biblical inspiration. RTB and AiG have much in common with their commitments to inerrancy and the rejection of human evolution. AiG, however, insists that the very nature of biblical inspiration be tied to recent creation and several specific scientific viewpoints.

---

83. Dennis Venema, "An Evangelical Geneticist's Critique of Reasons to Believe's Testable Creation Model, Pt. 1," BioLogos, November 6, 2010, http://biologos.org/blogs/dennis-venema-letters-to-the-duchess/an-evangelical-geneticists-critique-of-reasons-to-believes-testable-creation-model-pt-1#sthash.IlefxhFW.dpuf.

The mission of BioLogos places the promotion of evolution foremost, with details of pertinent biblical doctrines to be worked out in its light.

I believe AiG draws theological boundaries too narrowly and BioLogos too broadly. I have by far the deepest doctrinal concerns regarding the effects of BioLogos on the church. But I also have serious concerns about AiG's effect on the unity of the church.

THE THREE MAJOR CREATIONIST
MINISTRIES: DRAWING LINES

Reasons to Believe

The history of conservative Christians wrestling with Scripture and science makes clear that generations may pass before viewpoints coalesce on specific scientific theories. A few examples might include the law of faunal succession, glacial theory, and continental drift. More goes into acceptance of specific scientific theories than just analysis of objective data.

Therefore, I suggest RTB should consider halting the notion of tests to demonstrate the superiority of its model over its counterparts, including YECs. The difference is subtle but perhaps important, between presenting evidence for one's view, and presenting even a hint that another viewpoint should surrender. There can be no question that RTB has been the target of many unfair attacks by some YECs over the decades such as referring to it as evolutionist. I also have no expectations that those attacks will end any time soon. But I remain convinced that YECs should be encouraged to develop their models in faithfulness to their biblical convictions.

Answers in Genesis

If I believe YECs should be respected and heard regarding their biblical and scientific models, I also am convinced that some YECs draw the lines too narrowly. I believe the age of the earth should be a level-three issue. But one YEC leader told me the issue's importance makes it a "1.2" doctrine for him. Of course thinking of the issue that way does not fit Mohler's triage structure: (1) without believing this you cannot be considered a Christian; (2) you may be a Christian believing this, but regrettably we cannot do missions or education or church together; and (3) your belief differs from mine but that does not come between us. But my friend's "1.2" honesty explains the confused—and damaging—way some YECs handle the matter.

AiG's rhetoric has institutionalized for this generation the confusion about the importance of YEC. AiG's tone was first "constitutionalized" by Henry Morris but traces back to Price and the scriptural geologists. OECs are alleged to be enemies of God, thus allies of Satan. But in attempting to demonstrate this accusation, AiG leaders repeatedly overreach themselves. AiG uses the same science as do the "atheistic" OECs—but with reduced time scales, more speciation, and in considerable disagreement with some other YECs. AiG blames the downfall of the West, including the loss of faith and morality, on OEC without documentation and in the face of cultural historians. And, again without evidence, AiG blames the Chicago Statements for opening the door to more recent decay in the churches. To fix those problems, AiG unilaterally proposes a profound reformulation of the Chicago Statements that conflates interpretation with inspiration, excluding in the process even some YECs from being inerrantists. The Bible cannot be considered inspired unless the interpreter believes not only in recent creation, but also in particular scientific theories about the fossil column, Neanderthals, and the degree of speciation permitted in baraminology. AiG even argues the gospel itself must be linked to YEC or else be undermined. The easiest documentable example of overreach is the frequency with which AiG leaders claim to know the hidden motives driving OEC theorists: they are "trembling" before scientists rather than God's Word. Yet unless AiG leaders have received a remarkable spiritual gift, they are claiming to know something only God does.

Thankfully, most YECs I know neither believe nor approve AiG's rhetoric. One may believe wholeheartedly that the Bible teaches recent creation. And one may believe YEC without believing those who disagree are unwitting agents of evil. AiG may have well succeeded in convincing many to believe YEC. I have no problem with that, but am grateful AiG has not been nearly as effective in convincing YECs to use their divisive rhetoric.

I believe divisive rhetoric is the correct term to describe AiG's language as documented throughout this book. Why? If AiG's charges against OECs were believed and acted on, massive divisions in denominations and churches would follow. I have been a pastor or seminary professor for more than 35 years. I would consider it failure in the line of duty not to correct a Christian under my charge who believed doctrines that destroy the culture, church, family, faith, and the gospel. If I knew of a leader in my church, school, or denomination who believed in such destructive doctrines, I would take a further step. I would call for that person to disavow those doctrines. If they did not, I would have no choice but to bring charges for the removal of that person from leadership. Indeed, one denomination has struggled with whether to divide over YEC.[84]

Therefore, AiG needs to be more consistent. If it continues to use rhetoric which suggests the age of the earth is a level two doctrine, then it should also own the implications. In the first place, AiG should call for its supporters to kindly but firmly demand their pastors, professors, and denominational leaders disavow OEC. AiG should also call for denominations to disfellowship churches that refuse to recant OEC. But if AiG will not call for these actions, why not? If AiG does not really believe Christians should separate over the age of the earth, then it should recast its overblown language.

There is another reason AiG needs to take responsibility for the seriousness of its accusations. AiG places its followers under enormous pressure to act upon its rhetoric as a matter of biblical faithfulness. Most AiG followers likely cannot bring themselves to confront OEC pastors, seminary professors, and family members about their terribly evil-causing doctrines. Or even worse, an AiG supporter may work up the courage to demand their church, seminary, or denomination take action appropriate to the AiG charges.

Yet, if AiG supporters persisted in such a way as to be disruptive and divisive, I and many evangelical leaders would consider this applied aspect

---

84. The Presbyterian Church in America nearly divided over the age of the earth. On the details see "Report of the Creation Study Committee," PCA Historical Center, http://www.pcahistory.org/creation/report.pdf. AiG describes the PCA situation thus: "The PCA, like many other conservative denominations, is currently divided over Genesis. As in other churches, there seems to be a fundamental divide between the laity and the intellectual elites; most of the former favoring biblical authority and many of the latter insisting on the final authority of secular science with regard to the origin and history of the creation." See "Summary of a Response to 'PCA Geologists on the Antiquity of the Earth'," Answers in Genesis, https://answersingenesis.org/age-of-the-earth/response-to-pca-geologists-on-antiquity-of-the-earth/.

of AiG doctrine to be level two. In other words, a truly consistent AiG follower might rightly find themselves rebuked in a church or ministry for divisiveness, but not for believing the earth is young. A sad affair like this would not only be the responsibility of the person causing the division, but also AiG for misleading and motivating them in the first place.

BioLogos

Neither Darwinism nor theistic evolution is new, but a powerful and influential popularizing ministry urging evangelicals to get on board with them is. Neither does some of the material coming out of BioLogos appear like older versions of theistic evolution. Certain of their book titles make clear their target: *How I Changed My Mind about Evolution: Evangelicals Reflect on Faith and Science.*[85] The volume reads like a collection of Christian conversion testimonies, except the conversion is to evolution.

But this newly packaged evangelical version of evolutionary creation still raises deep concerns. Darwinism initially seemed to demolish natural theology by providing a naturalistic explanation for design in living creatures. Evangelicalism responded by strengthening its defense of the Bible. Yet BioLogos makes no commitment to full scriptural inspiration, thus it does not practice the conservatism principle. The question then for watching evangelicals: Will BioLogos be more prone to substantial doctrinal reformulations?

Again, since BioLogos is neither a church nor a denomination, it would be unfair to expect a unified theological vision. But that is precisely one of its biggest dangers. BioLogos unifies around evolution but only a fairly sparse doctrinal basis.[86] Its mission is to encourage evangelicals to realize that evolution can be accepted without theological worries. Yet how to construe important doctrines evolutionarily often seems to be a work in process, including how much to trust the Bible. The evangelical outsider might be forgiven for feeling like the message is: "Evolution is true, but we're not sure about all of the Bible, and we're hard at work now to figure out how to retain as much traditional evangelical theology as possible."

---

85. Kathryn Applegate and J. B. Stump, eds., *How I Changed My Mind about Evolution: Evangelicals Reflect on Faith and Science* (Downers Grove, IL: InterVarsity Press, 2016).
86. "About BioLogos," BioLogos, http://biologos.org/about-us.

To be sure, on some theological topics BioLogos presents a number of positions. This openness allows the organization to appeal to a broader range of evangelicals. But it also sends the message to the church that all of its options are acceptable, including those that conservative evangelicals will find most disturbing. Indeed, some BioLogos options appear to follow the trajectory liberals earlier adopted in response to evolution.

Conservative evangelicals will be especially nervous about the theological implications of the BioLogos belief "that God created humanity using the process of evolution and endowed us with his image."[87] Moreover, BioLogos holds that population genetics certifies that the entire human race cannot have descended from Adam. "At BioLogos, we are persuaded by the scientific evidence that human beings evolved, sharing common ancestors with all other life on earth. Furthermore, it increasingly appears that the genetic diversity among humans today could not have come from just two individuals in the past, but a population of thousands."[88]

And if the human species is not essential but rather evolved, how does this square with the doctrine of our being made in God's image? Denis Lamoureux answers: "Evolutionary creation contends that humans evolved from prehuman ancestors, and that the image of God and human sin were gradually and mysteriously manifested."[89]

Human evolution, then, apparently forces rejection of the traditional doctrine of the special creation of humanity, the fall, and original sin. In early response to Darwinism, theological liberals discarded the historical fall of Adam. Instead of the traditional view that humans degenerated from their created innocence, liberals argued that humanity evolved (fell) upward from its subhuman past with its animal appetites.[90] BioLogos entertains similar evolutionary notions of how sin might have entered the world, that "there was a gradual awakening to sin. That is to say, in the

87. "How Could Humans Have Evolved and Still Be Created in the 'Image of God'?" BioLogos, http://biologos.org/common-questions/human-origins/image-of-god.

88. "Were Adam and Eve Historical Figures?" BioLogos, http://biologos.org/common-questions/human-origins/were-adam-and-eve-historical-figures.

89. Denis O. Lamoureux, "The Evolution of an Evolutionary Creationist," in *How I Changed My Mind about Evolution: Evangelicals Reflect on Faith and Science*, ed. Kathryn Applegate and J. B. Stump (Downers Grove, IL: InterVarsity Press, 2016), 142.

90. Jon Roberts, *Darwinism and the Divine in America: Protestant Intellectuals and Organic Evolution, 1859–1900* (Madison, WI: University of Wisconsin Press, 1988), 136–45, 174–203, 211.

same way that each human individually becomes morally responsible for actions as he or she grows up, so too the species gradually developed an awareness of their sin. On this account, there is no stark before-and-after line, but rather a gradual 'coming of age.' . . . Perhaps God held *Homo* species 500,000 years ago responsible for some things; species 200,000 years ago for more; 30,000 years ago even more; and when the law was given to Moses, God held the people accountable in a new way."[91]

Likewise, evolutionary theory since Darwin has contended that human morality evolved from animal emotions. BioLogos not only promotes this gradualist origins of human morality,[92] but also an evolutionary account for belief in God. Thus evolutionary psychology has revealed "the (rather unsurprising fact) that, in the words of Oxford psychologist Justin Barrett, 'Belief in gods and God particularly arises through the natural, ordinary operation of human minds in natural ordinary environments.'"[93] Conservative evangelicals will wonder if BioLogos wants them also to consider an evolutionary account of Christian belief formation.[94]

---

91. Jim Stump, "Evolution and the Fall," BioLogos, November 04, 2015, http://biologos. org/blogs/jim-stump-faith-and-science-seeking-understanding/evolution-and-the-fall.

92. Loren Haarsma, "Does Evolution Compromise Human Morality?" BioLogos, January 14, 2013, http://biologos.org/blogs/archive/does-evolution-compromise-human-morality.

93. Michael Murray and Jeffrey Schloss, "Does Evolutionary Psychology Explain Why We Believe in God? Part 2," BioLogos, May 21, 2013, http://biologos.org/blogs/archive/does-evolutionary-psychology-explain-why-we-believe-in-god-part-2. Cf. Michael J. Murray and Jeffrey P. Schloss, "Evolutionary Accounts of Religion and the Justification of Religious Belief," in *Debating Christian Theism*, ed. J.P. Moreland et al. (New York: Oxford University Press, 2013), 254. For a similar but much fuller treatment on the origins of religion see Jeffrey Schloss and Michael Murray, eds., *The Believing Primate: Scientific, Philosophical, and Theological Reflections on the Origin of Religion* (New York: Oxford University Press, 2009). I understand that the apologetics point Schloss makes in these works is to defeat the naturalist's claim that if natural evolutionary processes produce belief in God, then those beliefs have no warrant. But my question is this: Would Schloss or BioLogos draw the line against evolutionary psychology should it claim a similar dispositional account for belief in Jesus?

94. The issues surveyed represent BioLogos views most disturbing to non-traditional evangelicals. But other issues could be mentioned that would have troubled Warfield as well as contemporary conservative evangelicals. For example, BioLogos makes clear that it accepts divine intervention in past and present salvation history, but the ministry seems fairly allergic to miracles occurring in natural history, that is evolutionary creation. "Evolutionary creationists differ with other Christians on the question of whether God performed miracles in natural history. Christians agree that God did miracles in human

In the end, BioLogos faces the same epistemological question as earlier theological liberals when they rejected the full trustworthiness of Scripture: How should we ground the knowledge of God? Unquestionably BioLogos leaders desire to be faithful to Christ and the gospel. But traditional evangelicals cannot help but be concerned when the ministry recommends an article urging readers to discern the Bible's scientific, historic, moral, and theological errors in the light of Christ's love.[95] Post-Darwinian liberals also sought to ground theology in Jesus Christ rather than the explicit teachings of the Bible. In actuality, human experience viewed through an evolutionary lens became their arbiter for deciding Christian doctrine.[96] BioLogos desires to help evangelicals no longer have to choose between faith and science. But some of us will feel BioLogos forces us to choose between their views and the Bible.

Understandably the ministry's leaders will view themselves in the Galileo tradition, and that their endorsement of evolution is similar to the heliocentric and age of the earth debates. I also understand my qualms with them appear similar to those of YECs with OECs. But one big difference stands out: BioLogos has abandoned the conservatism principle.

I would have no qualms with BioLogos were it strictly a scholarly society engaged in the study of science and theology, discussing and debating various hybrid models. Its talk of just having a conversation about evolution is no problem either. I personally view the BioLogos leaders I have met as warm-hearted followers of Christ. I certainly don't view them as enemies of God. They have treated me and my views with respect and

---

history, but natural history is different. . . . The evidence points to a God who chose to use regular chains of cause and effect to bring about life." See "Is There Room in Evolutionary Creation to Believe in Miracles?" BioLogos, http://biologos.org/common-questions/gods-relationship-to-creation/biologos-and-miracles. Some BioLogos leaders might still say they are not closed to the possibility of divine intervention in the evolutionary process. See Darrel Falk, "A BioLogos Response to William Dembski, Part 2," BioLogos, May 03, 2012, http://biologos.org/blogs/archive/a-biologos-response-to-william-dembski-part-2. Similarly, BioLogos pushes back against traditional efforts to use science to identify God's design in nature (e.g., Intelligent Design). See BioLogos Editorial Team, "Bad Science and Weak Theology?" May 25, 2011, http://biologos.org/blogs/archive/bad-science-and-weak-theology. Quote by Darrel Falk, former BioLogos president. Emphasis his.

95. See chapter 8.

96. Roberts, *Darwinism*, 126–28, 161, 166, 168–70.

grace. Indeed, BioLogos leaders have been kinder to me than some whose creationist views are closer to mine.

Yet just based on its extremely loose doctrine of the Bible, I could never recommend BioLogos as a constructive resource for the church. And that is what it seeks to be. The ministry seeks to popularize and promote specific scientific and theological proposals for evangelicals. The importance of a fully trustworthy Bible is so critical for evangelicalism that I believe this issue rises to level two of doctrinal importance. I could not in good conscience support pastors, seminary professors, or denominational leaders with similar biblical understandings. With its stance on Scripture, BioLogos will struggle to convince conservative evangelicals it harbors no theological dangers. Its endorsement of evolutionary based doctrinal changes of such importance as those mentioned above only reinforces those concerns.

Chapter 10

PATIENCE AND PEACE

The grass withers, the flower fades,
but the word of our God will stand forever.—Isa. 40:8

For now we see in a mirror dimly, but then face to face. Now I know in part; then I shall know fully, even as I have been fully known.—1 Cor. 13:12

THE WORD WAITS

Working through science-theology conflicts takes time. No matter how fast the pace of scientific discovery, major theological perspectives cannot and should not be flipped overnight. The more important the issue, the more careful needs be the deliberation. And that messy deliberation takes place among God's people cautiously seeking truth while remaining faithful to God's Word.

To see this, let us imagine pastors wrestling with the very first science-theology conflict, but in different times and places. A pastor trained in Wittenberg in the 1560s almost certainly was schooled in the new astronomy.[1] Master's-level students used advanced textbooks and received an even more sophisticated and extensive treatment of the new science. These texts stressed neither biblical arguments against a sun-centered universe nor a

---

1. Kenneth J. Howell, *God's Two Books: Copernican Cosmology and Biblical Interpretation in Early Modern Science* (Notre Dame, IN: University of Notre Dame Press, 2002), 39.

219

sense of urgency about believing the right things cosmologically. No one was taught to consider Copernicanism a theological heresy or was forced to hold heliocentric convictions secretly due to fear of authorities. The pastor's teachers considered Copernicanism on par with Ptolemaic astronomy as legitimate scientific theory,[2] but within a geostatic framework.[3]

Our pastor almost certainly would not have believed in a sun-centered universe with an orbiting and rotating earth. He would have learned too many good reasons to reject it. If German astronomers generally regarded heliocentrism with respect, most also considered it physically impossible.[4] Because Copernicus had used many Ptolemaic observational data, his predictions were not substantially more accurate.[5] And until Galileo's 1610 telescopic observations, no observational means undermined the old or supported the new theory.[6] With scientific hurdles and theological and commonsense problems to boot, our pastor would have been virtually irrational to believe in a motionless sun and a moving earth.

But now let us imagine a Lutheran pastor studying during the mid-seventeenth century in the university in Gdańsk, Poland. Discoveries by Kepler and Galileo supporting heliocentrism were introduced in Poland in the mid-1630s. This pastor would have certainly lived during changing times regarding astronomy. All his professors accepted the full compatibility of the Bible with scientific truth in general, and were under no compulsion to honor Rome's condemnation of heliocentrism.[7] Nonetheless debates were vigorous, and varied viewpoints likely were confusing to the student-pastor. Oppositions to heliocentrism often centered on its inconsistency with the

---

2. Robert S. Westman, "The Melanchthon Circle, Rheticus and the Wittenberg Interpretation of the Copernican Theory," *Isis* 66 (1975): 180.

3. Ibid., 191.

4. David C. Lindberg, "Galileo, the Church, and the Cosmos," in *When Science and Christianity Meet,* ed. David C. Lindberg and Ronald L. Numbers (Chicago: University of Chicago Press, 2003), 40.

5. So "if accuracy of prediction were the criterion [of a better theory], then Copernicus's work must be deemed a massive failure." Owen Gingerich, "The Copernican Revolution," in *Science and Religion: A Historical Introduction*, ed. Gary Ferngren (Baltimore: Johns Hopkins University Press, 2002), 97.

6. Ibid.

7. Barbara Bieńkowska, "From Negation to Acceptance (The Reception of the Heliocentric Theory in Polish Schools in the 17th and 18th Centuries)," in *The Reception of Copernicus' Heliocentric Theory*, ed. Jerzy Dobrzycki (Dordrecht, Holland: D. Reidel Publishing Company, 1972), 84–86.

Bible and the testimony of the senses. Heated exegetical debates swung between understanding the Bible literally or as phenomenal language addressed to ordinary readers.[8] More frequently arguments focused on the inconsistency of Copernicanism with Aristotelian physics.

But many Gdańsk professors who affirmed geocentrism actually praised Copernicus from an anti-realist perspective. Intellectuals also freely combined elements of the old astronomy and physics with the new astronomy. Besides Copernicanism, an array of hybrid systems vied for supremacy, all being geo-heliocentric. Some defended the traditional model of a motionless earth in the center of the universe with planets and the sun orbiting it. Others pictured a system with some or all planets orbiting the sun, and that system orbiting the earth. Some models even suggested that the earth rotated on its axis.[9] Understandably our Polish pastor-in-training would have struggled to sort things out.

So our pastor might have reasonably chosen one of several options. (1) Simply decline to take a position. Who could blame him for confessing lack of requisite expertise in either the science or the theology to choose a view? His teaching and preaching the essential Christian faith would have remained unaffected. (2) Choose the view of the professor(s) he deemed most authoritative. (3) Or simply retain the traditional geocentric view. Because of his professors' attitudes, however, he almost certainly would not have believed Copernicanism a heresy.

Finally, our thought experiment carries us to imagining a New England Puritan pastor in the late seventeenth century. By then "many Protestant scientists were Copernicans, and many Protestant theologians seemed indifferent to the issue."[10] Even before publication of Newton's *Principia* in 1687, heliocentrism was being widely taught and believed in the coastal lands of North America. Puritan ministers played the primary role in propagating the new science. Their most powerful medium was the almanac,

---

8. Ibid., 104–15.

9. Christine Jones Schofield, *The Geoheliocentric Planetary System: Its Development and Influence in the Late 16th and 17th Centuries* (unpublished Ph.D. diss., Cambridge University, Newnham College, 1964), 176–77, and Edward Grant, *In Defense of the Earth's Centrality and Immobility*, Transactions of the American Philosophical Society (Philadelphia: American Philosophical Society, 1984), 5–20.

10. Edward Davis and Michael Winship, "Early Modern Protestantism," in *Science and Religion: A Historical Introduction*, ed. Gary Ferngren (Baltimore: Johns Hopkins University Press, 2002), 122.

the most widely circulated literary form and only periodical of that time.[11]
Non-Puritan almanacs dominated, such as *Ames'* and Benjamin Franklin's
Poor Richard's, but the better almanacs of the late seventeenth century
were published by ministers.[12] These almanacs increasingly contained popular scientific essays, with astronomy being the most pervasive and popular topic. Christian leaders popularized Newtonian heliocentrism; biblical
passages formerly understood geocentrically were being reinterpreted
accordingly.[13] Though some pastors and their flocks continued to resist
heliocentrism during the Newtonian period, the exegetical skirmishes
were fast dying out.

Our New England pastor likely taught his flock that the Bible does not
conflict with the new astronomy. Because Holy Scripture speaks in the
everyday language of perception, he likely noted how it had previously
been misread geocentrically. A century and a half after the publication of
Copernicus's *On the Revolutions* the scientific community and much of the
American public believed it without hesitation. Another seventy-five years
would find even most of the recalcitrant exegetes as believers, too, and the
Copernican revolution would be complete.

The revolution had taken much time, much deliberation, and many
hybrid science-theology models along the way. The church's conservatism
principle demanded patience. The Lord was not obligated to clear up the
church's questions when it wanted answers, and the church was under no
obligation to decide on issues of which it was not certain. All the while the
unchanging Word of God remained for the church.

PROPRIETY IN HANDLING REVELATION

Christians have a responsibility to act properly in light of what they do and
do not know about the Word of God. First of all, Christians are obligated
to affirm certain beliefs. To deny the statement "Jesus is Lord" is to fail

---

11. Harry Woolf, *Copernicanism and Newtonianism in Early America,* in *The Reception
of Copernicus' Heliocentric Theory,* ed. Jerzy Dobrzycki (Dordrecht, Holland: D. Reidel
Publishing Company, 1972), 294–95.

12. Though *Poor Richard's* became popular because of its esteemed publisher,
Benjamin Franklin, *Ames' Almanac* was superior in many ways and enjoyed the widest
circulation. Ibid., 303.

13. Woolf, *Copernicanism and Newtonianism in Early America,* 296.

one's duty as a Christian. But most of us are under no obligation to pass judgment on the latest theory in particle physics.

Our confessional obligations do not always extend to complex details. For example, as faithful Christians we confess "Jesus is at the right hand of the Father." But revelational propriety might require we admit uncertainty whether Augustine's local view of the Father's right hand or the non-local view of John of Damascus is correct. We unhesitatingly and appropriately affirm Jesus' exaltation and session, but might just as appropriately realize we do not have enough biblical, theological, or philosophical reasons to make judgments about some of the details.

Science-theology controversies especially make evident the need for propriety in handling revelation. The complex relation between God's Word and his creation requires that Christians be careful with our confessional duties while being honest about our incomplete knowledge. So, for example, Christians feeling overwhelmed with the issues raised in this book are properly faithful in confessing their Creator God and any number of creation beliefs they believe the Bible teaches clearly. But those same Christians should feel no embarrassment to admit uncertainty about details other Christians seem so clear about. Not only do science-theology controversies force entire generations of Christians to wait on the Lord for solution, individual believers also have a normal progression of growth in knowledge. It is absolutely proper, and at times even required, to confess the truth about a matter. But revelational propriety also demands humble admission when we don't know and kindness toward those with whom we disagree.

So then, no Christian should ever feel compulsion to abandon confidence in the authority and complete truth of Scripture. Trusting in the Savior and his Word come packaged together to the Christian as a gift. Christians find rest in the Spirit-given conviction that no conflict exists between the truth of the Bible and God's creation. But scientific and theological theories, though necessary, never enjoy infallibility. Confidence in this basic principle provides believers with patience to wait in peace on solutions when faced with apparent conflicts.

CONCLUSION

Though only about a half century old, in conservative evangelical circles the age of the earth controversy feels like a major science-theology conflict on par with the Darwinian. One reason is that some leading YEC groups frequently and specifically link the age controversy to the Darwinian. Therefore, the debate takes on considerably more urgency among evangelicals with longstanding antipathy to evolution. Yet the battle against Darwinism was carried on for a century mostly by OEC anti-evolutionists, including the Old Princetonians such as Charles Hodge, the fundamentalists, and neo-evangelicals such as Carl Henry. Ironically, YEC initially gained credibility in OEC circles by appearing to be a new inerrantist version of anti-evolutionism with superior, even if confusing, scientific evidence.[14]

Evangelical voices of authority today urgently call for decisions on some extremely difficult biblical, theological, scientific and philosophical debates. Making matters more complex, an evolutionary creationist evangelical voice has been added to the mix. Many evangelicals feel forced to decide between well-known leaders or ministries, even though doing so may well lead to boundaries being drawn between them and other Christians.

These voices of authority are backed by enormous resources and popular support. Ignoring their calls for decision is not easy; fellow church members are being pressured to take a stand too. These popularizing ministries are specifically positioned to reach as many non-specialists as effectively as possible. Their presentations may contain complex and technical material beyond the training of their followers, but these ministries are not like evangelical scholarly societies, which have long debated the same issues without agreement.[15] Instead these ministries by design often present their viewpoints as long settled truths to those who have no way of knowing otherwise.

At present these creationist ministries present their evangelical audiences with a myriad of hybrid theories. The conceptual instability and emotional atmosphere suggest that those who are uncertain what to believe should trust their Bible and wait for further light on the details. Those Christians can trust that the God of truth will have the final say in the outworking

---

14. See chapter 6.

15. As we saw in chapters 4 and 8, societies such as the ASA, CSR, and ETS have never felt the compulsion to raise and expend significant resources to popularize specific controversial scholarly positions.

of history. But for those who believe they understand things rightly, they should humbly and patiently teach so as to nurture the unity of God's church. And if boundaries must be drawn, and at times they must, may they be outlined with exquisite Christian kindness and gentleness.

General Index

Adam, 90, 97, 178, 203, 209; and B. B. Warfield's view of, 195–96; and descent from, 214; and dinosaurs, 154; as historical, 24, 87, 180, 198; and the naming of animals, 137, 163; and his rib, 76

Affirmations and Denials Essential to a Consistent Christian (Biblical) Worldview (ADCW), 171, 178, 197n39

age of the earth, 13, 15, 21, 24, 212, 216, 223; and Answers in Genesis (AiG). *See* Answers in Genesis (AiG); and biblical inerrancy, 171–85; and compromise, 139; and the Creation Research Society (CRS), 90; as essential doctrine, 131–32, 144–45, 149–52, 154; and flood, fossils, and strata, 99–120 (ch. 5); and Ken Ham, 25; and the Presbyterian Church in America, 212n84; and Reasons to Believe (RTB). *See* Reasons to Believe (RTB); as salvation issue, 203–204;

and scriptural geologists, 124; and Terry Mortenson, 198

Agassiz, Louis, 79n25, 117, 117n.109

Agricola, Georgius: and *De Re Metallica (On the Nature of Metals)*, 104

American Civil Liberties Union (ACLU): and the Scopes Trial, 74–78

American Scientific Affiliation (ASA), 85, 86–90, 97, 172

animal death: and before the Fall, 97, 203–204

Anning, Mary, 112

Answers in Genesis (AiG), 13, 90, 94, 97, 124, 149, 176, 188, 206, 211, 214; and amending of Chicago Statements. *See* Chicago Statements; and Andrew A. Snelling, 152; and baraminology. *See* baraminology; and boundaries, 196–206; and conservatism principle, 209–10; and dinosaurs, 153–54; and Evangelical Theological Society (ETS).